Y0-DHW-779

BECOMING A KWOMA

AMS PRESS
NEW YORK

BECOMING A KWOMA

TEACHING AND LEARNING
IN A
NEW GUINEA TRIBE

BY

JOHN W. M. WHITING

With a Foreword by John Dollard

PUBLISHED FOR
THE INSTITUTE OF HUMAN RELATIONS
BY
YALE UNIVERSITY PRESS · NEW HAVEN
LONDON · HUMPHREY MILFORD · OXFORD UNIVERSITY PRESS

Library of Congress Cataloging in Publication Data

Whiting, John Wesley Mayhew, 1908-
 Becoming a Kwoma.

 Reprint of the 1941 edition published for the Institute of Human Relations by Yale University Press, New Haven.
 Includes index.
 1. Kwoma tribe. 2. Socialization. I. Yale University. Institute of Human Relations. II. Title.
 DU740.42.W47   1978   301.15'7'0995   75-35163
 ISBN 0-404-14178-1

Copyright, 1941, by Yale University Press

First AMS edition published in 1978.

Reprinted by arrangement with the original publisher from the edition of 1941, New Haven. [Trim size has been slightly altered in this edition. Original trim size: 15.1 x 22.9 cm. Text area of the original has been maintained.]

MANUFACTURED
IN THE UNITED STATES OF AMERICA

FOREWORD

THE problems of diffusion, or the horizontal transmission of culture, are widely known and have been well studied. The problems of socialization, or the transmission of culture from one generation to the next, have scarcely been isolated as legitimate or necessary objects of scientific research. The pioneer work of Sapir, Mead, Radin, Underhill, Hallowell, and Dyk, among many others, has brought the problem of socialization to the fore in the field of anthropology and given it the characteristic label of culture and personality. Some of these workers, especially Sapir, Mead, and Radin, have profited by contact with the Freudian stream of ideas concerning individual development. A knowledge of the relativity of culture has set the framework for problems of culture and personality in the widest sense; Freudian researches in our own society have suggested hypotheses to be tested on the data of primitive people. Mr. Whiting, like his forebears, has been heavily influenced by both of these intellectual movements and has utilized the problem setting which they propose.

In seeking aid from Freudian psychology, students of culture and personality have profited greatly. In taking over some of Freud's views and hypotheses, however, they have been exposed to a characteristic defect of the Freudian position. I am not referring to the defects usually attributed to Freud since I do not think he overemphasizes sex, nor yet that the term "unconscious" is meaningless. The defect I refer to is that there is no hypothesis in Freud's theory to explain learning. This limits the usefulness of Freud's work for anthropologists.

If the culture of a group is, from the standpoint of any one generation, an arbitrary set of patterns, and if these patterns are socially transmitted, some principles must be evolved on the basis of which this transmission can take place. The most promising hypothesis seems to be that put forward by modern learning theory. This theory must not be confused with the associationistic principles of conditioning which were derived from the Pavlovian experiments or with the earliest attempt to formulate a behavioristic theory by Watson. Pavlov and Watson have both made their essential contributions, but so also have Thorndike, Hull, and many others; the more recent systemization of Hull seems to bring the theory within the range of usefulness by social scientists who are concerned with human learning.

Sumner offered the dictum that the folkways and mores of the group are the habits of the individual. This statement ought to have been more helpful than it has actually proved. The difficulty seems to have been that Sumner had no conception of the laws of habit, and that, therefore, nothing could be predicted from his assertion. Linton has likewise affirmed that a culture is a set of habits, but this assertion merely raises the question, What is a habit? If one asks that, one comes directly to the need for the learning theory—for a systematic statement of how responses are evoked, how they are affixed to stimuli, how habits disappear, and what kinds of rewards are useful in building habits. The dictum that culture is a set of rewarded habits seems more useful. It promises to import into anthropology those principles from learning theory which may be helpful in determining the origins, transmission, survival, and disappearance of group habit.

Mr. Whiting's book is an exploratory research in this field. The first part of the book provides a description of Kwoma culture as it is brought to bear on children during their growth from infancy to adulthood. The data selected make the children seem real and lively. In the second part of the book an analysis of the behavior of the children in terms of learning theory is presented. Mr. Whiting has applied learning principles as they now exist and has made some significant innovations. The best, among the latter, are his discussion of how motivation is provided to get Kwoma children to learn, how the children are guided in what to learn, and how they are rewarded for having learned. Whiting finds that secondary as well as primary rewards and punishments play a great rôle in Kwoma teaching. While human learning must occur everywhere according to the same general principles, the details of the process probably differ from society to society. The responses rewarded vary endlessly, the stimuli to which these responses are pinioned are likewise different, and there must be as many systems of secondary reward and punishment as there are cultures. The work of anthropologists in this field will undoubtedly be of value to students of learning and teaching in our own society.

JOHN DOLLARD

CONTENTS

Foreword by John Dollard — v
Preface — xiii

PART ONE

I. Environment, Social Structure, and Personnel — 3
II. Infancy — 24
III. The Period of Weaning — 31
IV. Childhood — 38
V. Adolescence — 65
VI. Adulthood — 106

Illustrations — 168

PART TWO

VII. The Process of Socialization — 171
VIII. The Inculcation of Supernatural Beliefs — 202

Index — 223

ILLUSTRATIONS

View of lake and Sepik River taken from near Rumbima house tamberan.

Coöperative work group constructing the house of the ethnographers.

Work bee dragging the log for Yat's gong.

Uka holding lumps of sago flour at the market.

Mundik just after he had been beaten and bound for attending a ceremony tabooed to him.

Awa repairing a fish net.

Kum, the chief character in the Weaning Period.

Gwiyap, our best informant.

All illustrations follow page **168**

PREFACE

THIS monograph has two purposes: first, to present the data gathered on Kwoma culture, and, second, to present a theory of the process of socialization. In accordance with this dual purpose, the book has been divided into two parts, the first descriptive, the second theoretical. In the descriptive part, after an introductory chapter in which the setting of the study is presented, an attempt has been made to describe the culture as it unfolds itself to an individual born into Kwoma society. The cultures of infancy, of the period of weaning, of childhood, of adolescence, and finally of adulthood are described. The data in each of these chapters have been organized according to the drives[1] involved. Social habits related to hunger, elimination, sex, and pain have been described in that order. Since many customs are associated with several of these drives, this organization could not be strictly adhered to. Those habits motivated by acquired drives, such as fear, anger, the wish to help, and the desire for prestige, have been described where it seemed most appropriate. The second part opens with a chapter in which the various techniques of teaching observed at Kwoma are elucidated and defined in terms of learning theory. This is followed by a chapter which presents the results of an inquiry into the manner in which Kwoma children are taught supernatural beliefs. This inquiry is made in terms of learning theory, teaching techniques, and the conditions of the culture, the society, and the environment which exist at Kwoma.

The idea for this research was suggested by Professor John Dollard. As a result of attending his seminars, it became clear to me that, although culture was assumed by anthropologists and sociologists to be transmitted by a social rather than a genetic process, there was no adequate theory

[1] For the use of the concepts of *drive* and *acquired drive,* see chap. vii, pp. 173–174.

of this process. Furthermore, a survey of the anthropological literature indicated that with a few notable exceptions there were very few empirical data on primitive child training, although since this project was instituted considerable additional material has appeared.

The interest in child training and in pre-adult culture is relatively new in anthropology. Until the last fifteen years there were only scattered and casual references to primitive childhood in the ethnographic literature. Most of these reports merely gave a description of ceremonies at birth and naming and of initiation rites. Sometimes a description of the play group, or of children's games, and vague comments on how parents treated their children were also included. Infrequently fieldworkers like Kidd, Junod, and Milne[2] presented more detailed observations of the behavior of children in their monographs. Miller and Hambly[3] assembled the available data in comparative works on primitive education, which suffered from the paucity of good material.

The influence of Freud was responsible for awakening the interest of a number of anthropologists in the problem of child training. Malinowski[4] and later Richards[5] used data on primitive childhood to criticize certain aspects of Freud's theory and to verify others. Recently Kardiner[6] has used primitive data gathered by Linton to revise the implicit instinctivism of Freud and to verify his general theory of personality development. The pioneer in the gathering of data on primitive childhood, and one who has probably had the greatest influence on the later fieldworkers who have become interested in this problem, is Margaret Mead.[7] Her work was

[2] D. Kidd, *Savage Childhood* (London, 1906); H. A. Junod, *The Life of a South African Tribe* (Neuchatel, 1912); Mrs. L. Milne, *The Home of an Eastern Clan* (Oxford, 1924).
[3] N. Miller, *The Child in Primitive Society* (New York, 1928); W. D. Hambly, *Origins of Education among Primitive Peoples* (London, 1926).
[4] B. Malinowski, *Sex and Repression in Primitive Society* (London, 1927).
[5] Audrey Richards, *Hunger and Work in a Savage Tribe* (London, 1932).
[6] Abram Kardiner, *The Individual and His Society* (New York, 1939).
[7] Margaret Mead, *Coming of Age in Samoa* (New York, 1928); *Growing Up in New Guinea* (New York, 1930); *Sex and Temperament in Three Savage Societies* (New York, 1935).

Preface

also in part instigated by Freud's theories, and in part by the cultural relativism of Boas. She demonstrated unequivocally that personality and temperament are determined by child rearing, and vary from society to society. Other fieldworkers, notably Kluckhohn,[8] Du Bois,[9] and Gorer[10] have given further documentation to this point of view and in addition have made contributions of their own to the theory of the relationship between child training and personality development in primitive societies. Finally Erikson,[11] a practicing psychoanalyst, has turned his attention to this problem and has reported on fieldwork which he did among the Sioux.

Following Malinowski's functional approach to primitive education[12] a number of his students have given excellent descriptive accounts of primitive education. Outstanding among these have been Firth[13] and Evans-Pritchard.[14] In addition Fortes,[15] Hogbin,[16] Wedgewood,[17] and Raum[18] have written special accounts of primitive education from a functional point of view.[19]

Since but few of these fieldworkers had concerned them-

[8] C. Kluckhohn, "Theoretical Bases for an Empirical Method of Studying the Acquisition of Culture by Individuals," *Man*, 89, 1939; Paper read before Monday Night Group, New Haven, 1940.

[9] C. Du Bois. Papers read at Eastern Sociological meetings, 1940, and Yale Anthropology Club, 1940.

[10] G. Gorer, *Himalayan Village* (London, 1938).

[11] E. H. Erikson, "Observations on Sioux Education," *The Journal of Psychology*, VII (1937), 101–156.

[12] B. Malinowski, *The Sexual Life of Savages* (New York, 1929).

[13] R. Firth, *We, the Tikopia* (New York, 1936).

[14] E. E. Evans-Pritchard, *Witchcraft, Oracles, and Magic among the Azande* (London, 1937).

[15] M. Fortes, "Social and Psychological Aspects of Education in Taleland," *International Institute of African Languages and Cultures*, Memorandum XVII, 1938.

[16] I. Hogbin, "Education at Ontong Java, Solomon Islands," *American Anthropologist*, XXXIII (1931), no. 4, pp. 601–615.

[17] C. H. Wedgewood, "The Life of Children in Manam," *Oceania*, IX (September, 1938), no. 1.

[18] O. F. Raum, *Chaga Childhood* (London, 1940).

[19] This brief survey of the main trends of fieldwork on primitive childhood makes no pretense of completeness. For the most complete bibliography on the subject see J. Gillin, "Personality in Preliterate Societies," *American Sociological Review*, IV (1939), 681–702.

selves with the problem of the transmission of culture as a process, or had published their reports when this study was projected, it was determined to make a field study of the problem rather than a cross-cultural inquiry based upon the literature.

A preliminary field trip with Professor George P. Murdock to the Tenino Indians of Oregon demonstrated the feasibility of the project and provided valuable ethnographic experience. This work, however, indicated the desirability of choosing a tribe which was not "broken down" by contact with the whites. It proved difficult to study how Indians brought up their children when most of them were away at the government school learning the three R's.

On my return from this field trip, I found that Mr. Stephen W. Reed was also anxious to make a study of a primitive society. Together we picked New Guinea as an area which would best suit our requirements. The ethnographic literature concerning the island showed that the tribes were small and homogenous, government weakly developed, castes and classes lacking, and economic specialization slight. It seemed, therefore, that the criterion of simplicity would here be fulfilled. There was also a strange series of rites of passage, which, it appeared, would provide a contrast to our own culture. Finally, since New Guinea is one of the world's last frontiers—much of it, indeed, is still unexplored—we hoped to find a tribe which was little affected by contact with Europeans. Fortunately for us, Professor Richard Thurnwald was in New Haven at the time, and with his advice we were able to narrow our field to the Sepik River district of the Mandated Territory.

Since work with Professor Dollard indicated that the hypotheses developed by Freud were outstanding among the theories of socialization and since it seemed probable that the psychoanalytic method of interviewing might be useful in the field, I began a training analysis during the following winter. I worked under Mr. Earl Zinn for five months before leaving for the field.

Preface

Mr. Reed and I set out for New Guinea in the summer of 1936. We received extremely valuable practical help from Professor Hogbin at Sydney, and eventually arrived at Kwoma on October first. Mr. Reed collaborated with me until the end of February, when his project took him on a survey of the tribes of the Sepik area. I remained at Kwoma until the end of April, when I felt that, although my work was not complete, a period of diminishing returns had set in.

We used the usual techniques employed by anthropologists who work with the culture of a living society, combining participant observation with the questioning of informants. We kept a daily record of the events which occurred in the hamlet and of the happenings in other hamlets when we were able to observe them or were told about them. This record was scanty at first, but as our knowledge of the people and the culture grew the daily reports became fuller, until toward the end of our stay they contained some of our best information.

We also followed anthropological practice in establishing the reliability of our data, checking all statements with as many informants as practicable. In participant observation we employed a special criterion for discovering whether an act which we observed was customary or deviant. We found that if the act was customary, it would evoke no critical comment from those members of the society who observed it. On the other hand, if the act deviated from custom, the comments of those who observed it would reveal this fact. Thus, by paying especial attention to the spectators and recording their comments when an event occurred, we were usually able to determine whether or not an act was customary by the observation of a single instance.

The nature of the Kwoma settlement made our fieldwork difficult. The dwellings were loosely clustered in small hamlets of ten or a dozen houses each, so that it was impossible to find any vantage point from which to observe the life of the tribe as a whole. A further obstacle was the precipitous nature of the mountain on which the Kwoma lived. This made it hard for novices like ourselves to walk from hamlet to hamlet and therefore practically impossible to keep in touch with all daily happenings in the tribe. To visit the gardens which were on the edge of the tribe's territory was for us a day's task. For this reason most of our data were gathered from members of the hamlet in which we lived.[20]

The language barrier presented a considerable difficulty. Luckily, shortly before we arrived, a dozen or so of the younger natives had returned from working on European plantations or in the gold fields and could therefore speak pidgin English. We set about mastering this language and at the end of two months could speak it fluently. Although most of our information was obtained through this medium, we undertook also to learn the native language and by the end of a few months were able to speak it haltingly and understand everyday conversation. By the time I left, seven months after arrival, I was able to carry on an extended conversation, still haltingly, but well enough to exchange ideas and obtain information on the less recondite subjects.

On returning to New Haven I presented an analysis and description of the material gathered at Kwoma as a doctoral dissertation to the faculty of the Graduate School of Yale University. During 1938–39 a fellowship from the Institute of Human Relations enabled me to study stimulus-response psychology under Professor Clark Hull. The knowledge of learning theory gained from him and from Drs. Neal E. Miller and O. H. Mowrer seemed to me crucial for the development of an adequate theory of socialization; consequently as a member of the Institute staff I reanalyzed my data in the light of this theory and am here presenting the results. I have been much helped by suggestions from my colleagues, particularly Professors Dollard, Murdock, and Miller. Since I had little knowledge of learning theory before going into the field, crucial data were frequently not gathered, an unfortunate but unavoidable circumstance. It is hoped, how-

---

[20] The rôles which we played in the tribe and hamlet will be described in detail in the first chapter, as well as the informants from whom most of our material was gathered.

ever, that this pioneering attempt to apply learning theory to anthropological data will suggest methods of gaining a better understanding of the process of socialization.

JOHN W. M. WHITING

Institute of Human Relations,
New Haven, Connecticut.
June, 1941.

PART ONE

CHAPTER I

ENVIRONMENT, SOCIAL STRUCTURE, AND PERSONNEL

THE Kwoma live in the Mandated Territory of New Guinea on the Peilungua Mountains just north of the Sepik River and 265 river miles from its delta.[1] This small mountain system, not more than twenty square miles in area, is bounded on the south and west by the Sepik and a lake formed from a former oxbow in the river, and on the east and north by the vast, rolling watershed of the river which stretches to the foothills of the coastal ranges. It consists of a primary orographical feature in the shape of a letter *S* plus a series of short arterial ridges running off in all directions. From tip to tip as the crow flies the system measures a little over five miles in length. The slopes of these ridges are precipitous; in climbing it is often necessary to dig one's feet into the earth or hold onto vines to avoid falling. A dense forest of large trees covers the ridges and extends down to meet a sago swamp just above the level of the Sepik. The highest point, Ambunti Mountain, rises 1,520 feet above sea level.

The elevation of the Kwoma territory is not sufficient to cause any noticeable variation from the strictly tropical climate of the entire Sepik River Valley. The daily range in temperature, from an average of seventy-one degrees Fahrenheit at dawn to eighty-five in mid-afternoon, closely approximates the norm in the river villages. Humidity is high throughout the year. Some rain falls virtually every day and all-day storms are not uncommon, but the climate and precipitation are so uniform throughout the year that there is no clear-cut division into seasons. Gardens may be planted, cultivated, and harvested at any and all times of the year.

[1] The tribe is situated approximately four degrees and ten minutes south of the equator and one hundred and forty-two degrees and forty minutes east of Greenwich.

Although there is slight variation in the amount of rainfall within the annual cycle, during the months of December, January, and February the Sepik is in flood. This fact is of such importance to the river people that they divide the year into periods of high and low water. This seasonal periodicity is also noted by the Kwoma, but it is significant to them only in so far as it affects their commerce with the river people.

Cassowaries, wildfowl, hornbills, cockatoos, pigeons, and a great many unidentified species of smaller birds abound in the region. The only large mammal is the wild pig. The natives report that there were formerly wallabies in the region but that now there are none. There are several varieties of small tree-climbing marsupials. Many species of bats of different size despoil the fruit trees.

The flora of the region is tropical. The trunks of giant trees support a mat of foliage fifty to sixty feet in the air, so dense that the sun scarcely filters through it, except where the natives have cleared a garden or house site. The swamp land is full of sago palms whose thorn-studded spathes make passage difficult. Small stands of areca and coconut palms mark the sites of habitations past and present. Betel pepper vines cling to the pawpaw, breadfruit, and paper mulberry trees which the natives plant near each dwelling. Many varieties of yams, taro, and greens are grown as a first crop in Kwoma gardens; these are followed by a second crop of bananas and plantains of numerous varieties.

The Kwoma are short, stocky, negroid people with long heads, dark frizzly hair, medium thick lips, and skin color varying from light to dark brown.[2] The homogeneity in physical type is immediately apparent, although there is one family with two generations of strikingly aberrant members, whose skin is so blond that it sunburns. The so-called Papuan, or Semitic, nose-form occurs at random about as often as the dished type. Noses with straight bridges, however, are the most common.

[2] Their average height is five feet four inches, and their cephalic index is in the upper range of mesocephaly (71.7 to 83.6, average 77.4). These figures were taken from twenty adult males.

Environment 5

The Kwoma are a mountain-dwelling people. Except for the southeastern slope of Ambunti Mountain, site of the Ambunti Police Post,[3] they control the entire segment of the Peilungua Range which lies northwest of the Sepik. The territory they claim also includes enough of the sago swamps at the foot of these mountains to provide them with more than enough of the sago flour which is a staple in their diet. They are surrounded by swamp and river tribes. Living in the sago swamp somewhat to the northwest are the Amiki and Sowal people, and on a little group of hills to the northeast, separated by the swamp from the main range, live a half-dozen households who call themselves Yelagu. The Malu, Yambon, and Yessan, the river neighbors of the Kwoma, are linguistically and culturally distinct from the mountain people. When they converse with each other, each speaks his own language, which the other understands.

The Kwoma tribe consists of four subtribes: the Tangwishamp, the Urumbanj, the Koriasi, and the Hongwam.[4] Their territories are contiguous. The Hongwam, who dwell nearest Ambunti, were the group from which nearly all the data here presented were gathered, only a brief trip being made to the other three subtribes. These four subtribes, although speaking the same language and bound by not a few ties of trade and intermarriage, are distinct social entities and are not above carrying on head-hunting raids against one another.[5] More frequently, however, they will band to-

[3] While the fieldwork on which this report is based was being carried on, Ambunti was still a functioning administrative post. Since then this station has been moved to Marui, approximately thirty-five miles downstream, to facilitate communication with the District headquarters at Wewak.

[4] The terms "tribe" and "subtribe" have been adopted here although it might be objected that, since there is no political organization which unites these four groups, it is improper to call the Kwoma a tribe.

[5]   *Name Appearing on Maps and in*

Native Name	Australian Record Books	Population
Hongwam	Waskuk—Bangus	374
Koriyasi	Chissaraman (Shasherman)	116
Urumbanj	Urumbans (Urumbanji)	108
Tangwishamp	Tangunjambi (Taunjambi)	circa 300

Hongwam is referred to as Washkuk by M. Mead in *Sex and Temperament* and in "The Mountain Arapesh: 1. An Importing Culture," *Anthro-*

gether for raids against threatened or actual encroachments by non-Kwoma peoples.

Each subtribe is divided into several hamlets, most of which are clustered about a "house tamberan" or men's ceremonial lodge. A hamlet is usually named after its house tamberan. The arrangement of dwellings in a hamlet is determined by hereditary ownership of land and also by the fact that level sites are very few, owing to the precipitous nature of the mountain slopes.

The patrilineal sib is the primary descent group among the Kwoma. Although all the adult males of a hamlet are members of the same sib, the hamlets of a given sib are not necessarily contiguous, i.e., the descent groups are not completely localized. All the members of a sib theoretically descend from a common totem ancestor. Thus the three sibs of Hongwam subtribe are the *Wanyi*, who descend from a pig, the *Hayamakwo*, who descend from a great fish hawk, and the *Tug*, who descend from the sago palm. Each of these sibs has a great many subsidiary totems, some of which are claimed by more than one sib. These lesser totems are variously identified with birds, reptiles, fish, trees, plants, and parts of the human body.

Each sib is divided into lineages each of whose component families claims descent from a legendary hero. The men of a lineage usually build their dwellings in a cluster which forms part of a hamlet. A lineage is composed of several family lines whose members descend from a common grandfather. The men of a single family line also build their houses near one another. The smallest unit and the most compact is that formed by the sons of a father.

Thus a man remembers four ancestors in the male line: his father, his grandfather, a culture hero who is thought to have been his great grandfather, and, finally, his totem ancestor who lived—according to Kwoma myth—back at the

pological Papers of the American Museum of Natural History, Vol. XXXVI, Pt. III. The maps above referred to are: *Map of Sepik District* compiled by the Department of Lands and Mines, Rabaul, October, 1935, and *Sketch Map of Portion of Sepik District*, Sydney, 1935, Oil Search Ltd. Geological Survey.

beginning of the world. Each of these ancestors is shared by a descent group ranging in size from the children of a father to the descendants of a totem.

The Kwoma kinship system is of the Omaha type.[6] Parallel cousins are all classed as siblings while cross cousins are called *mother*[7] or *maternal uncle* if they are related through the mother (i.e., mother's brother's children), and *nephew* if they are related through the father (i.e., father's sister's children). Age distinctions are made between siblings of the same sex but not between siblings of the opposite sex. Thus a boy has two terms, *elder sibling* and *younger sibling*, to refer to his brothers but classes all his sisters as *sister*. A girl uses *elder sibling* and *younger sibling* for her sisters but uses *brother* to refer to her brothers. The same terms are used and similar distinctions are made between parallel cousins. In the parental generation the father and his brothers are divided into three categories: *father, younger uncle,* and *elder uncle*, while father's sisters are called by a single term, *paternal aunt*. Similarly a mother's sisters are classed as *younger aunt* and *elder aunt*, while her brothers are all termed *maternal uncle*. There are two terms for grandparents, *paternal grandparent* and *maternal grandparent*. All ancestors above this are called by a single term, *ancestor*. Own children and the children of *elder siblings* and *younger siblings* are called *son* or *daughter*. A man calls his sisters' children "*nephew*," and a woman calls her brothers' children "*niece*." Grandchildren and grandchildren of siblings are called *grandchild*.

The sons and sons' sons of the mother's brother are also called *maternal uncle*, and his daughters and sons' daughters are called *mother*. The children of a mother's brother's daughter or of a mother's brother's son's daughter (i.e., of a *mother*) are classed as siblings. The descendants of one's

---

[6] Described by L. Spier in "The Distribution of Kinship Systems in North America," *University of Washington Publication in Anthropology*, I, 69–88; and by G. P. Murdock (in MS.).

[7] Italicized terms are the nearest English equivalent to the native term and refer to Kwoma kinship categories. Terms not italicized are used in their English sense.

father's sister are also classified in a special manner: her children are called *nephew* or *niece* depending on the sex of the speaker. Her grandchildren are called *grandchild*.

There are special terms for *maternal uncle's* wife, *son's* wife and *daughter's* husband. The spouses of all other relatives are classed with the relative to whom they are married. Thus the wife of an *elder brother* is called *elder brother* and the husband of a *paternal aunt* is termed *paternal aunt*.

Affinal relatives are denoted by a relatively small number of terms. *Wife, wife's brother*, and *wife's sister* are the terms a man uses; *husband, husband's brother*, and *husband's sister* suffice for the woman. Both a man and woman use the same term, *parent-in-law*, for the parents of his or her spouse.

The Kwoma kinship system is extended to include two further categories: *friend* and *ceremonial father*. The category of *friend* is parallel to that of *brother*, i.e., a *friend's* father is called *father*, his sister is called *sister*, and his children are termed *children*.[8] The *ceremonial father* category similarly parallels *father*.

The Kwoma categorize one another not only with respect to their position in the kinship system, descent, and local groups but also with respect to their degree of maturation. There are three main divisions in the maturation hierarchy and two transitional ones. Persons are classified as infants, children, and adults. Each of these categories is characterized by a distinct culture. For example, an infant may suckle but a child may not; a child may play most of the day but an adult may not. Each of the three periods is characterized by relatively stabilized habits. The two transitional periods, weaning and adolescence, are, on the other hand, times of drastic and intensive learning and of the shifting of habits. The Kwoma have names for the persons in the three stable categories, but no particular terms for those in the transitional periods, relying rather on descriptive statements; for

[8] Friends are established at the time of initiation into adulthood. The *ceremonial father* relationship is established at the age-grade ceremony. See chap. vi, p. 106, and chap. v, pp. 65–68.

example, they describe an adolescent girl as one whose breasts are beginning to grow.

The Kwoma class a person as an infant as long as he still suckles. He remains in this category from two to four years, depending upon various contingencies such as his health or the birth of a younger sibling.[9] The weaning period, the transition between infancy and childhood, lasts from one to two years. A Kwoma is usually somewhere between four and six years of age before he is established as a child. The childhood category for boys runs from the end of weaning to the first initiation into the age-grade cycle, which roughly coincides with pubescence. A girl enters adolescence with the ceremony that is held at first menstruation. The period of adolescence extends from the end of childhood to a ceremony in which the boy or the girl is cicatrized. This takes place at about sixteen or seventeen, usually just before marriage for the boy and just after marriage for the girl. All persons who have been cicatrized are classified as adults.[10]

In addition to the maturation hierarchy, there is a system of age grades. A boy is initiated into the first of the four grades at adolescence, and into each of the next higher grades at approximately five-year intervals thereafter. While he is a member of each grade, he is permitted to wear a type of hair ornament which symbolizes his position.

In addition to the categories based on kinship, locality, and age, the Kwoma divide themselves into a variety of groups for the purpose of carrying out economic activities. A brother and sister before they are married, or a husband and wife after marriage, constitute a team to extract sago flour. The households of two or more brothers, or of a father

[9] Although a mother is theoretically prohibited from indulging in sexual intercourse while she is still nursing an infant, not all mothers abide by this rule.

[10] The aged also form a group which properly belongs in the maturation hierarchy. They have been arbitrarily excluded from this study. Old age begins technically when a person has gone through the age-grade cycle first as an initiate and then as an initiator. This puts it at approximately fifty years.

10   Becoming a Kwoma

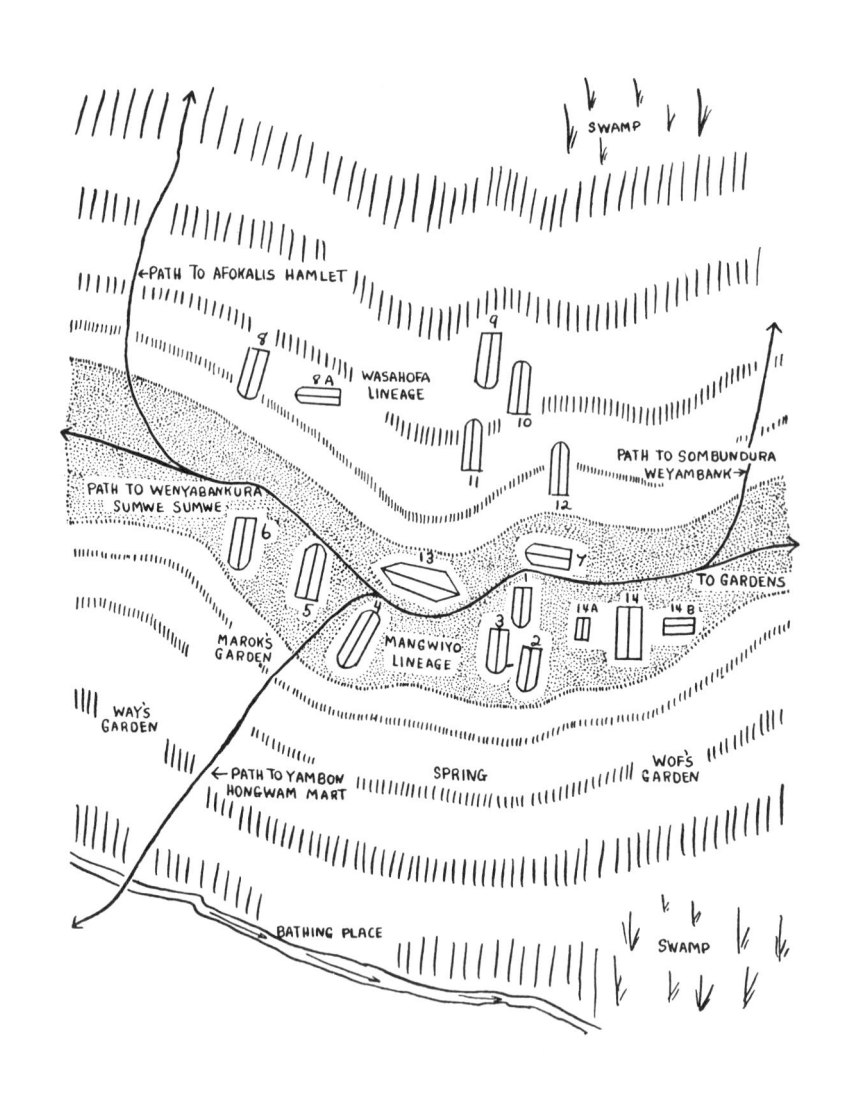

RUMBIMA HAMLET (by household)

Mangwiyow Lineage

1. Wof = Kaya = Chinuwa[11]
   Uka   Mey   Kum

2. Yowaka   Yawa

3. Mar   Gwiyap   Kwiya   Awa   Fit

4. War = Bora = Kuma   Kar = Difa = Yame   Kis = Amba = Sunga[12]
   Mano   Haya   Ham   Suw   Toka

5. Yat = Kafa = Gege
   Gwamp   Njan

6. Way = Mbwimbwi
   Famba   Gwanta   Merik   Kadowan

7. Marok = Dawi   Uka
   Afi

Wasahof Lineage

8. Waramus = Nawa
   (8a)   Mes = Yimba   Aya   Kwos

9. Afok = Kumwe
   Kawaf

10. Fokotay = Ngwiya
    Hambo

11. Daw = Huwena
    Kayamaka   Yawaka

12. Kwal = Gufo
    Angandim   Angeyamar

13. Rumbima house tamberan

14. Houses of investigators
    (14a and b)   Servants' quarters

[11] = denotes marriage, i.e., Kaya and Chinuwa are the two wives of Wof. Children are on the second line in each household, i.e., Uka, Mey, and Kum are Wof's children.

[12] War, Kar, and Kis are brothers. The children are those of War.

and son, form a gardening group who coöperate to raise vegetables. The coöperative work group is composed of a man who needs help in performing some major task, such as clearing a garden site or building a house, and those of his relatives who are willing to help him in return for the feast which he and his wife must provide for them. A larger coöperative work group consisting of men from all the hamlets of the subtribe, builds a house tamberan; and the men and women of the hamlet that is benefited provide the feast. The women of a hamlet unite in informal groups to carry on what little fishing is done.

The trading group meets on appointed days once or twice a week. It is composed of women from one or more hamlets in the sib who bring sacks of sago flour, their male relatives who go to protect them and to gossip, and men and women from the river tribes who bring fish.

Warfare, too, is carried out by a definitely constituted group. The raiding party consists of adolescent and adult males from one or more subtribes who unite for a head-hunting expedition. The whole subtribe, including women and children, is mobilized to greet the returning warriors and celebrate a victory dance and hold a feast.

Kwoma culture specifies who shall perform the necessary legal functions of the tribe. The final authority in disputes between members of different hamlets in the subtribe is a court held at a neutral house tamberan and attended by adolescent and adult males from the whole subtribe. Disputes between subtribes are settled by a court of the men of both tribes meeting on neutral territory. In none of these courts are there legal specialists; each man's opinion is valued in accordance with his prestige in the community.

Religious activities are performed by the yam cult. This cult is divided into three sections: *Yenama*, *Minjama*, and *Nokwi*. Every Kwoma boy in the subtribe is elected during adolescence to either *Yenama* or *Minjama;* young men of promise are inducted into both sections. *Nokwi*, the highest stage of the cult, receives only men who are of high prestige and who have taken a head.

THE LINEAGE OF MANGWIYOW[13]

Family line					
1	(Mangwiyow)				
2		(Yambasowak)[14] — (Ayamingay) — Yat (32)[15] — Njan (6 mo)			
		(Asanamp) — Minjarump) — Wof (45) — Mey (12)			
			(Yuw) — Yimba (18)[16]		
				Buka (10)	
			(Siyow) — Gwiyap (15)		
				Afi (8)	
				Kum (4)	
			(Meyik) — Kwiya (15)		
				Fit (10)	
			(Yaramp) — Mano (24)		
		(Dawangey)	(Cif)		
			Mar (18)		
			Awa (15)		
			Pamba (17)		
			Gwanta (15)		
3		(Sukangarat) — (Mokwot) — Way (46) — Merik (5)			
			Kad (6 mo)		
			Gwamp (6)		
4		(Hafagis) — (Wensungwiy) — Takawur (38)[17] — Mana (12)			
		(Yataminj) — War (34) — Haya (7)			
			Toka (6)		
			Suw (3)		
			Ham (7)		
			(Wonumar)		
			Kar (27)		
			Kis (25)		
5		(Nafwasiy) — (Wenyak) — Marok (25)			
			Uka (24)		

[13] Parentheses indicate that a person is dead. Numbers show approximate age. Female names are distinguished from male by vowel endings, a device for the reader's convenience, not a characteristic of Kwoma culture.
[14] The *brothers* in this generation are arranged from top to bottom in order of seniority, i.e., any man calls a *brother* above him in the list *older sibling*; he calls a *brother* below him in the list *younger sibling*.
[15] The shortened form of the names of living persons who appear frequently in the text has been used rather than the longer form. Thus the long form of Yat is Yataminj, of Wof is Wofaraga, of Mey is Meyamukw. The shortened form is used by the Kwoma in intimate address or reference.
[16] Females of lineage still living in hamlet are included in this table.   [17] Does not live in the hamlet.

Kwoma culture defines the persons who shall dispose of and mourn for the dead. The relatives of the deceased gather to place his body on a platform where it is exposed for several months. Then the members of the subtribe attend a second funeral, for the ceremonial disposal of the bones, and a feast, after which the adult males celebrate the end of the mourning period at the house tamberan with gong, flute, and dance.

These, then, are the variously constituted groups and categories of persons as defined by Kwoma culture. They provide the framework into which a child is born and in terms of which he has to learn to act.

The hamlet in which our house was built, and hence the one from which we gathered most of our information, is called Rumbima. It is situated on a mountain ridge near the geographical center of Hongwam subtribe. (See map.) The men of Rumbima claim descent from the giant fish hawk and hence belong to the *Hayamakwo* sib. They divide themselves into two lineages, the larger claiming descent from the culture hero Mangwiyow, and the smaller from Wasahof.

Mangwiyow is reputed to have had five sons, each of whom sired a family line. Our house was built among the dwellings of the living descendants of these five brothers. The oldest living male in the line whose houses were nearest us was named Wof (household 1, family line 2).[18] He dwelt a few yards from our hut with his first wife Kaya, his levirate wife Chinuwa, his adopted son Mey (a nephew), his adopted daughter Buka (a niece), and his stepson Kum (Chinuwa's son by her former husband). Wof is a man of about forty-five[19] whose skin is grey and scaly from tinea. He has the reputation of being a powerful sorcerer.

Adjacent to Wof's house is the rather dilapidated dwell-

[18] Households are presented both on the map and on the household chart. Family lines may be found on the lineage chart.
[19] Since the Kwoma had no method of counting years, the ages given are rough approximations based on the physical appearance of the individual and on his estimated age at the time of the tribe's first fleeting contact with Europeans, the members of the Behrmann expedition of 1913. (See W. Behrmann, *Im Stromgebiet des Sepik* [Berlin, 1922].)

ing of Yowaka (household 2), an old woman who cannot walk because of a great sore on her leg but who makes up for that with her sharp tongue and loud voice. She is the widow of Yaramp, Wof's first cousin, and the mother of Mar (see household 3). With her lives Mar's betrothed, Yawa, a rather unattractive and lazy adolescent girl.

Yowaka's son, Mar (household 3, family line 2), the owner of the third dwelling in this cluster of houses, is a tall gangling youth who has not adjusted very well to Kwoma society. He shows marked anxiety about expressing himself sexually and aggressively, and appears unable to measure up to the standards of behavior set by the culture with respect to these drives. With him live his adolescent sister Awa; two of his father's brother's children—Kwiya, an adolescent girl, and Fit, a boy of eight or nine; and Gwiyap, an adolescent nephew of Wof's.[20] Gwiyap, perhaps my best informant, is a lad just past puberty. He is not yet fully grown but is extremely intelligent, very active, and has learned to speak pidgin English fluently.

Just across the path from these three houses is that of Marok (household 7, family line 5). With him live his wife Dawi, his married sister Uka,[21] and his adopted daughter Afi, the real sister of Gwiyap. Marok is in his middle twenties. He is the only male of his age group in the hamlet who did not leave for a time to work for the whites. For this reason he is also the only one who speaks no pidgin English.

About fifty yards down the path from the houses of Wof and Marok is a dwelling shared by three brothers with their wives and children (household 4, family line 4). War, the oldest, a man in his thirties, is a cleanly built, thick set person with a somewhat cocky air. He has the highest status in the community, being renowned as a head-hunter, singer,

[20] It is unusual for an unmarried adolescent to be in charge of a household. This came about as a result of the death in rather quick succession of the fathers of Mar, of Fit, and of Gwiyap. Actually, Wof and Yowaka kept a sharp watch over the household. The three houses were near enough together so that they could do this quite effectively.

[21] She is living with her brother while her husband is away on a three-year contract to work on a white man's plantation.

dancer, and man of great personal courage. He had two wives, Bora and Kuma, but Bora left him during my stay in the hamlet, taking with her her young daughter Toka. By Kuma he has had three children: Mana and Haya, girls of approximately eleven and eight, and Suw, an infant son. Ham, a nephew, about seven years old, also lives in the household. Kar, the next younger brother, is an intelligent young man in his middle twenties who returned from working in the gold fields just before our arrival and who speaks pidgin English fluently. He has two wives, Difa and Yame, but no children. Kis, the youngest brother, like Kar, worked out a three-year contract in the gold fields and speaks pidgin English. He also has two wives, Sunga and Amba, but no children.

Down another fork in the path, a few rods from the house shared by War, Kar, and Kis, stands that owned by Yat (household 5, family line 1), a stocky, volatile man a year or so older than Kar. He is the only man in the hamlet who has learned pidgin English working in the gold fields and has also taken a head. He has two wives, Kafa and Gege, and one son, Njan (John), born shortly after my arrival at Kwoma. There are no other members of Yat's line living in the hamlet.

Very near Yat's dwelling is one owned by Way (household 6, family line 3), a rather spindly, sneaky man in his forties, who has some reputation as a sorcerer. With him live his wife Mbwimbwi, his two adolescent daughters, Famba and Gwanta, and his two young sons, Merik, just weaned, and Kadowan, a few months old. Way also has taken care of his nephew, Gwamp, ever since the latter's father, Takawur, was driven from the hamlet for attempting to rape War's wife.

About fifty yards down a steep path from Way's house is the dwelling of Waramus (household 8, family line 7), who is about fifty and the oldest man of the hamlet. He is slightly cross-eyed and has a reputation for sorcery equal to that of Wof. With him live his wife Nawa, his eighteen-year-old son Mes, his sixteen-year-old daughter Aya, a young son Kwos, a boy of about eight, and Yimba, who is the wife of Mes and

THE LINEAGE OF WASAHOF

Family line

6 (Wasahof)——(Hokungay)——(Mbondunk)——Fokotay (35)——Hamb (7)
                                                     ——Kawaf (2)
                                       ——Afok (30)———Yawa (15)
                                       ——(unknown)

7 ——(Eleyaf)——(Hokwaw)——Waramus (50)——Mes (18)
                                      ——Aya (16)
                                      ——Kwos (8)

8 ——(Afokwalump)——(Hafaduk)——Daw (36)——Kayamaka (7)
                                       ——Yawaka (5)
                            ——Kwal (34)——Angandim (4)
                                       ——Angemar (1)

a niece of Wof.[22] Mes has started to build a house for himself and Yimba near that of his father. There are no other members of Waramus' line dwelling at Rumbima.

A short way down the mountainside from Marok's house is the dwelling of Kwal (household 12, family line 8), a quiet, hard-working man of approximately thirty-two. He is married to a woman named Gufo and they have two boys, Angandim, a young child, and Angemar, an infant. Kwal's older brother, Daw (household 11, family 8), lives in the adjacent house with his strapping wife Huwena, and two girl children, Kayamaka and Yawaka. These two families comprise the second line of the Wasahof lineage.

Two brothers head the third and final line of the lineage of Wasahof. They live together a little farther down the path which passes by the last two households described. Fokotay (household 10, family line 6), the elder, is a jovial but rather ineffectual man of forty. He is married to Ngwiya, and has only one child, a little girl called Hambo. Afok (household 9, family line 6), a few years younger than Fokotay, has a keen sense of humor and is somewhat more forceful than his older brother. Except for those who have worked for Europeans, Afok is the only adult who has made any attempt to learn pidgin. Although he has learned only a little, he seems to get considerable pleasure from the attempt. He lives with his wife Kumwe and their infant son Kawaf. Yawa, Mar's betrothed (household 3), is also a descendant of this line, her deceased father being a brother of Fokotay and Afok.

The Wasahof lineage thus numbers only fifteen living persons.[23] Six wives swell the group to twenty-one. The Mangwiyow lineage has thirty members and thirteen wives. This makes a total of sixty-four persons living in Rumbima hamlet. Persons from the other five hamlets were interviewed primarily to check information gathered at Rumbima. The Mangwiyow lineage provided more material than did the Wasahof lineage, both because it was larger and because we

[22] A theoretically incestuous marriage.
[23] This does not include the women who have married and left the hamlet.

were more closely associated with it. All our best informants —Yat, Kar, Kis, Mar, Mes, Gwiyap, and Mey—spoke pidgin English, and all were of the Mangwiyow lineage with the exception of Mes. They also acted as interpreters when those who spoke only Kwoma were questioned. Gwiyap, Mar, Mey, and Mes were hired as house and shoot boys so that they were virtually always around. This permitted a great deal of unobtrusive questioning and observation of their behavior.

A short statement of the social positions in which the Kwoma placed the investigators may be useful in order to indicate the direction of the biases and lacunae in the data. At first we did not fit into any of the simple categories into which they had divided Europeans. A summary of the history of Kwoma contact with whites will clarify what being white meant to them. The first contact was in 1913 when the Kwoma killed a police boy[24] connected with the Behrmann expedition, for raping one of their women. A Kwoma was shot in reprisal. From this time until the Australians brought them "under control" in 1928, the Kwoma had little contact with Europeans. Since then they have come only occasionally in touch with white recruiters, traders, missionaries, and Australian government officers.

According to their own retrospective accounts, the first conception which the Kwoma had of the whites was that they were unnatural beings. They called them *ngamba* (ghost), a word which is also used to refer to a person who commits some heinous crime. It corresponds roughly in meaning to the English words "inhuman," "monstrous," or "unnatural"; and it would appear that this feeling persists, to some extent, to the present day. After I had been living at Rumbima for about six months, I came back from bathing at the spring below Mar's house without bothering to put my shoes on. Awa and Kwiya were sitting under Mar's porch. I had become quite friendly with these two girls, as I had frequently gossiped and joked with them on my almost daily

[24] Natives trained by both the former German and present Australian territorial governments to act as constables under the orders of a white officer.

visits to Mar's house. They had never seen me without shoes on, however, and when they saw my white feet they shuddered and turned away, indicating strong revulsion and horror. Mar told me afterward that the girls were sure that I was a ghost after they had seen my feet.

Another event that was important in determining the attitude of the Kwoma toward Europeans took place in 1928. Two Australian police boys, while foraging for food at Hongwam, met and raped two Hongwam housewives. The husbands and relatives of these women attacked and killed the two police boys. When the Australian officer in charge of the district discovered the murders, he visited the tribe with a squadron of police boys, killed about twenty of the natives,[25] cut down their orchards, and burned their house tamberans. The natives who escaped fled into the bushes and swamps. The patrol officer built a house and stayed with his entourage until he had enticed the natives to return to their territory and had established order. During this time he tried to make clear to the natives that they had been punished for homicide and that, if they had grievances, they should bring their case to the "government" and not take the law into their own hands. He also let it be known that the Australian government was ready to punish anyone convicted of head-hunting or sorcery. Despite this warning, the Hongwam carried out a successful head-hunting raid a few years later. The patrol officer again visited the tribe; however, he could not discover the actual culprits, and so merely gave the assembled people of Kwoma a severe lecture threatening dire consequences similar to those of 1928 if there was any further evidence of head-hunting. He also forced a group of Kwoma, including Gwiyap, Mar, and Fit, to witness the hanging at Ambunti of some river natives who had been convicted of taking heads.

When we arrived at the government station at Ambunti on our way to Kwoma, the patrol officer stationed there sent a police boy to Hongwam to order all the adult males to come to the station and carry our luggage over the mountain.

[25] Seventeen of those killed appear on the genealogical charts.

About a dozen of the Hongwam obeyed this command but said that it was impossible to take the luggage by land. The patrol officer scolded them because more had not come and told them that they lied about the road being impassable. He explained that two white men were coming to stay with them for a long time to learn their language and customs. He then ordered them to return home and gather as many men as possible the next afternoon at the foot of the mountain, where we would land after taking the river route by canoe, to carry our baggage. The patrol officer decided to go to Kwoma with us because it was an appropriate time to make his yearly visit to the tribe and because there was also a special matter to attend to. Several Hongwam natives had signed a contract to work on a plantation but had bolted back home before their time was completed. It was the patrol officer's job to make them fulfill their contracts. We were accompanied into Kwoma territory, therefore, by the patrol officer and a company of police boys. On the day after our arrival he commanded all the natives to assemble at Rumbima house tamberan near which we had camped. When they arrived he took the annual roll call and recorded births and deaths. He scolded the natives because many of them had not responded to the assembly summons. He said that the excuse of being away in their gardens was not sufficient and unless they all came on his next visit there would be trouble. Then he asked where the four runaways were. No one knew. He said that if they came with him to fulfill their contract all would be well, but that if they did not they would be hunted out and put in jail. In response to this threat one gave himself up, but the other three remained hidden. The patrol officer then announced to the assembled tribe that we had come to study their language and customs and were going to stay a long time. He ordered them to build a house for us and warned them that if anyone harmed us he would be severely punished by the government.

In order to complete the description of the status of a white man in Kwoma culture, it should be noted that white recruiters had on several occasions visited the tribe in person, or else had sent native emissaries, during the previous decade, and had enticed a dozen or more of the young men to leave with them to work either on plantations or in the gold fields. The old men had strongly opposed this because it put a great economic burden on them to have so many able-bodied men leave the tribe. Mothers feared that their sons would never return alive, sisters were left without brothers to help and protect them, and the young women were left with fewer lovers. On the positive side, however, the families of the recruited boys were given axes, knives, plane irons for adz celts, and other European articles which were extremely valuable to the Kwoma who had hitherto known only tools of stone, wood, and bone. Then the young men came back from their work with more tools and with money with which to buy pigs and shells from the river natives as well as with many tales of the wonders of white technology and the peculiarities of white customs. Yat, Kar, and Kis were the only ones to go from Rumbima.

When we arrived, therefore, white men were classed in two categories: government agents and recruiters.[26] The former were dangerous; the latter both annoying and useful. Since we arrived with the patrol officer, we were first classed as "government." Furthermore, since we came at a time when the patrol officer was trying to force runaways to return, many of the people of Hongwam believed that we were special emissaries sent to bring these fugitives to justice. It was not until we had lived in the community for four months that we even saw these young men. On the other hand, since we brought many boxes of supplies and trade goods, we were classed in part as recruiters. In fact, the older men continually warned us not to entice young men to leave the tribe with us. Wof put it: "Don't take Gwiyap and Mar to America with you. We need them to help with the work of the hamlet." Their fears came true, for when I left with a recruiter, Gwiyap, Mar, Mes, and four other boys "signed on" with

[26] The Kwoma had had so little contact with missionaries and traders that these people hardly formed distinct categories.

him. As a result, none of my Kwoma friends would speak to me or bid me good-by.

In so far as we were included in the social structure of the Kwoma, we were known as *masta bilong Rumbima*. This meant that we belonged to the Rumbima hamlet of Hongwam subtribe, a natural consequence of the position of our house and the frequency of our contacts with Rumbima people. We were also placed in the kinship structure, being assigned to the Hayamakwo sib, Mangwiyow lineage, and Asanamp family line as younger brothers of Wof. Logically this should have made us *older brothers* to everyone else of the parent generation in the hamlet, but actually we were called *younger brother* by most of them. Those of the first descending generation called us *elder* or *younger uncle*, except Mey, Gwiyap, and Mar who frequently called us *father*. The fact that we were not married, but were apparently older than any unmarried Kwoma should be, made our position in the maturation hierarchy somewhat anomalous. We were sometimes classed as adults and sometimes as adolescents. The latter tendency was accentuated by the fact that we did not know the culture but were learning it.

With this short account of the environment and of the various groups into which the Kwoma divide themselves, with this indication of our chief informants and brief description of our position in Kwoma society, the task of describing the habits which a Kwoma learns as he passes from stage to stage along his life cycle may now be undertaken. The framework presented in this chapter has but limited meaning for the infant, more for the child, and gains full significance only when adulthood is reached. The following chapters are an attempt to present the culture as it unfolds to the maturing individual at Kwoma.

CHAPTER II

INFANCY

KWOMA infants[1] up to the time they are weaned are never far from their mothers. It is, in fact, very seldom that they are not actually in physical contact with her. Having turned over most of her household duties to her co-wife or some female relative, the mother may hold the child all day and give it her undivided attention. She sits either on the earth floor or on a bark slab under the porch of the family dwelling with the baby nestling on her outstretched legs. At night the infant sleeps cuddled by her side. Whenever she has to move, she carries the child with her cradled in her arm, sitting on her neck, or, less frequently, straddling her hip. The hours that she spends sitting, however, far outnumber the total time spent in standing or walking around with the baby. This is especially true during the first few months, when she considers it dangerous to the child's health to leave the house. If the child appears robust at the end of three or four months, the mother may venture out to the house of a neighbor to visit and show off her infant, but she will not go beyond the limits of the hamlet until the fontanel hardens. This precaution results from the belief that infants are especially susceptible to sorcery before this time and that they should therefore not be subjected to undue risks. For the same reason any visitor except a close relative is unwelcome in a house where there is a newborn infant. Two children were born in the hamlet during my stay, but I was not allowed to see either of them until they were about three months old.[2]

Hunger produces one of the earliest and most persistently

[1] The infants from whom most of the data were obtained were Yat's son Njan, who was born a few weeks after my arrival, Way's son Kadowan, who was born a few weeks after Njan, and Suw, the son of War, an infant who was slightly over three years of age, but retarded by yaws and malaria.
[2] This made the observation of infants extremely difficult and accounts in large part for the paucity of data in this chapter.

recurring discomforts that an infant experiences. The mother keeps her breast constantly available, so that for the most part the infant is able to satisfy this drive by merely exercising the innate sucking reflex. He does learn, however, that certain preliminary behavior is useful in bringing satisfaction more quickly and efficiently. He learns to turn his head to take the nipple in his mouth, to stop sucking from one breast when it becomes dry, and finally even to lift himself from a prone position to a vantage point from which he can suckle. Suw, one of the older infants of the hamlet, had learned to do all these things very adeptly. Kadowan and Njan, whom I first observed when they were three months old, depended almost entirely on the mother to lift them to the proper position, to help them get the nipple into the mouth, and to change the breast for them at the proper time. Nevertheless they already manifested some of these instrumental acts in incipient form.

Suw, who was almost old enough to be weaned, had learned to grasp other objects besides his mother's breast and to put them into his mouth. At times he even crawled about the porch floor in order to examine things which caught his interest. One of his first responses to these objects was to lift them to his mouth. Compared to ourselves, the Kwoma are exceptionally permissive toward this type of behavior. I once saw Suw with the blade of a twelve-inch bush knife in his mouth and the adults present paid no attention to him. As a result of such trial-and-error investigations, the child learns to discriminate between the edible and inedible. Mother's beads, father's adz, or brother's pith ball not only do not satisfy hunger but sometimes even hurt one's mouth.

Toward the end of infancy the Kwoma mother begins to prepare her child for weaning by introducing foods other than milk into the diet. At first she bends over and transfers masticated food from her mouth into that of her child. Later she gives him a spoonful of soup or a bit of gruel. Even infants as young as Kadowan and Njan were given a small piece of pork to chew on; this probably served both as nourishment and as a pacifier.

Bladder and colon tensions give an infant little trouble. He simply evacuates when the pressure becomes strong enough. The mother makes no attempt at toilet training while the child is still an infant; she simply learns to anticipate his bowel and bladder movements, quickly lifting him from her lap and holding him over the earth floor. The feces are then wiped up with a leaf. Sometimes the mother does not lift the child quickly enough and he urinates on her leg. In such cases the leaf is again used, and the child is not held accountable for the mistake.

A mother prevents her infant from smearing. This indeed is the only act for which I observed a Kwoma infant punished. One afternoon Suw defecated on his mother's leg. She moved him aside and called to an older child to fetch her a leaf. While this was being brought, Suw began dabbling in the feces and put some in his mouth. The mother contorted her face and said: "You must not play with feces; they are bad."[3] She rather roughly yanked Suw's hand from his mouth and held it. After I observed this case, I asked several informants whether it was a usual occurrence. They all insisted that it was not, maintaining that feces are naturally disgusting and even doubting that I had seen Suw behave in this manner. The fact that I did observe this behavior shows that, unless Suw was an exception, the disgust reaction is not so strong or innate as my informants believed it to be and indicates the probability that it was the product of cultural conditioning.

I have no direct evidence concerning the sexual behavior of Kwoma infants. I did not observe any infant masturbating; but I was only able to watch them during the afternoon visiting hours so that the evidence is inconclusive. However,

[3] The word used in this connection is *kafwa sek*, which is a term meaning bad, nasty, disgusting, rotten, and the like. A facial expression of disgust usually accompanies its use. *Kafwa* is a word which refers to a white substance reputedly used by certain sorcerers to poison their victims. I was once shown the flyblows on a dead dog and told that this was *kafwa* and proof that the dog had been killed by sorcery. *Sek* may be related to the verb *seka*, which means "to grow." The punishment in this case applied to eating as well as to playing with feces and was thus a restriction on eating habits.

the general permissive attitude which a mother exhibits toward her infant suggests that she may also allow it freedom to discover this mode of gratification. On the other hand, the fact that older children are not permitted to masturbate in public might influence the mother to prohibit this type of behavior in her infant as well. The fact that both Kum and Merik, boys who were in the weaning period, fingered their genitals without being punished suggests a permissive attitude toward masturbation as perhaps the more plausible assumption.

Although a mother tries to protect her infant from pain inflicted by the natural environment, frequent experience with suffering is unavoidable. It is practically impossible for her to ward off the clouds of hungry mosquitoes that are continually present. The extreme temperature variations are often unpleasant. In the afternoon, with humidity at a maximum and the temperature around ninety degrees, the heat is stifling. By contrast, a damp foggy morning with the temperature at seventy is uncomfortably cold; I would shiver in a thick sweater while the natives huddled by their fires. Teething is another source of pain which every infant must endure. Yaws and malaria are prevalent diseases at Kwoma. Informants told me that no one ever grows up without contracting the former. Certainly few youths or adults can be seen who do not bear scars of yaws sores. The infant's physiological immaturity makes him for the most part dependent on his mother to help him cope with these natural pains just as he depends on her to feed him.

Crying is selected as the most effective response which a Kwoma infant can make both to pain and to hunger. It constitutes an injunction to the mother to discover the source of the trouble. Her first response is to present the breast. If this fails to quiet him, she tries something else. If she believes that the child is crying because he is too hot, she moves him away from the heat of her body. If she thinks he is cold, she cuddles him. If his crying calls her attention to a mosquito on him, she brushes it off and scratches the bite. If she suspects that sores from yaws are hurting him, she tries to move him into a more comfortable position. If he seems to be crying because he is sick, she tries to distract his attention by crooning to him, rocking him gently, and patting him. One mother, by putting a stone in a tin can, had invented a rattle which she used in these circumstances. Each time a mother reacts to her child's crying by discovering and removing the source of discomfort, she rewards this response in her child. The situation in Kwoma is such that, for the young infant, crying is followed by the alleviation of pain more frequently than is any other response.

When the infant begins to talk, he learns an even more efficient technique for securing help. A mother does not always know the trouble when her infant cries, but his words elicit immediate and appropriate help. A Kwoma infant who has learned to speak may say, "Mother, my back itches," or "I am cold; warm me." The mother rewards these demands by removing the source of discomfort. This indicates one of the advantages of learning language and hence why an infant is motivated to do so.

Thus during infancy the response to discomfort which is most strongly established is that of seeking help by crying or asking for it. Responses such as approaching the breast, moving to avoid pains, and other independent acts are also established. They form a basis for later learning, but hold a less important position in the response repertory of an infant than that of seeking help.

A motive which becomes strongly established during infancy is the wish to be near to and touch the mother. Almost all the pains and discomforts which an infant experiences are reduced while he is either sitting in his mother's lap or lying by her side. He is fed there, he sleeps there, and he is warmed and cooled, scratched and petted there—always while in bodily contact with his mother. The following case indicates the strong attachment that an infant has for his mother's lap and how loath he is to leave it. Mbora one afternoon was teaching her infant son Suw to venture from her lap. She was rolling a ball a little way from her and then putting Suw down and gently urging him to retrieve it. He crawled a few feet toward the ball and then returned to his mother. She took him back into her lap and rocked him in her arms and patted him for a while. She then asked someone for the ball and let Suw play with it. Then she rolled it away again and told him to go get it. This time he retrieved the ball and was again rewarded. During weaning, as we shall see, the strength of this desire to touch and be near the mother is even more clearly demonstrated.

An infant's reaction to the social environment is pleasant but limited. Except for smearing he is rarely punished.[4] Since, moreover, almost all his needs are satisfied by the help of his mother, he inevitably develops a strong attachment to her. By comparison, other persons are relatively unimportant in his life. His father sometimes picks him up and holds him for a few minutes to display him to a visitor, but he soon returns the child to his mother, especially if he starts to cry. A mother never entrusts her young infant to an older brother or sister to hold, even for a short while, unless she is near to supervise. Next to the mother herself, her co-wife cares for a child more frequently than any other person. It is she who usually holds the infant when the mother needs a short respite from the constant care. The only other persons who are allowed to touch the child are its grandparents, its father's *brothers* and *sisters*, its *mother's brothers*, and the spouses of these persons; but to be held by them is a rare occurrence. The mother stands out as by far the most important figure in the infant's life—a person essential to his very existence.

Sickness is the chief source of anxiety for a Kwoma infant. The mother, successful in bringing about the reduction of other discomforts, knows no efficient means of coping with most of the diseases which her child contracts. Indeed, one method employed to cure minor ills increases the infant's pain instead of reducing it. If he complains of a headache

[4] Masturbation and biting the mother's nipple may be two other exceptions to the rule of complete facilitation. All informants stated firmly that an infant is never punished.

or stomach-ache, the mother cuts the skin on his temple or belly and allows blood to flow from the wound.[5] In this sphere, therefore, an infant experiences pain without anticipating any possibility of its reduction except by slow and natural means.

Very few aggressive responses are established during infancy. The infant is not big or strong enough to alleviate pains by removing the source. Loud crying is, however, established at this time. A parent will say, "The infant is cross."[6] Nevertheless, a mother helps her infant even if he is crying angrily. In fact, the louder he cries, the more effort she expends trying to aid him, so that aggression is rewarded rather than punished. Infants also gain some success in the technique of killing mosquitoes, an act classed as aggression in Kwoma culture.[7]

As regards prestige, the Kwoma infant enjoys in a sense the most dominant social position that he will ever attain. His every command is obeyed, and all his wants are attended to. For the remainder of his life he can only expect to have his commands obeyed after he has, by the expenditure of considerable effort, gained a position of high prestige.

---

[5] Such pains are supposed to be caused by an accumulation of bad blood. This theory will be described below. See chap. iv, p. 64.

[6] *Wejowa,* "to be cross"; or *owambato,* "to speak angrily."

[7] The Kwoma term for killing a mosquito is *yogisa fiju,* "to fight a mosquito." *Fiju,* "to fight," is the general term for aggression.

CHAPTER III

THE PERIOD OF WEANING

WEANING marks the end of the infancy period.[1] It is a gradual process for which the mother prepares the infant by substituting solid foods for milk and by coaxing the child to spend more and more time on the floor of the porch rather than sitting in her lap. When she eventually decides that he is mature enough, usually during the second or third year, she prevents further breast feeding. She chooses the time in accordance with the adequacy of her child rather than his chronological age, a sickly child being weaned later than a healthy one. Several informants stated that infants stop breast feeding of their own accord, but others said that the mother stops the flow of milk by daubing her nipples with the sap of the breadfruit tree, a thick, viscous fluid, which is used by the natives as glue. If the infant is very persistent in trying to continue to suck, the mother may tell him that a *marsalai*[2] has taken the place of her milk, sometimes emphasizing this story by placing a leech on her breast.

After he has been weaned, the child must learn to depend entirely on the diet of his parents. He becomes adept at drinking soup from coconut-shell bowls, learns to munch the sago briquettes which his mother has cooked for the family, and begins to eat meat with his sago just as his parents do. He also learns that he cannot eat whenever he is hungry, but

[1] Wof's stepson Kum supplied most information on this phase of the process of socialization. He was a bright lad between four and five years old. Merik, Way's son, was also in this period. He was an unhappy child of about Kum's age, who seemed to resent the birth of his younger brother Kadowan.

[2] *Marsalai* is the pidgin English term for a class of huge supernatural beings who dwell in the swamps surrounding the tribe. These monsters usually take the form of great snakes or crocodiles. The belief in these monsters is widespread both in New Guinea and in Australia (cf. M. Mead, "The Marsalai Cult among the Arapesh," *Oceania,* IV [1933], 37–53).

must wait until his mother prepares a meal at the regular time.[3]

Cleanliness training begins at approximately the same age as weaning. The mother is comparatively gentle in teaching her child toilet habits. She tells him that adults go outside near the garbage heap[4] to urinate and that he is big enough to do likewise. Similarly, she points out that adults do not defecate in the house but in the household latrine.[5] She takes the child with her to the latrine and holds him while he relieves himself until he has learned to do this without assistance. When I asked an informant whether a mother punishes her child if he persistently defecates in the house, he answered: "No, of course not. He is her own child, isn't he? Why should she punish him? It is her duty to clean up after him if he defecates in the house." Although this may express the theoretical position of the Kwoma native, in actual practice the infant is more recalcitrant, and the mother less patient, than the statement would indicate. One morning I heard Kum's stepmother scolding him for defecating inside the house. She was telling him that he had been very naughty and that he must come and clean up the mess. The boy, however, had hidden somewhere in the underbrush, and repeated calls did not induce him to return. Gwiyap and Mey, his older *brothers*, were sent in search of him but were unable to find him. Half an hour later he reappeared unconcernedly. By this time the stepmother had cleaned up the mess, and her anger had cooled enough so that she administered only a mild scolding.

Both Kum and Merik, the only two boys in the hamlet in the weaning period, habitually fingered their genitals, and often stood with one hand on the penis. This may have been a habit which they were learning at this time or it may have

[3] Children of this age may be given a cold sago briquette between meals.
[4] The garbage heap is usually close by the porch of Kwoma dwellings and in sight of those who sit there so that no one can steal sorcery material (food leavings) from it without being observed.
[5] Each household has a specified spot, usually marked by a tree, or some such landmark, and situated a few rods from the house, which the members of the household use as a place of defecation.

been one that they had already learned during infancy. In any case neither parents nor older siblings scolded them for this behavior although it was often done in their presence. Kum showed considerable interest in the genitals of other males,[6] staring at those of his father and older brothers. Perhaps the discovery of his own penis as a source of gratification stimulated his interest in the genitals of others.

While a child is being weaned he must learn many new and independent habits for coping with pain. He has to warm himself by the fire rather than by contact with his mother's body. He must suffer the pain from pressure against his yaws sores, or change his position until the pain is relieved. He no longer has someone to brush the mosquitoes from him but must deal with them alone. He must go down to the spring with his older siblings and wash himself with cold water instead of being gently bathed by his mother with warm water. When it rains he must run into the house if he wishes to keep dry.

When a child is weaned he may no longer sit in his mother's lap by day nor lie by her side at night. This is apparently felt as the most severe frustration experienced at this period of life. No longer is it possible to attain the vantage point from which all drives have hitherto been satisfied.

Kum's behavior indicated an especially strong desire to be near his mother and to touch her. When she came back from work in the evenings he would usually clasp and hug her leg. When she left in the morning he would cling to her, begging to be taken with her. When she sat in the house making a net bag or cooking a meal, he would stand beside her and often lean against her shoulder. Chinuwa, the mother, would never allow him as much contact as he seemed to want. When he hugged her leg or leaned against her side she might tolerate it for a moment, but would soon push him away and tell him to stop annoying her. Kum reacted to one of these rebuffs by

[6] Both men and women in Kwoma society go naked with the exception of some of the young men who have, within the last few years, adopted the custom of wearing laplaps (calico wrap-around skirts) from their contact with Europeans, and a few of the younger women who have recently procured blouses from white traders.

throwing himself on the ground screaming with rage. On another occasion he wept silently with his forefinger in his mouth. Usually, however, he would move away a little, look at his mother, and then move cautiously toward her again, as though in a state of conflict. Merik exhibited similar behavior, but to a less marked degree. His mother had not respected the prohibition against cohabitation while still nursing, so that his infancy period had been cut somewhat short by the birth of a younger sibling. His behavior seemed to indicate that he had already learned that he could not hope to regain his infantile pleasures, but that he was not yet mature enough to turn to the childhood play group.

With weaning, then, many of the demands which the Kwoma child has learned to make during infancy become no longer successful. His mother no longer responds in the same helpful way to many of his requests. His demands to be taken into her lap, scratched, patted, or warmed, are now ignored. When she no longer heeds his demands, he becomes more vociferous. Unless he is in serious danger, however, she still does not cater to him. He then reverts to the earlier response of crying. When this fails, he tries other responses in his repertory. For example, one morning Kum's mother put on her net bag to go to the swamp to collect sago. Kum, observing her, said, "Mother, I want to go too." "No," she replied, "you must stay at home." Kum repeated his request more vigorously, but his mother did not heed him. Then he began to cry, but still without success. His crying increased in intensity until he was screaming. His mother, having finished her preparations, started down the path. Kum ran after her and clasped her leg, trying to hold her back, and shrieking. When she disengaged her leg he threw himself on the ground and rolled over and over in the grass.

If a child is too vociferous and persistent in his demands, he is actually punished. One morning Kum was calling to his mother, who was a short way down the mountainside gathering firewood: "Mother, come! I am hungry. Mother, come! I am hungry." She answered at first that she would be home shortly. Kum kept on shouting until finally his mother stopped answering him. Then he began to wail. His older *brothers*, who were playing ball a short distance away, told him to be quiet. His stepmother, who was working in the house, after several times telling him to hush, finally gave him a scolding.

During the weaning period a child continues to receive help from his mother if he is in grave danger or sick. If he contracts malaria or some other serious disease, she will take him back into her lap and minister to him. If he has a headache or stomach-ache, she attempts to cure him by phlebotomy. When Kum once got lost in the forest, his mother and both his *brothers*, guided by his cries, searched until they found him and brought him home. Thus a child must learn to discriminate between serious dangers and minor pains. Demanding is still successful as a response to the former situation, but it is necessary to discover a new mode of coping with the latter.

Parents and older siblings teach a child to anticipate pain. They point out dangers so that he may avoid them before he is hurt. They warn him about snakes, scorpions, nettles, and other objects in the natural environment that may injure him. He soon discovers that if he does not heed their warnings, the predicted pain does follow, and so he learns to heed them.

Parents and older siblings extend their warnings to include supernatural dangers. They tell the child that huge, snakelike monsters which cause storms dwell in the swamp, and that it is dangerous to go near their dwelling places. This danger is brought within the sphere of experience of the child when his mother tells him that a *marsalai* occupies her breast and vivifies the story by putting a leech on it. A child is also warned during the weaning period not to venture out at night, for this is the time when ghosts are abroad; and not to go too far from the house unless accompanied by an older person, for if he does a sorcerer may kill him.

A child at this age also learns that people as well as the

natural environment may inflict pain upon him. His parents push him around, scold him, and sometimes even spank him.[7] They strike hard enough to give meaning to their commands and scolding, but not hard enough to injure him. His older siblings also scold and punish him. He learns to respond to punishments with two special forms of behavior: obeying and escaping. He learns that if he does as he is told he will not be punished. He also learns that if he runs away when someone threatens him he is less likely to be hit. Kum was playing with a broom one afternoon and started to take it out from under the porch. His older *sister* noticed this and told him to bring it back, starting toward him threateningly. Kum dropped the broom and ran. The *sister* did not pursue him.

Thus during the weaning period, except when he is in serious danger, a child is forced to give up demanding as the preferred response and must learn new and independent habits. He is aided in this learning by warnings from his parents and older siblings. These warnings are extended to include beliefs about supernatural dangers. Finally, it is during this period that a child begins to experience pain from other persons and learns to obey commands and to escape from threats.

Weaning greatly increases a child's experience of anxiety. His desire to sit in his mother's lap and his fear of being pushed away and scolded for it, the desire to suckle and the belief that there is a *marsalai* in his mother's breast, the wish for his demands to be heeded and the punishments he receives for crying, all are anxiety-producing sources of conflict. As has already been shown, obeying, escaping, and learning new habits are the means by which he reduces these anxieties. Sickness, however, remains an unresolved source of anxiety.

Aggression still plays a minor rôle in the life of a Kwoma during the weaning period. In some ways aggressive behavior is less successful at this time than it was during infancy. Although the child becomes more adept at killing mosquitoes

[7] Kwoma parents customarily spank their children by striking them between the shoulder blades with their open hands. They do not hold the child, but chase him if he attempts to escape. The child is usually able to elude the parent after one or two blows have fallen.

and eliminating similar minor dangers, he is now punished for becoming angry with his parents, as was shown by the scolding received by Kum for crying loudly for his mother.

In the realm of prestige, the Kwoma child during the period of weaning plunges from the very top to the very bottom of the social hierarchy. Most of the commands which he issues are now ignored, and the help which he expects is denied him. Furthermore, he has to learn to obey the commands of others during this period. His control over his social environment is at a minimum.

CHAPTER IV

CHILDHOOD

WHEN the child[1] has relinquished his attempts to recapture the preferred habits of infancy, his mother gives him a little bag which she has netted for him and his father the betel-chewing accoutrements to go with it. They tell him that he has become a little man. He now turns to the play group and spends his time playing games with other children, roaming in the forest, and participating to some extent in adult activities. The sexes avoid each other from this time, the boys and the girls forming separate play groups.

The widening of a boy's contact with the environment necessitates new discriminations about the edibility of things. While playing in the forest he comes across luscious-looking berries which may cause his death if he does not know that they are poisonous. Kwoma boys play a game in which they kill lizards and snakes and cook and eat them in a playhouse[2] in the jungle. Some of these reptiles are good to eat; others are poisonous. The parents warn the child about the objects that are poisonous. When I went for a walk with a native, he would frequently point out some class of objects to be avoided. Children were as likely to teach me as adults. Once a little girl of eight was scathing in her comments about me because I did not know that a certain berry was not good to eat. Although I observed no specific example of an older sibling using this technique on a younger one, I feel confident that it occurred rather frequently. In any case, the training

[1] Mey, Fit, Kwos, Gwamp, Ham, and Hamb—boys, and Afi, Buka, Haya, Toka, Kayamaka, and Yawa—girls, constituted the personnel of the childhood age group of Rumbima hamlet. Mey, Fit, Kwos, and Ham spent much of their time running in and out of my house and playing near by and therefore provided most of the observational data on the boys in this age group. Afi and Buka, who lived in houses next to mine, provided most of the data on girls.

[2] A rough bough hut which children construct for play.

of Kwoma children is very effective in this respect. Errors and warnings sharply differentiate the things in the environment which may, and those which may not, be eaten, with the result that Kwoma children show a remarkable knowledge of the local flora and fauna.

Parents provide their children with a general formula to keep them from eating harmful food. The formula is: if you do not know a thing is good to eat, do not try it. I have no data on how this fear of strangeness is transmitted to the child, but I did observe the fact that children generally reacted with fear to strange objects and persons.

A Kwoma child learns that, in addition to things naturally inedible, there are also foods which are made poisonous by sorcerers. Boys and girls are told never to eat food given them by a stranger or a non-relative, for it may be poisoned by the insertion of a magical white powder. As an example of parental training on this point, Wof refused to allow Mey and Fit to eat at my house because I bought bananas, pawpaws, yams, and other vegetables from people of other hamlets. He also warned us not to eat this food, for we might have enemies in the tribe who would try to poison us. Another illustration of the manner in which this eating restriction is inculcated occurred when Marok's dog died. It was his best hunting dog, and both he and his wife and sister were very fond of the animal. When it died, they wailed as they would have done for a member of the family. It died early one morning, and the women mourned throughout the day. By afternoon flies had gathered about the dead animal and laid their eggs upon it. Mey, Fit, and Buka were with me when Marok pointed to these flyblows and told me that this was the poisonous white powder which sorcerers use. This was definite proof, he said, that someone had tried to poison him or one of his family, but that the unfortunate dog had eaten the food instead and died as a result. All the children of the hamlet soon knew the imputed cause of the dog's death, and it is probable that this knowledge served to strengthen their fear of food not prepared by relatives.

A child is warned about another type of sorcery which also

pertains to food but is concerned with how and where a person can safely eat rather than with what he can eat. A child is taught to be very careful with his crumbs and other food leavings. He is warned that, if someone steals such material and performs a certain magical rite upon it, he will sicken and die, and that, therefore, he should be particularly careful if he eats anywhere but in his own house. It is difficult for a thief of sorcery material to steal leavings from the floor or rubbish heap of your own dwelling because he would be killed on the spot if he were caught at it, but a sorcerer can pick up food leavings left in the forest with little danger of discovery. Since relatives may not sorcerize one another, one may eat in their houses if one is careful, but parents warn children never to eat in the house of a non-relative, for a crumb may fall, no matter how careful they may be, and non-relatives are not to be trusted. A child is warned that his blood is another material which must be kept from the hands of sorcerers: therefore, if he cut himself, he should take care to catch or wipe up the blood in a leaf which he should burn or hide in a safe place. He is also warned that his blood "goes into" any animal that he kills, so that he must be careful not to spill the blood of such an animal.

A child does not have to be warned frequently about the dangers of sorcery because his parents show such fear of it.[3] Whenever anyone is sick in the hamlet, practically the only subject of conversation is sorcery. Adults speculate about the identity of the sorcerer and curse those whom they suspect. Everyone is worried and emotional. The almost hysterical reaction of his parents to sorcery impresses the seriousness of the danger upon the child so vividly that it is not difficult to teach him to be careful.

In addition to learning that he may not eat things naturally poisonous nor food contaminated by sorcery, the child is conditioned against eating food which belongs to someone else. In other words, he comes face to face with the property

[3] Emotional attitudes as well as overt habits are subject to imitation. See N. E. Miller and John Dollard, *Social Learning and Imitation* (New Haven, 1941), chap. xiv.

concepts of the culture, and must learn to respect them. As an infant, he suffered no such restriction, for no food that was available to him was prohibited on these grounds. During the weaning period he received some training in this respect, but it is especially during childhood that this learning takes place. In contrast to discriminating between things on the ground of their edibility, this restriction on behavior is not supported by natural characteristics such as hardness, bitterness, or poisonousness; it is a man-made prohibition, and must be inculcated entirely by means of social rewards and punishments.

A Kwoma child learns that he cannot eat any food that he sees, but that he may do so only if he has regarded certain property rights.[4] Several times a week his older sister or his mother brings a net bag laden with fruit and vegetables back from the garden. Bananas, plantains, spinach, coconuts, yams, and taros are emptied out on the porch floor to be stored or cooked. The child soon discovers that he cannot help himself freely from this pile of food. If he does so, his mother or sister scolds him: "Don't take those bananas; they were picked from So-and-so's tree and we are going to use them in soup." Sometimes he is told that certain fruit or vegetables come from his own tree or from his own plot in the garden; in this case, his mother is not cross with him if he takes some, but says: "Those are your bananas, but it is your turn to contribute to the family pot. If you eat them now, we won't have enough for the soup." On other occasions he may begin to help himself to a breadfruit that his older brother has just roasted for a between-meal snack, and get a kick or blow and a volley of abuse from this brother when he is discovered. On the other hand, he finds that if he first asks if he may share the snack, his brother usually gives him some.

After considerable trial and error of this kind, as well as after explanations and examples from parents and older sib-

[4] Property rights in respect to tools, toys, etc., follow the same formula as property in food; but since Kwoma children have few toys or tools, it is with respect to food that property rights are primarily learned.

lings, the child learns that all the vegetables which come from a certain plot in the garden, and the produce of certain trees, belong to him. He learns that he can take and eat this food without interference, except that he must contribute his share to the family soup pot when his mother asks for it, and must share with his brothers and sisters when requested, if he expects them to reciprocate. He also learns that other persons in the household are usually willing to share their food with him if he asks permission and that sometimes he may even properly help himself without asking. The circumstances which determine when one should ask for food and when one may take it without asking were too subtly shaded for me to appreciate. I can simply record that Kwoma culture contains both these customs and that children learn to distinguish between them.

A child learns that persons outside his household are much more severe with him if he takes food without asking than are his own parents and siblings. Fear of sorcery makes a man suspicious even of his *brother's* children, and if they take food without asking for it, he may suspect their intentions.[5] A child is therefore even more careful to respect the property rights of the other members of the hamlet than he is of those of his household mates, and, as we have seen, this avoidance receives support from the sorcery complex.

The *maternal uncle* holds a unique position with respect to property rights. A child has the right to take any food that he wishes from this relative and need only announce the fact to him. In so doing, however, he incurs the responsibility of paying a considerable amount of shell money to him at the time of the age-grade ceremonies.

Since a Kwoma child can get food belonging to another person without being punished only if the owner gives permission, he develops varied techniques of begging. No stigma is attached to begging for food, and one may even wheedle or beg after an initial refusal. A hard-luck story which may be

[5] Although there is a taboo on sorcery between relatives, suspicious action from a relative arouses the fear that the taboo may be broken.

entirely false is permissible, as is a huffy reaction implying, "Well, you are no friend of mine, then."

Children also develop the technique of thieving. They discover that if they take food secretly and then deny that they have done so, they can, if they are adept enough, escape the usual punishment. If they are caught stealing, however, they will be even more severely punished by the owner than if they openly took the food. Despite the greater punishment, most children develop the art of thieving. Mar and Gwiyap both told me that when they were children they stole tobacco, areca nuts, and other foodstuffs from their parents and carried them to the forest playhouse to enjoy.

Since the stealing of food leavings is a necessary step in carrying out the form of black magic most frequently practiced by the Kwoma, some parents are reputed actually to train their children in the art of stealing. Mey, according to his *brother*, Gwiyap, was being thus trained by Wof. The frequency with which he stole things from me and the technique which he employed tend to support this statement. One evening when he thought I was not looking, he took some of my cigarette papers from the table. I accused him and he blandly denied that he had taken them, showing me his empty hands to prove it. I looked under the table and saw that he had dropped the papers and attempted to kick them out of sight. On another occasion he asked me for some tobacco and I refused. A few minutes later he pulled an areca nut from his pocket and said that someone had attempted to sorcerize him and that if I looked carefully at the nut I would see the tiny holes where the poison had been inserted. It was by mere chance that I glanced up from my examination of the nut to see Mey quickly withdraw a handful of tobacco from the tin. He had invented the sorcery story to distract my attention.

However adept the child may become in begging and stealing, he must learn at this time that as an adult he cannot live by these means alone; he must acquire prescribed work habits in order that he may be able to wrest food from the environment when he assumes the responsibility for supporting himself and his dependents. Thus, during childhood, he begins to participate in the hunting, gardening, and collecting occupations of his parents.

Even as an infant a Kwoma has begun his training in working for food by learning to clamber to his mother's breast. Later, during weaning, habits of helping himself to food and eating have been developed. Now the whole cycle of planting and harvesting, hunting and fishing, collecting and processing, unfolds before him, and little by little he learns to participate in one or another segment of these activities.

A child learns that most of his food must be cooked before he can eat it and that if he wishes to eat between meals he must learn this technique himself. At any time of the day boys may roast a bunch of plantains or a breadfruit. Sometimes they build up the fire on the hearth of their mother or older sister, but more frequently they cook their snacks in groups of two or three in the forest. They learn to cook by watching and imitating their mother, and by trial and error. Girls, in addition to this, are specifically trained. They are told by their mothers what to do and criticized if they do not do it correctly. Boys also receive some specific training if they try some of the more complicated dishes such as gruel or soup. Both girls and boys are expected to help their mother when she is cooking the main meal, standing ready to pass her a utensil or to fetch the bamboo water container. She is severe with her children for negligence in helping her, scolding them if they do not carry out her orders. Kaya, for example, severely reprimanded Mey for bringing her the old mixing sticks when she wanted the new ones.

Since water and firewood are necessary for cooking, a supply must be kept constantly to hand. This is woman's work, and consequently does not affect the boys.[6] A girl in the childhood age group accompanies her mother to the spring and brings back a small bamboo of water, and also forages for firewood with her mother. Older girls, though still in the childhood age group, are often given the responsibility of

[6] A boy will occasionally help his sister fetch water or firewood as a favor to her, but not as a duty.

Childhood

getting the wood or water on days when their mothers are busy with some other task, and are punished if they do not. One day Buka forgot to get firewood, and Wof, her father, beat her for her negligence, when he returned and found none.

Children of both sexes participate in the work of gardening[7] by helping to clear the site. It is their duty, together with the women and old men, to clear the ground of underbrush while the adult men are in the treetops lopping off the branches. In contrast to some of the other gardening tasks reported later, children are expected to help with this work and are scolded by their parents and older siblings if they do not. Toward the end of childhood the boys are allowed to climb some of the smaller trees and try their hand at "man's" work.

In the process of breaking the ground and planting, the children usually accompany their parents to the garden site and watch the work. The older children sometimes help by putting the seed beside the hills. The younger ones, on the other hand, are likely to get bored and to retire to the edge of the forest to play. Children are forbidden actually to put seed yams in the ground, for only an adult who has been elected to *Nokwi*[8] may do this. When the yam shoots break the ground and it is time to hang stringers up which the vines may climb, the family again goes to the garden, the women carrying the split liana stringers and the men draping them from tree limbs. The older girls help their mothers by carrying a small bundle, the boys their fathers and older brothers by keeping them supplied with lianas. If the boys get tired of this and wish to play, the men carry on by themselves. Ham and Mey, for instance, on one occasion helped for about an hour and played during the rest of the morning. Weeding is the responsibility of adult women, and girls only help if they wish to. When the yams are harvested the children render more effective assistance, the boys in picking

[7] Gardening and other economic tasks in which the child participates will be described in more detail in succeeding chapters.
[8] *Nokwi* is the highest stage of the yam cult.

up the yams that have been dug, the girls in carrying the harvest home.

Kwoma parents develop their children's interest in the work of gardening by setting aside a section of garden for each of them. The section is carefully marked off with bamboo poles laid end to end on the ground, and its produce is put in a separate bin in the family storehouse as the child's private property.

Children do not participate in the process of extracting flour from the pith of the sago palm. This is a task which requires the coöperation of one man and one woman, and the technique has been so worked out that a third person would be a nuisance rather than a help. Children often go with their parents and watch, but do not actually crush or wash the pith until they are big enough to do the whole job, that is, not until adolescence.

Hunting is restricted entirely to men. Boys begin as soon as they reach the status of childhood, chiefly killing snakes and lizards. They usually kill these animals with sticks or stones, but sometimes capture them with a noose tied to the end of a stick, an implement which they manufacture themselves. Bows and arrows are known to the Kwoma, but they are poorly constructed and rarely used. A boy's father usually makes him a small bow and some bird darts, and the boy then tries stalking birds. He never attempts a shot unless he can get within a few feet of the bird, and even then the poorly constructed arrow shot from a crude bow is likely to go wide of the mark. Despite the poorness of the weapons, some boys become remarkably adept at stalking. Mes, an adolescent who had won a name for himself as a good stalker, became my shoot boy. He had, of course, never fired a gun in his life, but I instructed him in its use and he took about a dozen practice shots at a target. On his first foray for pigeons he brought down three with only four shells.

It is not until adulthood that a Kwoma may become a hunter of big game. A child is taught a healthy respect for wild pigs, and is not allowed to play with a spear, the principal hunting and fighting weapon, as it is considered too dangerous. Children compensate for the taboo against the use of real spears by playing several dart-throwing games. A favorite sport of this type consists in tossing a pawpaw[9] up a slope and attempting to transfix it with a sharpened bamboo dart as it bounds down. In another common game, children toss a rock into the air and try to hit it with stones before it falls to the ground. As a result of such games, they become very adept at hitting moving objects, a habit which stands them in good stead when they become old enough to go pig-hunting.

Kwoma children participate in caring for the domesticated animals of their parents. They are given a small pig of their own to tend which they must feed, habituate to the dwelling, and teach to come at their call. Parents often give their child a puppy to pet and care for. A child calls his pets by the kinship term for *son* or *daughter;* the other members of the family refer to the pet by kin terms which accord with this relationship.

Fishing is considered by the Kwoma rather as a sport than as a serious activity. Girls participate in what little is done, often simply scooping fish from a swamp pool or mountain stream with their hands. Although men do not deign to waste their time fishing, boys sometimes accompany their mothers and sisters to the stream and join in the fun. Even as children, however, they feel that they somewhat demean themselves by doing this.

Children watch their parents make tools but do little such work themselves. Boys sometimes help their parents by fetching materials for various utensils, and girls begin netting bags before they reach adolescence, but otherwise toolmaking is restricted to older persons.

In general, the Kwoma child discovers that it is necessary to work to get food, and learns, in part by observation and in part by participation, the techniques that have been developed in the culture for producing it. He is forced to assume responsibility for some of this work, is allowed to help with

[9] A tropical fruit about the size, shape, and consistency of a small muskmelon.

other tasks if he wishes, and is definitely debarred from still others. Although this work is directed toward the satisfaction of hunger, the children cannot always appreciate this and must be coerced. A Kwoma does not take full responsibility for many of the tasks until adolescence; then he learns by experience that no work means no food. The coercion, as we have seen, consists in scolding or beating the child for not doing the tasks expected of him, and in warning him of the dire consequences which follow an undesired act.

Cleanliness habits are usually already established by the time a boy or girl reaches childhood. Informants stated that if a slip occurs it is the child's own business except that he is forced to clean up after himself. The following example indicates how sanctions actually operated in a case of enuresis. One night, when the mosquitoes were very bad, Buka, a girl about eight years old, slept with her mother, older sister, and younger brother in the screened room in my house. The next morning I found a puddle on the floor. Soon after breakfast the two young girls came in shamefacedly and offered to clean up. They lied to me, saying that Kum had wet the floor and that they were going to punish him for it. While they were carrying out the rug, their *paternal uncle* came in, scolded Buka, and beat her. She cried and ran home. The uncle then told me that it was Buka's own business if she wet the bed as long as she cleaned up after herself. He said that he would not have scolded her if she had done it at home, but wetting my floor was an insult to me which must be punished. Several of the onlookers referred to the act as that of an infant and said that she was old enough to know better.

Sexual conditioning begins in earnest during childhood. A boy is punished for looking at the genitals of any female. He is scolded and even beaten if he does this, the person at whom he looks usually being the one who does the punishing. Informants stated that learning takes place primarily with respect to the mother and sisters because they are the females with whom the boy comes most frequently in contact. When a woman scolds a boy for staring at her, she tells him that he should not look at her genitals because they are her private

Childhood

property.[10] From this time on a male must avoid looking at the genitals of any woman except those of a lover or wife.

The sexual response for which a boy is most severely punished during childhood is that of tumescence in public. Any female who observes a boy with an erect penis is expected to beat the member with a stick. It is usually the boy's older *sister* who takes the responsibility for inflicting this punishment. I never saw this punishment actually administered, but I did observe boys with erections on two occasions. While playing at my house one morning Ham had an erection. His older *brothers*, Gwiyap and Mey, noticed it and teased him about it. They told him that he should be ashamed of himself and warned him not to let any females see him that way. On another occasion Fit was observed by his playmates with an erect penis and was similarly teased. Shortly after this I was visiting at Fit's house. His *brother*, Gwiyap, began telling his older *sisters*, Awa and Kwiya, about what had happened to Fit, illustrating the story in a joking manner by putting a stick between his legs. Awa and Kwiya laughed at Gwiyap but they scolded Fit. "You had better not let us catch you that way or we will beat you. What are you, a baby? You should be old enough to control yourself." Fit was much discomfited at this. He denied the truth of Gwiyap's story, told him to shut up, and finally left the house sullenly. Kwoma inculcation on this point is apparently very effective for I observed no adult, and, in fact, no other child with an erection.

A boy is also restricted from fingering his genitals. Anyone who observes a child touching his penis scolds him for it. They tell him that he should not do it because this part of his body belongs to his future wife, and that masturbation will cause injury to his penis. The training is effective enough to prevent the child, who during the weaning period was allowed to touch his penis, from persisting in this habit. I did not observe any boy child manipulate his genitals, and

---

10 *Enji mbumbowi*—"My something." This expression is also used to establish property rights, thus bringing the act in context with offenses against ownership and property.

boys of this age even refrain from touching them while urinating.

I cannot say whether this prohibition also prevented private masturbation. I asked Ham, Fit, and Mey, all of them boys in the childhood group, whether they played with their penises when they were alone. All of them denied it with considerable embarrassment. They hung their heads, pretended not to understand me, and changed the subject as quickly as they could. This embarrassment suggests that they were guilty about masturbation, but it does not indicate whether they actually did not masturbate or whether they did and were afraid to admit the fact.

Boys who have not seen one another for some time rush together, throw their arms around each other, and hug and pat one another and rub one another's cheeks with their lime gourds. They exhibit this behavior with boys of their own age and sometimes with older men, but never with a female. Such an embrace is permitted between the sexes only when they are both aged and related. Mey, Fit, and Ham frequently chose to sleep together in my house rather than at their homes. They were often joined by adolescents. Although this was attributed to the advantage of mosquito proofing, they usually slept huddled together and often with their arms around one another.

Kwoma boys frequently play a game with sexual connotations: one boy chases another, throws him down, and simulates copulation with him. Other boys in the group then take advantage of the aggressor and pretend to copulate with him until four or five boys line up in this way all laughing and yelling with enjoyment. Then, when the bottom boy has broken free and the chain disintegrates, there follows a hubbub in which each boy calls another his wife and claims to have impregnated "her." Adolescents often join the game, and, when they do, the children have great difficulty defending their "honor." When this game was the fad, one or another group of boys played it almost every day for a period of over a month.

Boys often tease one another sexually when they sleep

Childhood

together. In a manner similar to that associated with the "homosexual" game, each claims that the other is his wife and will have a child by him. On one occasion Ham slept in the mosquito net with Wysep, one of my houseboys, when the latter's wife was away. The next morning Gwiyap and Mey began teasing Ham, saying that they suspected that Wysep had had sex relations with him and that pretty soon "his belly would swell up." Ham hotly denied the accusation, but the kidding persisted until Ham retired from the scene.

As far as I could observe, there was very little genital contact established either in the games or when the boys slept together. Sodomy is believed to be unnatural and revolting, and informants were unanimous in saying that anyone who would submit to it must be a "ghost" and not a man. Although this sanction theoretically applied only to the person who played the passive rôle, it seemed to be effective in restricting the practice.

The sexual training of a girl during childhood differs somewhat from that of a boy. Although she is punished for masturbating, in a manner similar to that of the boy, her conditioning differs in other respects, the most marked contrast resulting from the fact that the difference in her anatomy relieves her from the punishment which a male receives for having an erection in public. On the other hand, she is scolded by parents and older siblings for exposing herself unduly. She is taught to sit modestly with her legs stretched out together before her, and never to draw her legs up or sit with them apart. She is also warned not to lean over when a man is behind her unless she is wearing her net bag hanging down her back. Furthermore she is told that a modest girl should step aside from a path if she sees a man approaching and stand with her back to the path until he has passed. She should not address him until he has gone by, at which time she may speak to him over her shoulder. When a girl is immodest, however, she is punished much less severely than is a boy. She is rarely more than scolded for such a lapse. The girl is also treated more leniently than the boy in that she is not restricted from looking at the genitals of the other sex.

Kwoma culture defines this as immoral only on the part of the boy.

Although a Kwoma becomes considerably more independent on entering the status of childhood, he still relies upon his parents in cases of serious injuries or sickness. If he has a bad boil, a parent or older sibling will lance it for him with a bamboo knife. They treat his sores by irrigating them with warm water in which certain herbs have been cooked. The cooked herbs are used as a sponge and the medicated water is squeezed over the sore. They pick away the proud flesh so that the wound does not heal over too quickly, and force the child to sit quietly in the sun so that its rays strike the sore. When a child suffers from an ache in the stomach or head or from a sprained and swollen joint, one of his parents will practice phlebotomy upon him as they did during the weaning period. Parents react to serious sickness in their children by specialized anti-sorcery behavior to be described later. A child coöperates in these activities, but the responsibility rests with the parents.

A child's environmental horizon widens upon his entry into childhood. When he ranges into the forest with his playmates and accompanies his parents to swamp and garden, he comes into contact with aspects of the environment which may be injurious. He learns to cope with them more and more by himself. Sometimes he discovers that aggression, at other times avoidance, is the more appropriate response. He kills scorpions, lizards, and small snakes which threaten him, but learns to avoid the larger animals. If a large snake appears on the path, he will walk around it. He keeps away from places where he may meet wild pigs or crocodiles. He learns not to step on sago bark unless the thorns have been removed and therefore to take care in walking in the mud of the swamp. He learns which of the bushes and shrubs in the forest bear nettles and which can be walked through with impunity. He learns to predict when a storm is coming so that he may return to the house before it begins to rain.

A child's parents and older siblings continue to help him avoid these dangers by warning him. In consequence, a child may learn to avoid or kill a scorpion even though he has never been bitten by one. So it is with other dangers, especially the more serious ones; if children were permitted to learn to avoid wild boars or crocodiles by actually experiencing pain from them, the society would soon disappear. Parental warnings come true frequently enough so that children usually heed them.

A child is not permitted to show excessive fear of his environment. If he is too afraid of a small snake or lizard to kill it, or if he is afraid to walk in the swamp lest he be pricked by a thorn, his older *brothers* will tease him and his parents will scold him. An overanxious child is usually called a "baby" in a derogatory manner.

The warnings of parents and older siblings include supernatural dangers. A child is taught that certain glens, springs, rocks, and trees are dwelling places of *marsalai*, and he learns the names of the supernatural beings who inhabit them. He is warned that, if he goes too near one of these places, the monster will cause a violent storm and high wind that may blow down the dwelling of his parents, or it will "shoot" a sago needle into his foot for disturbing it. Such a needle, although invisible, is very painful and can be removed only by adult operators who have mastered the special magical technique. Actual storms and unseen needles are used to impress the validity of these beliefs upon the child. Whenever there is a severe storm, the adults in the hamlet speculate as to who has disturbed the *marsalai*. Was it Yat who was clearing a garden too near to the rock in which Kumbundum dwelt, or was it Wof who went hunting near the bog inhabited by Kurumbukwas? Similarly when a child reported that he had a pain in his foot which felt like a thorn but which he could not see, his parents would say: "There, you see. You have been 'shot' by a *marsalai*. We told you to beware of disturbing them."

A child is warned that he should not go near the house tamberan while the yam-cult ceremonies are being held. He is told that at this time the adult men of the tribe consort with *marsalai*. He is warned that although men can do so with impunity, it would be extremely dangerous for children and women to be near the scene. In fact, a child is told that he would die if he entered the house tamberan at the time of a ceremony. Cases are cited to the children of women and children who had joined the men at this time either willfully or by mistake and who had died as a result. The initiated tell the children that the gongs, trumpets, flutes, water drums, and bull roarers that they hear at the time of a ceremony are the voices of the *marsalai* who are present. Hints that these are man-made sounds come seeping down from adolescents and the careless remarks of adults, so that the child has a fairly accurate knowledge of the ceremonies before he ever participates in one. Despite his scepticism about the origin of the sounds, he nevertheless is awed whenever a ceremony takes place, and takes care not to venture near the scene. Furthermore, he takes care not to reveal to the adults that he has any suspicion of what really goes on.

Despite a child's awe of these meetings of the yam cult, he senses the excitement which prevails in the whole subtribe before a ceremony takes place and eagerly looks forward to the time when he will be old enough to attend them. He hears his father, *uncles*, and *older brothers* talk excitedly about the coming event, he sees them carefully paint their faces, comb their hair, don their best ornaments, and depart for the house tamberan. Then he hears the rhythmic harmonies of the gong orchestra, the high-pitched shouting of the singers, and the weird and plaintive flute melodies. These thrilling sounds burst out sporadically during the whole day, increase in tempo and intensity as night falls, and continue unabated as long as he stays awake. Stimulated by these events, Kwoma boys make toy gongs from bamboo nodes and try to imitate the gong rhythms; they hum mimicries of the ceremonial songs; and they form miniature groups to practice the shuffling dance steps. Since they are not supposed to know these things, they do them in their forest playhouse or at times when there are no adults present.

Parents and older siblings also warn a child not to trespass in another person's garden lest he break out with boils. They tell him that the owner of a garden usually casts a spell on it so that anyone who enters it will be afflicted in this way.

Ghost lore is taught during childhood. The child is told that the spirits of the dead live on a mountain at the edge of the tribal territory, where they lead a topsy-turvy existence. They go by canoe on land and walk upon the water; they sleep by day and venture out at night. Often they assume the shape of a bird or beast. After dark they are attracted by whistling. They frequent a corpse, especially just after death. A child is warned that a ghost is dangerous, and is taught that it is the wish of ghosts to take his soul to the land of the dead. Close contact with them is therefore also dangerous,[11] and a child is told not to go near a burial platform. Sometimes ghosts appear in nightmares and struggle to take the soul of the dreamer. Sometimes they possess people and make them irresponsible for their actions. In these cases a child is taught to be aggressive toward the ghost. When a person is possessed or has a nightmare, those who are present at the time, children included, beat the air with sticks and shout curses and commands at the ghost in order to frighten him away.

A child is punished if he does not heed the warnings of his parents and older siblings. This holds in both the natural and the supernatural spheres. Since I did not know the culture, I was, in a sense, in the status of a child. One day when I was walking in the swamp with Kar and Gwiyap, they pointed out a water hole that was supposed to be the dwelling place of a *marsalai*. I poked my walking stick into it. Kar shouted at me to take it out, then told me very seriously of the danger of doing such a thing. Gwiyap joined in the scolding.

The following case illustrates strikingly the punishment of a child for not heeding a warning. When some of my shotgun shells spoiled, I cut off the shot and lit the powder, which went off with a puff and amused the natives. Kwos, one of the

[11] The belief that all death is due to sorcery is somewhat contradictory to this. The Kwoma are not very specific about the mechanism of death, but unless a person is sorcerized a ghost cannot succeed in taking the soul. Ghosts are nevertheless feared.

children in the hamlet, saw me doing this, stole some shells, and tried to do it himself. His older brother, Mes, saw him and told him that shells were dangerous and that he had better not fool with them. Kwos paid no heed. He tried to light the shell, but it did not go off and he looked to see what the trouble was. At that moment the powder exploded, seriously burning one side of his face and closing one eye. Mes scolded him severely: "I told you not to play with those shells. Why didn't you heed me?" His father also scolded him: "You will probably go blind, but it is your own fault. Why didn't you heed your brother? He told you not to play with the shells." No one in the hamlet expressed sympathy for Kwos's injury; everyone blamed him.

The number of punishments that a Kwoma receives from other persons increases markedly in childhood. He is frequently beaten and scolded by his parents and other persons of their generation. They order him to do household chores and scold him for being lax about them. They shout at son or daughter, nephew or niece, to stop yelling and rushing around the house when they are resting or trying to carry on a conversation. They scold the child for snooping into cult secrets, for not helping a *brother* who needs aid, or for damaging the household property. One afternoon Ham was wandering about under the porch of Wof, his *paternal uncle*. The latter, irritable because of an argument that he was having with his wife, roared at Ham to sit down. Ham dropped as though he were shot, and Wof began scolding him severely. He accused Ham of being a little thief and of trying to steal something. Ham began to cry and as soon as he dared got up and ran home. The incidents of Wof beating his daughter for not getting the firewood, and that of Kwiya scolding Mey for not passing the proper mixing sticks, have already been reported.

A child is kicked and beaten, scolded and teased, by his older siblings even more than by his parents. Older siblings imitate their parents, commanding, scolding, and punishing their younger *brothers* and *sisters*. Older *sisters* punish a boy if they see him with an erection, a girl if she sits immodestly.

Older *brothers* scold younger *brothers* for showing a precocious knowledge of cult affairs, or for not heeding their warnings and younger *sisters* for annoying them or for not carrying out their household chores properly.

A boy is most frequently hurt by his older *brothers* in the course of games. The most popular sport consisted in kicking a pith ball up a slight slope against the side of a house and then, when it rolled down, kicking it back up again. In this, as well as in the dart-throwing and "homosexual" games, the older and bigger boys tease the younger one and knock him out of the way when he interferes. They order him to retrieve the ball or the pawpaw when it bounds into the bushes, or to throw the target rock for them. In the "homosexual" game it is the smaller boy who is usually at the bottom of the pile and who is called "wife" by the older boys.

A child becomes adept at avoiding punishment from older persons by obeying, escaping, lying, and being secretive. He learns that if he does not do what he is told, a blow will follow; that if he persists in doing what he is told not to do, he will be beaten. Thus he not only learns to obey commands, but also to anticipate the commands, that is, to follow custom. He also learns that, if he has disobeyed, he can often escape punishment by running away from the person who has issued the command, or by lying if someone accuses him of doing something wrong. Finally, he learns that he can do things of which the older people disapprove, if they do not observe him. He therefore learns to be secretive. Smoking in the bush house is one example. Masturbation may be another. A child also learns secretly to beat cult-gong rhythms, being careful that no older person is present when he practices. Kwoma parents do not punish a child for lying or being secretive; they only punish him if the misdemeanor is discovered. Children therefore become very adept in these arts of deception.

A child has his first success in social aggression toward his younger siblings. They, being smaller than he, are easily overcome when they threaten or interfere with him. When they get in his way in games, it is not difficult to shove them aside nor dangerous to command them to get out of the way. If they jostle him when he is about to throw a dart into a pawpaw, he can kick or beat them without fear of effective retaliation, and he is rewarded for doing so when they thereafter keep out of his way. If younger *brothers* or *sisters* take some food which he intends to eat, he can force them to give it back if he catches them at it or prevent a future recurrence by punishing them after the event. When younger siblings tag along despite his wish to be with boys of his own age, he can command them to stay behind and back up the command with a blow if he is not heeded.

Such is the success of aggression toward younger siblings that a child often expresses it even when they do not threaten or annoy him. Kwoma boys and girls continually tease their younger *brothers* and *sisters* and order them about apparently for the pure joy of it. Presumably by so doing a child both reassures himself that he is in a position to be successfully aggressive toward these younger children and at the same time finds expression for the aggression generated by older persons which he usually dare not manifest.[12] Thus he gains practice in expressing aggression toward persons who are not responsible for producing it—a type of response which he frequently employs in later life.

Toward the end of childhood, when social aggression has been greatly strengthened by success with smaller persons, a child may sometimes express it toward those older than he. If he does so, he usually escapes immediately afterward. It is, so to speak, "hit and run" aggression. Fit's feud with his older *brother*,[13] Mey, exemplifies this. One morning Mey was teasing Fit as they were eating breakfast. Fit lost his temper and cursed Mey by telling him to cohabit with his sister. Mey

[12] As soon as a child learns to be aggressive in response to a threat, this behavior tends to assume ascendancy over avoidance, because in the former case the goal of the activity in progress need not be given up, whereas in the latter it often has to be. Thus a child should develop a wish to be aggressive toward his parents rather than to obey them, but, since he dare not do so, he takes it out on his *brothers* and *sisters*.

[13] Mey was only slightly older and bigger than Fit. I should guess twelve and ten as their respective ages.

returned the taunt, whereupon Fit hit him on the head with his fist. Mey scrambled up, grabbed a burning brand from the fire, and ran after Fit, who had started to flee. Mey managed to strike Fit twice on the back before the latter made good his escape. The next day Mey reported that Fit had stolen or destroyed the contents of his (Mey's) net bag and fled to his mother's house in another hamlet.[14] Fit did not return for a month. All went well for about two weeks thereafter. Then one afternoon the two began wrestling at a time when Fit had a razor blade in his hand. Fit lost his temper in the scuffle and cut a deep gash in Mey's lip. He then ran away, but, hearing indirectly that Mey did not bear a grudge, returned after a couple of hours. Two weeks later Fit stole a knife from Mey and again ran away to his mother.

A child is sometimes aggressive even toward his mother and father. For the most part, he expresses it indirectly in such ways as grumbling under his breath when he receives an order from them, or insulting them behind their backs. Sometimes, however, the tendency to aggression becomes strong enough to overcome fear of retaliation. Gwiyap reported that, when he was a child, he had been infuriated with his father for scolding him, had seized a spear, and had attempted to run it through his parent, but someone present had prevented him from carrying out his purpose. He also told of an occasion when he had struck his stepmother. She had been sitting by the fire cooking and had asked him to pass her a ladle. He delayed in doing it, and she began to scold him. He became angry at this and "punched her in the nose." She picked up a stick to beat him with, but he ran away. Mey reported a similar story of an occurrence several years before. He said that he was lying on a platform which was built shoulder high on the limb of a tree in front of his house. He had a sharpened stick in his hand and was lying in wait for his mother because he was angry with her. Finally, she came close to the platform and he jabbed her several times as hard as he could on her head and shoulders. According to

[14] Fit's father had died, and his mother had married a man of another sib.

Mey's story, the blows knocked her down and gave him a chance to scramble off his perch and dash away. His mother chased him, but he had too great a start. Both Gwiyap and Mey reported that they stayed at a *paternal uncle's* house after these incidents until their parents' anger had cooled. When they returned, they got a scolding but were not otherwise punished.

A child is taught to be polite, not aggressive, toward those of his relatives who do not dwell in the hamlet. He learns to behave properly toward his *mother's brother*, his *mother's sister*, his *father's sister*, and their children. A child's parents teach him to greet[15] these persons and to address each of them by the appropriate kinship term. Although these relatives seldom command a child, he is expected to obey them when they do. Not only is a child punished by his parents if he is rude to one of these relatives, but he is warned that unless he behaves nicely toward them, they will "break relationship"[16] with him. Then they will be like non-relatives, and he may no longer visit them with the expectation of a warm welcome. He may not eat food at their house lest they sorcerize him. Finally, he can no longer avail himself of the special privileges that his relationship to them implies. To the young child this threat of a broken relationship has little meaning; he is polite to his uncles and aunts because he has learned that it is expedient to obey his parents. As he becomes older and discovers that he may help himself to the produce of the garden and sago plot of his *mother's brother*, and that his *father's sister* gives him something to eat whenever he visits her and treats him just as does his own father but never scolds him, the threat of the loss of these privileges begins to become meaningful and he takes care to behave properly toward them.

A child also learns to behave appropriately (i.e., to be polite and friendly, not aggressive) to the children of his

---

[15] Greeting consists of repeating an abbreviated form of the phrase, "You and I may eat together without fear of sorcery."

[16] Any kin relationship may be broken, in which case the two persons behave toward one another as non-relatives. This will be described in more detail in later chapters.

father's *friends*.[17] His parents teach him that these children are his *friends*. He is told that he can visit and play with these children without fear of sorcery, and that he should be nice to them when they come to visit him.

A child is taught to fear and avoid non-relatives,[18] as has already been mentioned in connection with sorcery. He is also warned that they are dangerous for reasons other than sorcery. Non-relatives, he is told, not only do not help and protect him as his relatives do, but may even have little compunction about hurting him. In addition to warnings, the child receives many object lessons from the bitter exchanges of insults and threats of violence which occur not infrequently between the adults of the hamlet and those not related to them. He learns, on the other hand, that non-relatives belong to the same subtribe as his own family and that therefore there is a limit to their danger. He comes to understand that they and his relatives have a considerable community of interest; that they will stand together against aggression from outside; that they participate jointly in ceremonies and court meetings; and, finally, that a complicated web of kinship bonds interlaces the whole subtribe and holds it together. A boy learns the names of non-relatives. If he meets one of them he may exchange a brief greeting and gossip for a moment, but, in contrast to a meeting with a relative, he is reserved and anxious. He never enters the house of a non-relative unless accompanied by an older person, and seldom plays with unrelated children.

A child is taught that foreigners[19] are even more to be feared than non-relatives. Not only will they sorcerize him without shame, but they have little respect for his life or limb. He is told stories of head-hunting raids, and most Kwoma children actually experience a raid in which some acquaintance or relative is killed and decapitated by a group of foreigners seeking prestige.

[17] A ceremonial pseudo-kin relationship established at the time of initiation to adulthood.
[18] Unrelated members of the subtribe.
[19] A member of another subtribe who is not a relative by marriage.

Social sanctions as well as fear of retaliation play a part in determining the manner in which a child will react to pain from the social environment. Custom as well as natural expediency dictates when it is appropriate to be aggressive, when submissive. Custom also specifies the manner in which either of these responses may be expressed. Members of the community stand ready to punish deviations from custom.

A child is punished for being too submissive. If he runs away when he has a right to retaliate, members of the hamlet who observe such action scold him for being cowardly. If he is afraid to join in the childhood games, he is teased for acting like a baby, especially if he runs away when both he and his brother are attacked. An instance of this occurred when Gwiyap, Mey, and Fit were playing the "homosexual" game. Gwiyap caught Fit and threw him down, and Mey ran away. The boys' uncle, Yat, who was watching, scolded Mey severely for running away when his *brother* needed help. "If your *brother* is in trouble, it is your duty to fight for him."

Children are punished for being inappropriately aggressive. If a child is aggressive when he should be submissive, or more aggressive than the circumstances warrant, he is called to task by members of the community who observe it. Kwoma children may tease, punish, or scold a younger sibling, but may not actually injure him. A child is continually being lectured about the great value which his relatives will have for him throughout his life in terms both of defense and of economic aid. Parents say: "You and your *brother* are 'one blood.' If you hurt him, you hurt yourself." For a boy, the sanction against hurting a *sister* is more severe than that against hurting a *brother*. An aggressive act which, if made toward a *brother*, would pass unnoticed, is punished if made toward a *sister*.

The reaction of the community to the fight reported above between Mey and Fit illustrates the operation of the social sanction on aggressive behavior. Several older *brothers* of the two boys were sitting around the breakfast fire when the fight started. Their reaction was one of laughter and of egging the boys on. Soon after I asked Gwiyap, who had been present, if the boys' parents would scold them for fighting. He said: "No indeed; fighting is a good thing. A person who is afraid to fight can never be a big man in the community." When Fit stole the contents of Mey's bag, the latter's *paternal aunt* told him to wait until Fit came back and then do the same thing to him. When Fit did return, I asked Mey if he had carried out his *paternal aunt's* suggestion and he said, "No, my father told me that after all Fit was my *brother* and that I should forgive him."

Kwoma boys and girls thus learn during childhood to avoid punishment by running away, obeying, hiding, lying, and being polite. They learn to fight, tease, annoy, punish, scold, retaliate, insult, and threaten as ways of being aggressive. They become aware that the source of pain or danger, whether it be man or animal, is the most important thing to know in deciding whether to fight or flee. Finally, they discover that if they are inappropriately aggressive or too submissive they will be punished by other members of the community.

Prestige is a motive which in Kwoma society is closely allied to aggression. The advantage of being old and big is strongly impressed on a Kwoma boy. He can successfully command his younger *brother* to perform tasks for him and to get out of his way, but he must submit to similar commands from his older *brothers*. The contrast is even more marked if he compares himself to his father and *uncles*. Not only are they continually commanding and punishing him, but they are also able, because of size and social sanctions, to do things which a boy would like to do but cannot. Kwoma language indicates that the wish for prestige is largely derived from the struggles between siblings during childhood. The term for a man of high prestige is *harafa ma malaka*, which means "big older brother man," while persons are often derogated by being referred to as *karaganda yikafa*, "little child." It is not surprising, therefore, that Kwoma children exhibit a strong desire to grow up.

Kwoma culture provides the boy with a system of beliefs according to which he can hasten the process of growing up.

He is taught that growth depends upon the renewal of blood, and that food produces blood, which promotes growth as long as it is fresh. When blood has been in the system for a time, however, it begins to grow stale and finally rotten, and then growth ceases until the bad blood is removed from the body. It is furthermore believed that the best method of removing this bad blood from the system is through the penis.[20] As might be expected, children with a strong wish to grow up and with a method which they are told will accomplish it, take this means even though it is painful. Boys frequently go into the bushes and scrape their penises with nettle leaves so that the blood may flow out. For some reason that I could not discover, perhaps because penis scraping was associated with masturbation, boys performed this act only in private and were ashamed if they were discovered. One day Gwiyap, seeing that Mey had left his net bag lying in my house, opened it and pulled out a bundle of nettles. When Mey came in, I asked him about the bundle. He became very embarrassed and said, "Oh, just something of mine." When Gwiyap began to tease him about it, he ran from the house.

It would perhaps be more appropriate to describe this complex in terms of the fear of not growing up rather than in terms of the wish to grow up. The following cases suggest that this is probably the way in which Kwoma boys think of it. Fit asked me if I had performed this rite when I was a child, and when I answered that I had not, his mouth dropped in amazement. "How did you grow up, then?" he asked. Gwiyap, who was also present, settled the matter by explaining to Fit that white men are different from Kwoma. On another occasion Ham asked me the same question and was equally amazed at my answer. Apparently Fit had told him what I had said, and Ham had asked me to make sure that Fit was not teasing him.

[20] This belief concerns health as well as growth, and, as has already been shown, phlebotomy is practiced in the case of sickness, in order to "let out the bad blood."

CHAPTER V

ADOLESCENCE

ADOLESCENCE[1] begins for the Kwoma boy with his initiation into the age-grade cycle, for the girl with a ceremony at the time of her first menstruation. Adolescence is a relatively short period, lasting from one to three years. It is a time of transition from the established habits of childhood to those of adulthood. The attainment of a maturing physique brings with it the necessity of learning to do many of the economic tasks which are not expected of a child, and the increase in the strength of the sex drive makes childhood sexual satisfactions no longer adequate, thus throwing the youth into new learning dilemmas. Next to the weaning period, adolescence is the most turbulent time in the life of a Kwoma individual, a period marked by the learning of many new habits and the facing of many new problems.

The rites which the Kwoma girl undergoes at the time of her first menstruation are a strictly feminine affair. The men know little about them, and do not pry. Male informants stated that, since men kept cult secrets from the women, it was only proper that the women should be permitted to keep their secrets from men. Women were silent about the rites.[2] For these reasons, I was only able to gather that the rite included a period of seclusion and that the initiates were given ornaments in which they paraded as a part of the ceremony.

A Kwoma boy is initiated into the age-grade cycle in an

[1] Gwiyap was the only adolescent boy of Rumbima hamlet. Mar was in a somewhat anomalous position between adolescence and adulthood. He had already received his keloids of manhood but was not yet married. Examples from his life have therefore been included both in this and the following chapter. There were five adolescent girls in the hamlet: Kwiya and Awa, in Mar's household; Gwanta and Famba, the daughters of Way; and Aya, the daughter of Waramus.

[2] Had it been possible to establish better rapport with women, more information concerning these rites and other aspects of female life could have been obtained.

elaborate and protracted ceremony which takes place approximately once every five years. For this reason, a boy's initiation may not correspond exactly with his physiological pubescence. If he is within a year or two of pubescence when a ceremony is to be held, his father and paternal uncles tell him that he is big enough to join. They do not force him to enter at this time, but they make it clear to him that he will not have another chance for five years. Thus a courageous lad may undergo initiation before pubescence, while others may be too frightened to respond to the first call and may consequently not be initiated until some time after the onset of puberty.

The whole subtribe participates in the age-grade ceremony, and all the boys from every hamlet who answer the call go through the rite together. The initiates gather in the early afternoon and march to a stream at the foot of the ridge. Each initiate is then chosen by an unrelated man who has already completed the cycle, and who thereby becomes the boy's *ceremonial father*. This older man slashes the tongue and penis of his *ceremonial son*, and then rubs salt or ashes in the wounds. The blood is allowed to flow down the stream out of the territory. Following this, the initiates of the previous three grades are cut in the same way by their *ceremonial fathers*, each grade submitting separately and in order of age. The sponsors and the youngest grade of initiates then go to the house tamberan, leaving the three older grades behind at the stream. The men tell the women, who are waiting at the house tamberan dressed in grass skirts,[3] that the other initiates have been killed, whereupon the women wail. By this time it is late afternoon, and the initiates who are present dance until dark, when the other three grades appear bearing torches. They dance around the house tamberan until the torches have gone out, whereupon the women join in a dance which continues throughout the night. On this occasion ceremonial sexual license, within the limits of the incest taboos, is permitted to everyone but the youngest initiates. At dawn the women return to their homes to

---

[3] This is the only time that women wear clothes other than their net bags.

cook and the men go to the bush. Here each *ceremonial father* gives his *son* an ornament which symbolizes the latter's grade. The youngest grade receives a bamboo phallocrypt and a plaited belt to hold it in place. The other grades receive decorative combs of increasing elaboration. In the afternoon the women gather again at the house tamberan with the food they have cooked, and the initiates parade in front of them wearing their ornaments. After the meal, a dance similar to the one of the previous night begins and continues throughout the night, again accompanied by sexual license. On the following morning all ceremonial debts are settled; young men pay their *maternal uncles* shell money for the privileges they have gained from the relationship, and young husbands the bride-price which they owe their wives' relatives.

Following this prolonged rite, the youngest grade goes into seclusion in a small house erected near the house tamberan. They must avoid being seen by women for about two months. Food is brought to them by men, and they must wear the phallocrypt whenever they leave the house. The boys engage in hunting competitions during this time, but otherwise do not perform any economic tasks. A small ceremony marks the end of the seclusion period, when each boy puts his phallocrypt over a growing bamboo shoot, which in time splits the ornament and is supposed to symbolize and induce magically the growth of the lad's penis.

The ceremonial scraping of penis and tongue is related to the childhood custom of penis scraping performed by boys in private. Not only the act but also the stated purpose is the same. The Kwoma explanation for the ceremony is that it is to promote growth in the boys—"to help them grow up," as Kis explained to me. The splitting of the phallocrypt thus really symbolizes the purpose of the rite. Although the private rite of childhood produces no change in status, the age-grade rite does result in a marked advance in social position. After it, a boy becomes an adolescent and gains the privileges and immunities which Kwoma culture grants to persons in this category.

Once a Kwoma has passed through the initiatory ceremony he learns new restrictions on eating, assumes new economic responsibilities, and acquires new work habits. Although adolescents are for the most part subject to the same restrictions as children, eating at the same times and consuming the same food, there are some special food taboos which now apply for the first time. A boy may not eat fish for several months after his age-grade initiation. His blood, following the ceremonial cutting, is believed to flow down the stream into the lake and finally into the Sepik River, so that it contaminates the fish caught there. The taboo is thus supported by the Kwoma belief that to eat food contaminated by one's own blood is dangerous. Another restriction is the "voluntary" abstention by adolescent boys and girls from eating sago gruel for the period between the first and second funerals of a close relative. A third new limitation upon a boy's eating habits is associated with his sexual behavior. It is believed that if a male eats food cooked by any female with whom he has had sexual intercourse, he will sicken and perhaps die.[4] Sickness is believed to result not only from eating food contaminated by one's own blood, but also from eating food contaminated by one's own sperm. When a woman cooks, any sperm which she has recently received is thought to contaminate the food. For these reasons an adolescent boy takes care not to get the harmful sperm back into his system by eating food cooked by a girl with whom he has philandered.[5]

When Kwoma youths have attained the status of an adolescent, they must assume new economic responsibilities. While they were children, their parents provided all the sago flour that was needed by the household, but now both sexes must share in the labor of collecting and preparing this staple. Since this is a task which involves the coöperation of a man and a woman, a *brother* and *sister* form a team and they produce together a supply of flour to supplement that prepared by the mother and father. It is the boy's duty to

[4] This taboo also applies to adults with the exception of food cooked by a wife.
[5] The effects of this belief on the sexual behavior of the Kwoma will be discussed later.

Adolescence

cut down the palm tree and remove a section of bark. The girl then crushes the pith, and the boy washes and squeezes it in a trough which he has constructed, allowing the milky juice to flow into a bark container set below the trough. A fine flour settles to the bottom of this container, and the water flows off. After a long morning's work a couple will have produced a sixty or seventy pound deposit of flour. The boy pours off the last of the water and wraps up the flour in a spathe. The girl places this bundle in her net bag and carries it up the mountain path to the dwelling on her back. The division of labor in sago making is maintained in part by the belief that, if a woman should do the man's part of the process, especially that of washing and squeezing the pith, the flour would be inedible.[6]

An adolescent girl takes the responsibility for cooking part of the family meal, presiding over a fireplace of her own instead of merely helping her mother. She prepares the vegetables for soup, boils sago flour, and roasts the meat. She and the older children share the meals which she cooks, thus relieving the mother from the task of providing for the whole family. The mother generally continues to cook for herself, her husband, and the smaller children. If there are two adolescent girls in a family, they usually share one fireplace and coöperate in the cooking. A girl must keep herself supplied with firewood and water.

At adolescence boys and girls must assume new gardening duties and become more specifically associated with the gardening group, which consists of from one to three adult *brothers* and their families.[7] They take their place in the gardening group of their father or, if the father has died, of a *paternal uncle*,[8] and begin to perform adult gardening

[6] Mar and Gwiyap, my houseboys, broke this taboo, a circumstance which will be discussed in chapter viii.

[7] There were six gardening groups in Rumbima hamlet, headed, respectively, by (1) Wof and Marok; (2) War, Kar, and Kis; (3) Yat and Way; (4) Waramus; (5) Afok and Fokotay; (6) Kwal and Daw. Gardening groups will be discussed in more detail in chapter vi.

[8] Gwiyap and Mar joined the gardening group of Wof and Marok. Mar, in addition, had to care for a garden which had been started by an older brother who had recently died.

tasks with the adult men and women of the group. Adolescents do not, however, have much voice in matters of agricultural policy, such as choosing the proper site, or determining the time of planting.

One of the principal duties of a boy is to assist in clearing sites by climbing trees and lopping off branches; he was not allowed to do this as a child because of the physical dangers involved. He also helps in preparing the yam hills and in planting tobacco, taro, and spinach, but he may not put seed yams in the ground until he has become a member of *Nokwi*, the third section of the yam cult, which does not occur until adulthood. When the yam plants break through the ground, he works with the gardening group at the task of hanging stringers of split bamboo from the dead limbs of the trees which stud the garden and pegging these stringers beside each hill. If the garden is near the hamlet rather than in an outlying district, he helps his father build a fence around it to prevent the village pigs from ruining the crop. He works with the adults at harvest time, helping to dig out the yams and to store them.

An adolescent girl does the work of an adult woman in her father's garden. She performs her share of the labor of preparing food for the workers, especially when a feast must be provided for a work-bee. She helps her mother carry the seed yams and the liana stringers to the garden. It is her duty to keep her section of the garden clean of weeds and to help her *sisters*, *mothers*, and *aunts* weed the sections belonging to her father, *brothers*, and *younger sisters*. The most arduous part of her labor is the transportation of the harvest. She carries from fifty to seventy-five pounds of yams in her net bag miles over the steep, slippery paths from the garden to the hamlet, where they are stored in small houses especially built for the purpose.

Adolescence entails no change in the fishing habits of the girls nor in the hunting habits of the boys. These activities continue to be undertaken primarily for sport. A boy is not permitted to hunt pigs until he has become a man. Nowel, an adolescent, deviated from this custom and set out to spear a pig. He managed to drive his spear into the side of a wild boar but the animal charged at him. Nowel sidestepped the beast but the handle of the spear struck him and gave him an ugly bruise on the forehead. The day after this experience he stopped at my house. Yat, Wof, and War happened to be present and asked Nowel how he had come by the bruise. When he told them, they blamed him instead of sympathizing. They said that it was a wonder that he had not been killed and asked him if he thought that he was already a man that he should have attempted such a thing.

Adolescent boys are not expected to make the tools necessary for their economic pursuits. Although each has an adz which he uses as a tool of all work, it is made for him by his father or *paternal uncle*. The lime gourd and stick, which a boy uses for preparing betel for chewing, are also made and given to him by his father or by his *paternal uncle*, the net bag, which he uses as a carryall, by his mother or his sister. Indeed the following case shows that they are prevented from manufacturing tools. Mes and Mar decided to make a canoe together. They cut down the tree and began hollowing it out under the direction of Nambomai, a river native who was working for me. When War heard what these two boys were doing, he forbade them from continuing the work. He said that they were not old enough. As soon as War was out of hearing, Mar and Mes protested that it was none of War's business and that they were not going to obey him. They worked on the canoe one more day and then gave it up. The canoe was never finished. Adolescent girls, on the other hand, are expected to produce tools. They make net bags both for themselves and for their brothers. They carry out the entire process, stripping the bark from the proper tree, preparing it, rolling it into thread on their thighs, and netting it; women's bags are voluminous, men's smaller. Adolescent girls also make bark-fiber fishing nets.

These economic activities are all in some way associated with the satisfaction of hunger. It would be inaccurate, however, to assume that these customs are maintained by this drive alone, for sex also plays a part in impelling Kwoma adolescents to perform their economic tasks. One of the criteria by which a girl chooses a man for a lover or a husband is his ability as a worker. Other things equal, the more industrious a boy is, the more he is sought after by the girls. Lazy lads are shunned. Mar, who was considered to be very lazy and a poor worker, was not at all popular with the girls.

Industriousness on the part of the girl is an even more important criterion of attractiveness than for a boy. The big, strapping women, who could carry large loads of produce or firewood up the mountainside, and who could labor tirelessly, were the females that caused Kwoma men to smack their lips and make lewd comments. Marok's sister, Uka, a powerfully built woman, was considered the most attractive girl in the hamlet. Her strength and industriousness were always mentioned as attributes of her desirability. Indeed, after her husband left to work on a plantation, Marok had some difficulty in preventing her suitors from ignoring her marriage and taking her to live with them. She needed pressure from relatives to keep her in line. Yawa, on the other hand, exemplifies what happens to a lazy girl. Before she went to live with Mar as his betrothed,[9] she was affianced to another young man. The engagement had been arranged by her parents, but the boy and his family would not accept her because she was so lazy. They treated her with such contempt that she returned home. With Mar she fared little better. He once complained to me: "Yawa is no good. She is terribly lazy. When she is getting firewood, she just brings tiny twigs. When she gets sago flour, she cuts down the smallest palms. If she attempted a big one it would take her from dawn until after dark. I have never had intercourse with her and I never will, even if she stays here the rest of her life. If I did and she had a baby, I would have to pay the bride-price. She is not worth any."

Laziness is directly punished by social disapproval, industriousness rewarded by social esteem and prestige. The cases of Mar and Yawa also exemplify the application of these sanctions. After Mar had delayed hanging stringers in his

[9] Girls live for a few months with their parents-in-law before marriage.

garden for almost a week, Gwiyap reprimanded him severely for his negligence, "You will not have any yam crop at all if you continue being so lazy." Other members of Mar's family and even less closely related persons began scolding him to his face and talking behind his back until he finally did the work.[10] Yawa suffered similar criticisms for her laziness. Not only did her negligence contribute to her lack of sexual gratification, but whenever she shirked her duties of gathering firewood or extracting sago flour both Mar and his *sisters* were openly critical of her. Thus economic work habits, although they are instrumental to the production of food and are thus primarily motivated by the hunger drive, are also culturally connected with both sexual satisfaction and the avoidance of punishment.

Pubescence brings with it a new sexual status for the male. His sexual drive, increasing rapidly in potential intensity, forces him into new learning dilemmas. He discovers new modes of gratifying the impulse, although he also persists in most of his previously learned habits. In addition to the prohibitions imposed during the weaning and infancy period, he must learn new restrictions against the behavior which will most immediately and directly reduce his sexual tension. He must also prepare for adult status by beginning to plan for marriage, since every adult Kwoma must marry.

There is some evidence that adolescent boys masturbate. Gwiyap reported that he stimulated his penis to the point of orgasm while in bed at night. He stated that he did this only when he was unobserved by others, which was not very often owing to Kwoma sleeping arrangements.[11] He was somewhat loath to give me this information and did so only after I had established strong rapport with him. He had previously denied it. Since all others whom I questioned denied masturbation, Gwiyap's behavior may have been aberrant. On the other hand, I was unable to establish such an

---

[10] Mar, as will be described later, had had a nervous breakdown the last time he had gone to his garden, so that his fear of returning was very strong. Considerable social pressure had to be applied to overcome this fear.

[11] The whole family sleeps in the enclosed room of the dwelling on separate bark slabs.

intimate relationship with my other informants. This, together with the fact that Gwiyap was, as far as I could determine, a normal Kwoma youth, tends to support the view that his behavior was typical rather than aberrant.

A Kwoma youth usually has had experience in sexual intercourse before he marries. He must acquire this experience in the face of danger from the relatives of the girl, who try to keep her chaste, and he must exercise the greatest secrecy lest they discover the relationship. He arranges a tryst with the girl at some secluded place in the bush, which they approach from different directions so that no one will see them together. Trysts are usually arranged at a chance meeting on a path or at the market. The boy must be careful, since merely to be seen talking to a girl is enough to arouse suspicion. The belief that ghosts frequent the paths after dark operates to prevent the boys from using the cover of night for assignations with girls in other hamlets.

Rape is defined by the Kwoma as sexual intercourse with a girl who is unwilling. It is much more dangerous than philandering because, in the native mind, it combines antisocial sexual and antisocial aggressive behavior. If caught in the act of raping a girl, a boy is in danger of being killed by her relatives unless he is able to escape to his own hamlet, where he will be protected by his own relatives; even then he is not safe from the long arm of sorcery which the relatives of the girl may use against him. A case of rape usually eventuates in a "court case"[12] as a result of which the boy pays an indemnity to prevent retaliation from the girl's relatives.

The strong negative sanctions on rape lead a boy to exercise extreme caution in his love making. If he approaches a girl to ask her for a date, and if she has a grudge against him, she may cry out that he is trying to rape her. Consequently, it is customary for a boy to wait for the girl to take the initiative, assuring himself that she wants him before he makes any advances. The boy does not remain passive, however. If he is interested in some girl, he carefully makes up

---

[12] The court system will be described in chap. vi, pp. 161–162.

his face, combs his hair, and nowadays also dons his gayest laplap, and either walks past the girl's house or down a path where he is likely to meet her. He also plays an active part by resorting to love magic. He tries to put scrapings from a fingernail of his left hand or blood from the left side[13] of his penis into the lime gourd or cigarette of a woman whom he desires. If she ingests these magical substances, it is believed that she will have an uncontrollable sexual desire for the man who gave them to her.

In his sexual activities a boy also runs the risk of making a girl pregnant. If this should happen, her relatives try to force her to name the father of the child. If she names a particular youth as the father, he will be forced by her relatives either to marry her or to pay them an indemnity in shell money. Threats of sorcery or violence are employed to bring about the marriage or extract the payment. The reason given for the indemnity is that if a girl has had a child before marriage no one will pay a full bride-price for her. If a boy is willing to marry the girl anyway, he is not greatly inhibited by the fear of making her pregnant, although there is some social stigma attached to such an event. If the girl is unattractive, however, this factor assumes greater importance.

The danger from the relatives of a girl has certain consequences in controlling an adolescent boy's general behavior toward a girl as well as in determining his mode of sexual behavior. Breaches in etiquette with respect to females become much more serious than they were during childhood. We have seen that, if he stared at the genitals of his mother or sister as a child, he was scolded by the female at whom he stared; when he reaches the age of puberty such behavior is defined as specifically sexual. If he now stares at a girl, her relatives classify the act as a sexual advance and react to it accordingly. To be sure, they do not react as strongly as to an actual liaison, but they usually criticize him and may even insult and threaten him. Even staring at a girl's body in gen-

---

[13] The only explanation that I could get for the idea that the left side is important was that work is done with the right hand, and that this, for some reason, made the left side preferable in sexual matters.

eral, and not specifically at her genitalia, may lead to suspicion, if it is more than a quick identifying glance. A boy must restrain his eyes even when the girl's relatives are not present, for she may report his breach of etiquette with similar results. For these reasons we had considerable difficulty taking photographs of females. As the Kwoma women phrased it, a photograph "caught" their genitals and made it possible for them to be looked at without the possibility of social control. After we had taken several pictures of women in ignorance of the prevailing sentiments, we were told by both the women and by their relatives to take no more.

To avoid the sanctions against looking, a boy either keeps his eyes fixed on the ground or sits or stands with his back to a woman whenever he is in her presence. If he happens to be sitting facing a path down which a woman is walking, he must arise and stand with his back to it until she has passed. He may not speak to her until she has passed him; when they are both back to back he may speak to, but must not look at, her. Whenever he meets adult females on a path, they turn aside and stand with their backs to the path until he has passed. He must keep his eyes on the ground and must not stop and talk to them until they are behind him. If a boy goes visiting, he must be very careful in his behavior. He may only quickly glance under the porch to note who is there and must then keep his eyes on the ground until he has found a seat facing away from the women, when he may gossip with them over his shoulder.

An adolescent boy must obey these rules with respect to all adolescent and adult females except those who live in his own household, with whom he need not be so elaborately careful. His behavior toward them does not differ appreciably from that which he learned during childhood; he may not stare at their genitals, but he is not restricted from looking at them in general. When no one else is around and when a girl has made sexual advances toward a boy, he may look at her. In fact, this is defined as part of the preliminaries to sexual behavior. Just as boys avoid the sanctions against sexual intercourse by having affairs in secret, so they develop techniques of furtive looking. Both Gwiyap and Mar, whenever they met an attractive girl, could and would report her appearance in detail, including a description of her breasts and genitals, although they had apparently obeyed all the precepts of Kwoma etiquette and kept their glance averted.

Boys often start their love making with their *sisters*. All the females of one's own sib and generation are termed *sister*, whether they are patrilineal parallel cousins of various degrees, or actually unrelated. It is theoretically taboo to cohabit with any related female, but in practice it depends on how closely she is related, the taboo being the more effective the closer the relationship. The factor of proximity[14] seems to lead a boy to choose his *sisters* rather than a non-relative with whom to learn to cohabit. He has a greater opportunity for arranging trysts with girls of his hamlet, since he is normally more frequently in their presence and he is not so conspicuous when he talks to them as when he speaks to a girl of another hamlet. Furthermore he runs less risk of being severely punished if he is caught, because there is a taboo on aggression between members of the same hamlet. Finally, he can more easily trust a *sister* not to claim she has been raped than he can a girl whom he knows less well and who has no reason to protect him against the consequences. Boys apparently resolve the conflict between the incest taboos, the advantages of proximity, and the prohibitions on intra-sib aggression by choosing the girls of their hamlet who are most distantly related.[15]

Gwiyap's exploits constitute a good example of the philandering of the Kwoma adolescent. He was a lively youth just past pubescence. One evening about a month after my arrival at Kwoma, I asked him if he had ever had sexual intercourse. He looked embarrassed and said noncommittally that he did not know. His confusion led me to suspect that

[14] Owing to patrilocal residence and patrilineal descent, all the girls of the same generation in the hamlet are *sisters*.

[15] I have no information on what would happen if a girl became pregnant as a result of an affair with a *brother*. Probably she would claim that she had been impregnated by a non-relative.

he had had sexual experiences, but feared punishment or disapproval if he confessed, so I told him that boys of his age in America had intercourse and cited several examples. He was much interested, and asked if the girls' fathers would be cross if they found out. I told him that the boys kept it a secret. Then he wanted to know what would happen if one of the girls should have a child. I told him that Americans had a means of preventing pregnancy. He expressed his amazement at this, and the subject was dropped. The next night, however, when we were discussing other matters, he brought up the subject again and mentioned six girls, three of them his *sisters*, with whom he claimed to have had sexual relations. One of them was Awa, Mar's sister. He recounted his experiences with great gusto, but warned me not to tell Mar about them, especially about his affair with Awa.

About two months later Gwiyap appeared with his hair combed and a new laplap around his waist and told me that he had a date that afternoon with Famba, a girl of his own generation and lineage, whom he addressed as *sister*. After playing ball for a while with some of the other boys, he departed. That evening I asked him how he had fared. He answered that his "shitnothing" *brother*, Fit, had followed him to the tryst. He had told him not to come and finally had chased him back with a stick, but when he finally met Famba he had not dared do anything because he was afraid that Fit had sneaked after him and was spying.

Two weeks later while I was sitting with Gwiyap in front of my house, Kwiya came by carrying firewood. She was a girl of about the same age as Gwiyap who lived in the same house and belonged to the same lineage. As she passed he exchanged bawdy remarks with her, as is the custom between *brother* and *sister*. Then he said to me that he thought he would go to America with me when I left because so many girls liked him and asked him to cohabit with them that he would certainly get in trouble if he stayed at Kwoma. He then recounted his sexual experiences. There was Kwiya, the girl who had just passed, and Awa, Mar's sister, both of whom were his household mates. Then there was Famba,

Way's daughter, who was of his lineage, and Mes' sister, Aya, who was of the other lineage of the hamlet. The only girl on his list whom he did not call *sister* was Gwimpi, an attractive girl of about his age who belonged to another sib and whom he said he intended to marry. I asked him about Gwanta, the only girl of the hamlet in his age group who was not on his list. His face fell, and he said that she did not like him. Then he brightened and remarked that she was no good anyway. He went on to say that Mes' sister, Aya, was the best of all because she had a very large vagina. Again he cautioned me not to tell Mar about his escapades. I asked him what Mar would do if he found out and he replied: "He would beat me. No, he would not beat me, but I would be much ashamed." Two afternoons later he came in looking very proud of himself and boasted that he had just cohabited twice with Awa in their house. Mey came in as he was talking and Gwiyap stopped short, explaining later that he did not want Mey to know for fear he would tell Mar.

Toward the end of my stay at Kwoma, Gwiyap began an affair with Gwanta, the girl who had previously turned him down. One afternoon he came to my house greatly excited, saying that he had met Gwanta on the path and that she had told him that she was willing to have intercourse with him. He had given her younger brother two razor blades and told him to give one to Gwanta and keep the other himself, and to come and tell him when Gwanta went to the spring to get water so that he could meet her there. He said that he intended to ask her to come and sleep under Wysep's mosquito net. When he met her later that afternoon in her house, she agreed to this proposition; her younger brother said that he would come, too. Gwanta told him that he could not, asking him how many people he thought a mosquito net would hold.[16] Gwiyap also reported that she had refrained from calling him by his name.[17] Later in the evening I asked him if

[16] Gwiyap was apparently very indirect in his remarks so that neither the mother nor the brother of the girl suspected anything.
[17] It is the custom for engaged persons not to address one another by name.

he thought that Gwanta would really come. He said that he did not know, appearing less enthusiastic than before. Then he said that he intended to sorcerize Way and marry Gwanta. When I pointed out that she was his *sister*, he said, "Oh, that does not matter; she is not my real sister; just a sister nothing." The next day he reported that she had not come. On the following day a recruiter came and Gwiyap "signed on" to work on a white plantation and left the tribe.

A Kwoma boy, despite his disregard of some of the incest rules, respects them with reference to his real sister. All informants agreed that sexual intercourse with a real sister never occurred. This, of course, is not proof of the absence of brother-sister incest, but it does indicate its rarity. On one occasion when Gwiyap was telling me his sexual exploits, I asked if he had ever had intercourse with Afi, his real sister. He became very serious and said: "No, indeed! She is my real sister. These other girls that I have told you about are my 'sisters nothing.'[18] If I had sexual intercourse with her, I would be terribly guilty.[19] These other sisters are all right."[20]

Unmarried youths do not as a rule philander with married women. Besides the fear of retaliation from the husband, the factor of age may also play a part in this restriction. There is a strong feeling that a man should not marry or have sexual relations with a woman older than himself. Gwiyap even

[18] *Sumwe sumwe mowe*—"nothing sister"—classificatory sister; *mowe sakana*—"sister of the same seed"—real sister.

[19] *Homba,* as nearly as I could discover, is the word which the Kwoma use to describe guilt or shame. They have another word for fear or anxiety. While the origin of this "guilt" may be quite complicated, the punishments that a boy receives as a child for having an erection in his sister's presence, and for looking at her genitals, probably play a part in producing the feeling. It was this word which Gwiyap used to describe what his feelings would be if Mar should find out about his affair with Awa.

[20] A myth supports the Kwoma attitude toward brother-sister incest. "Once upon a time, long, long, long ago, a father and mother went to the swamp to collect sago flour. Their children, a boy and girl, stayed at home. They had sexual intercourse. When the parents came home, the girl told them what had happened. The father was very angry and killed his son. Since then brother-sister incest has been forbidden." Although in real life a father would probably not kill his son for this crime, because sons are an asset, the myth, which is often told, probably exerts an inhibitory effect on sexual behavior between brother and sister.

felt this with respect to a girl who was only a few years his senior, maintaining that he was not interested in her because she was too old for him.

A boy gains prestige from his sexual exploits. Although he must be careful not to tell anyone who might inform the girl's relatives, he frequently boasts of his conquests to those of his *brothers* with whom he is most intimate, unless, of course, the girl happens to be closely related to them. A lad who enjoys the reputation of being a successful philanderer gains the respect of his fellows. Although seldom praised to his face, he receives added motivation from hearing others complimented for their successful exploits.

A youth normally does not marry until he has undergone the ceremony which makes him an adult. He begins courting, however, during adolescence, and he is subject to all the restrictions which control the choice of a mate. Although a boy may successfully engage in secret philandering with a *sister*, open courtship and marriage would bring their relation under public obloquy. Incest and other marriage restrictions, therefore, influence a boy's choice more strongly in courtship than in philandering. His selection must be made from a relatively small number of persons. The prospective bride should be slightly younger than he, but must be already pubescent. She must be a member of some sib other than his own and not closely related to his *mother's brother, mother's sister, father's sister, sister's husband, wife*,[21] *friend,* or *ceremonial father*. Finally, she must be unmarried.

The Kwoma give a number of different reasons for their restrictions upon marriage between relatives. One of their rationalizations stems from their theory of reproduction. They believe that the foetus develops from a combination of the sperm of the man and the blood of the woman. They further believe that if a man and woman with the same sperm-blood combination should produce a child, he would be sickly and apt to die. This idea is related to their theory that the renewal of blood is necessary to growth and health. Since

[21] A man may not marry a relative of his first wife while she is still alive.

relatives belong to the same sperm-blood strain, they should not marry. Although members of the same sib are not necessarily related in the biological sense, the idea of their relationship is extended by the assumption that every member of a specific sib is descended from a single common totemic ancestor. The degree of similarity in the sperm-blood strain in two persons is thought to depend upon the number of generations back to their common ancestor—common parents being the closest, a common totemic ancestor alone the most distant. Relatives in the female line are included in this theory, but only the children of the biological siblings of the mother are considered to be related. *Friends* are brought in line with this theory as a result of being scarified at the same time, so that their blood is mixed on the bark slab on which the operation is performed. The close female relatives of a *friend*, therefore, should not be married. Since the *ceremonial father* scrapes a boy's tongue and penis at the age-grade ceremony in order to purge him of bad blood and stimulate his growth, their blood too becomes associated. In consequence, a boy should not marry the close female relatives of his *ceremonial father*.

The Kwoma also believe that the marriage of relatives breeds in-group antagonisms. The relatives of the bride must often bring strong pressure to bear on the groom in order to collect the bride-price. Implied threats of sorcery are not at all uncommon, and insults are usual unless the payment is promptly made. If such bickering should take place between relatives, it would weaken the power of the in-group, and therefore should be avoided if possible. When the bride-price is paid, on the other hand, the families of the boy and the girl become "safe" with one another, and thus if they were previously unrelated, the in-group is extended. If the two families are already related, this advantage is not gained.

Despite these sanctions, marriages not infrequently occur between relatives, most commonly between *brothers* and *sisters*. This deviation from the Kwoma ideal follows in part from the factor of proximity as described in connection with philandering. Such a marriage may, in fact, result from a liaison. Those who break the rule are most frequently neurotic individuals who dare not or cannot get a spouse from without the sib; this was the case with Mar and his betrothed, Yawa. Susceptibility to sorcery, that is frequent sickness, is regarded as an excuse for breaking the rule, since it is believed to be dangerous for such a person to have contacts outside the sib. Out of eighteen cases, only one marriage and one betrothal were between relatives. Both cases were between *brother* and *sister*, and in both there was no known blood connection.

Theoretically a boy's parents decide whom he shall marry. They discuss with the parents of a girl of the proper age the advantages of a marriage between their children, and often exchange small presents to formalize the betrothal if it is mutually agreeable. There is no set occasion when betrothals take place; usually they result from an informal conversation at the market or in the house tamberan. There is no prescribed age for betrothal. Parents usually do not arrange a marriage for their child until he has reached the age of puberty, although a betrothal may be agreed upon even during the infancy of the parties primarily concerned. There is nothing particularly binding about a betrothal. The exchange of gifts is balanced, so that, if the engagement is broken, neither family is the loser. Although betrothal binds neither boy nor girl to marriage, it is important enough so that they seriously consider one another as mates and only break the engagement if, for some reason, they feel a mutual antipathy.

More marriages result from actual courtship, which follows approved rules, than from betrothals arranged by the parents; sometimes they result from philandering. The woman takes the initiative in courting as well as in philandering, for here too the youth fears retaliation from the girl's relatives if he is too forward. Courtship is carried on during chance meetings on paths, or in visits to the house of the girl on the pretext of seeing her father or brothers. On these latter occasions the boy does not even speak to the girl, but shows off by making witty conversation with her brothers or parents. There is sometimes a sort of indirect conversation between the boy and girl when they both talk to the same person, and some of the bolder youths may even address the girl directly. In such cases, however, neither should mention the name of the other as this would be a breach of etiquette.

Mar's courtship of Aya exemplifies the sanctions directed against marriage with a relative. Mar and Aya were members of the same hamlet, but not of the same lineage. Despite the taboo on intra-sib marriage, Aya's brother had already married Mar's sister. Mar's betrothed, Yawa, was also a member of the same sib, so that if he married her and Aya he would be marrying girls who were related to one another as well as to himself, another reason for not courting Aya. The fact that Mar was neurotic presumably made his courtship somewhat atypical. The affair started when Aya asked Gwiyap if he wanted to marry her. He replied that he was too young but that his brother, Mar, was looking for a wife. Aya seemed to like this suggestion and offered some fish that she had bought to Mar's aunt. The latter refused to accept them and told Aya that she should know better than to make advances to a boy in her own sib. This rebuff did not stop the couple. Mar gave Aya a razor blade to show that he was seriously interested in her, and they made plans to marry despite the disapproval of their elders, even if they had to elope. Aya's father, Waramus, finally got wind of the affair and told Mar, in no uncertain terms, to stop courting his daughter. As a result of this tirade, Mar had what seemed to be a nervous breakdown. He believed that his sickness resulted from being sorcerized by Waramus. He was in bed for more than a week, stayed home for another week, and did not recover his full strength for almost a month. During this time, the affair with Aya lapsed.

When Mar had fully recovered from his sickness, he began thinking of Aya again, but this time he was more careful in his approach. He talked the matter over with his *paternal uncles* (his father was not alive) and convinced them that it would be all right for him to marry Aya if Waramus would agree to it. In discussing the matter, they weighed the pros and cons carefully. The principal arguments against the match were that the two were of the same sib and that Mar was already engaged to a girl of his own hamlet. Mar and his supporters countered that, although he and Aya were of the same hamlet, they were of different lineages and were not very closely related. "Close enough to make their offspring sickly," argued those who were opposed to the match. The fact that Mar's sister had married Aya's brother was brought up as precedent, but was discounted because they had not as yet had any children. Someone suggested that it was probably because they were so closely related that they had had no children. A telling argument in favor of the match arose from the fact that Mar had not received the bride-price for his sister, and that if he married Aya this would cancel the debt, thus relieving a situation which usually leads to trouble —unpaid debts within the hamlet. Another argument in favor of the match was that Mar was lazy and susceptible to sorcery (the Kwoma way of describing a neurotic), so that he might have difficulty in finding a girl who would marry him. It therefore seemed advisable to allow him to accept any girl who would have him. Mar rebutted the argument that he was already affianced to a girl in the sib by saying that she was no good and that he would never marry her. The upshot of the whole discussion was that Mar's *paternal uncles* agreed to support him if Waramus was willing. One of Mar's *paternal uncles* sounded Waramus out and discovered that, although he was not pleased with the idea, he would agree if Mar paid him a certain amount of bride-price in addition to canceling the debt owed for Mar's sister.

Mar was delighted with the prospect that the marriage might take place, and he became very friendly with Aya's brother. They went hunting together, helped each other gardening, bleached one another's hair, and even began to build a canoe together. Mar made plans to elope with Aya because he did not have enough money to pay the bride-price in advance as Waramus insisted. He arranged with two of his *sisters* to go fishing with Aya. He was to meet them, and then he and Aya would go to their bush house until Waramus calmed down. He was very anxious about this plan, and kept asking me to support him if he got into trouble as a result of it. He was afraid that Waramus and his son would seize one of his *sisters* in retaliation.

On the eve of the planned elopement one of the more influential of Mar's *paternal uncles* withdrew his support, saying that Waramus was a notorious sorcerer and would undoubtedly sorcerize Mar if the latter carried out his plan. This was enough to deter Mar. Gwiyap was contemptuous of Mar's vacillation, and said that if he had wanted to marry Aya, he would have done so long ago, Waramus, *uncles*, or no. He told Mar that he was too afraid of talk. As a matter of fact, Mar did delay too long, for shortly after the elopement fell through a white recruiter came to Kwoma, and Mar escaped the conflict by signing a contract to work for three years on a plantation.

The sexual behavior of adolescent girls has in part been covered in the foregoing consideration of male adolescents. In some respects it differs from that of boys. I was able to discover nothing about the private sexual life of adolescent girls, nor of their homosexual behavior. They do not, however, either masturbate in public nor indulge in any open sexual relationships with other females.

The sanctions against immodest behavior increase in intensity when a girl becomes pubescent. Whereas young girls are only mildly scolded for assuming immodest postures, adolescent girls are severely criticized for such behavior. A girl is told that immodest behavior is interpreted as a sexual invitation and that consequently if she is immodest she will be considered a loose woman and her chances of a good marriage will be spoiled. Usually the sanction does not appear in this rational form, but simply as a command from a parent or other relative to be more careful. A properly modest Kwoma girl never sits with her legs apart or knees drawn up, but stretches her legs out close together with knees unbent. She takes care never to bend over in the presence of men unless she is wearing her net bag hanging down her back,[22] and never to leave the hamlet unless she wears her bag. When she meets a man on the path, she must step aside with her back to the path and must not speak to him until he has passed her.

A girl, like a boy, normally has her first experience in sexual intercourse during adolescence. She, too, must be secretive in this behavior, but for reasons quite different from those which force a boy to hide his philandering. The only danger which a girl faces from a non-relative in her sexual adventures is that of rape or of being aggressively attacked. In contrast to the boy, she stands in no danger of punishment from the relatives of her lover if she is discovered. Her own relatives, particularly her brothers, are the ones from whom she must hide her behavior. It is they who try to prevent her from philandering because, if she gets a reputation for being loose, and particularly if she becomes pregnant, her value as a potential wife is decreased and her brothers will be unable to get such a high bride-price when she marries. The Kwoma rationalization for the bride-price is, in fact, that it is a payment by the husband to the brothers of his wife for having kept her pure and unblemished up to the time of her marriage. Since a brother uses the bride-price paid for his sisters to buy his own wife or wives, it is not a matter of indifference to him if his sister loses her reputation. If a girl becomes pregnant, therefore, she may expect a severe scolding and perhaps a beating from her father or brothers.

The pressures exerted upon an adolescent girl lead her to solve her sexual problem in a somewhat different manner from the boy. As has already been shown, it is she who makes the advances rather than the boy, which she can do since she runs no risk of punishment from the boy's relatives. A second consequence of the differential sanctions is that, since the girl risks punishment from her own relatives, it is more danger-

[22] The woman's net bag is hung from the forehead down the back and when empty reaches almost to the knees. It thus functions as an article of clothing as well as a carrying device.

ous for her to philander within the hamlet. From this it would be expected that she would be less likely to violate the incest prohibitions than would a boy. Since my only data on the sexual affairs of adolescent girls were obtained from male informants, it is impossible to check this deduction.

By the time a Kwoma has reached adolescence he has learned to cope with most of the environmental dangers. He continues to react to these with either aggression or avoidance, depending on circumstances, previous practice, and the dictates of custom. With his increase in size, however, aggression comes more and more to replace avoidance as a response to a threat of pain. Animals and reptiles which loom large to him as a child now seem less ferocious. He kills them instead of fleeing from them. The adolescent likewise depends less upon his parents and relatives to help him cope with sickness. He now attends to his own sores, instead of asking his parents to treat them. When he has a headache, stomach-ache, or sprained joint he sometimes bleeds himself, but more frequently requests a brother to make the slashes for him, returning the favor when his brother needs to be bled.

A boy comes into more direct contact with the sorcery complex during adolescence. Philandering and increased motility bring him into greater danger from this source; and he now must support the adults of the hamlet in anti-sorcery behavior when one of his relatives falls sick. He does not take the lead in this aggressive reaction to sickness, but discusses with the adults the probable identity of the sorcerer and attends, but does not participate in, the sorcery court.[23]

Adolescents still believe that ghosts are dangerous and simultaneously avoid and curse them. They are still nervous whenever they have to venture very far from their dwelling in the dark, but they dare go farther at night than do children. They keep at a distance from burial platforms and the "land of the dead." They are jumpy about strange noises at night, and take particular care not to whistle at this time.

[23] The anti-sorcery complex will be described in detail in chap. vi, pp. 137-8.

One evening I started whistling when Mar and Gwiyap, two adolescents, were in my home. They told me to stop, warning me that ghosts would come if I persisted. I continued to whistle in order to discover what their reactions would be. They pleaded with me to cease and finally bolted for home.

A marked change takes place in a boy's reaction to *marsalai* when he reaches adolescence. At about the age of puberty he is initiated into the first stage of the yam cult.[24] He must first decide whether he wishes to join the *yenema* or *minjama* section. Although it is presumably up to him to make this choice, his father, older *brothers*, and *paternal uncles* exert considerable pressure upon him. It is their wish to keep the hamlet about equally represented in each section and they therefore see to it that such a balance is maintained by influencing the adolescents who are ready to make their choice.

After a boy has decided which section he will join, he is taken into the forest, where a rude hut has been constructed at a sufficient distance from the hamlet, so that women cannot hear. Here the young men of the hamlet who have recently been initiated meet to practice gong beating and flute playing.[25] Their practice is overseen and criticized by older men, the parents and *uncles* of the novices. On the first occasion that a boy attends one of these practice meetings, he is told that the sounds that he has heard as a child during ceremonies are man-made and not the voices of *marsalai*. He pretends to be surprised because theoretically he should not know what in fact he already does. He is also told at this time that he must not in any way reveal this secret to any child or female, and he is warned very seriously that the mere knowledge of the secret of the cult may kill such persons. Then, during sporadic meetings over a period of sev-

[24] Boys are sometimes initiated into the cult a year or so before physiological pubescence. It has seemed more expedient, however, to describe it in this rather than the previous chapter. This initiation should not be confused with the age-grade initiation.
[25] The spot for the camp is picked near a variety of tropical tree which has flange-like roots. These roots ring out when beaten and are used as a substitute for gongs.

eral months, he is given some instruction in gong beating and flute playing, so that he may show his prowess at the coming initiation. Most of the time, however, he watches those who have already been initiated, but who have not yet fully mastered the techniques, practice the complicated rhythms, and then tries to copy them.

On the day of the ceremony, the beating of the house tamberan gongs begins early in the morning. Meanwhile, the boy who is to be initiated prepares himself for the event. He carefully combs his hair and paints his face in the prescribed manner. About mid-morning he is led near the house tamberan by his sponsor,[26] who warns him that when he enters the building he will see the *marsalai*, who will be on an altar in the center of the dance floor. The sponsor especially warns the initiate not to look up at the altar too quickly lest the shock kill him. The lad is then left waiting with other boys who are to be initiated while the sponsor goes to tell the men already there that the initiates are about to appear. At this, the gongs, flute playing, and singing cease abruptly, and the men prepare to produce special sound effects to impress the initiates. The sponsor returns for his initiate and leads him up to the house tamberan. A screen of sago fronds hides the inside of the building from view. Gongs and flutes burst into a deafening roar as the initiate is made to stoop and enter an opening in the screen. The sponsor holds the initiate by the arm and dances with him around the altar. The men shout and dance around with them. The gong beaters and flutists play wildly. Someone just outside the house tamberan whirls a bull-roarer, and the sponsor shouts in the boy's ear that its sound is that of the wings of a *marsalai*. For the first two rounds the boy keeps his eyes fixed on the ground; then his sponsor tells him to look up at the altar, where there is a stylized representation of a human head carved from wood and painted with designs in black and white. The boy is told that this too is a hoax, that it is made

[26] I am not sure how a boy's sponsor is determined. In any case, he is a member of the appropriate cult section and of the parental generation.

Adolescence

of wood, but that the secret must be carefully guarded from the women and children. The sponsor then thrusts a roasted yam into the boy's hand and leaves him to dance by himself in the circling ring of men as he eats it.

The boy's dream of participating in the cult ceremonies is thus finally realized. From now on he may take his turn in the gong orchestra, taking care not to make a mistake lest he be shouted at and teased by the older men, and hoping to gain their praise for a perfect performance. Although adolescents are usually only permitted to beat the gongs while the simpler rhythms are being played, those who have shown a special aptitude during the practice sessions and who make no mistakes during their first few performances at the house tamberan may be permitted to try their hand at more complicated rhythms. Although few adolescents gain the skill necessary for a public performance on the flutes, they can put to use the secret dance practices of their childhood as they skip around the altar, their hands above their heads, their eyes on the wooden figures, and their bare feet rhythmically slapping the earth floor in unison with the other dancers. They may also join in the chorus which the dancers shout after each of the song leader's verses. Finally, they may squat with the adults as they drop out of the dance to smoke cigarettes, chew betel, and gossip.

The unfolding of the hoax of the cult does not destroy a Kwoma boy's belief in *marsalai;* it simply verifies his suspicion that the *marsalai* do not palpably visit the house tamberan at the time of the cult ceremonies. He still believes in the existence of these supernatural beings and does not doubt that they live in their special dwelling places and cause storms or "shoot" sago needles when they are disturbed. He is also impressed with the fact that these *marsalai* are responsible for a successful yam crop, and that the chief purpose of the yam cult ceremony is to insure their coöperation in producing a bountiful harvest.

An adolescent reacts toward his younger *brothers* in much the same way as he did during childhood. Indeed, a specific advantage of the age-grade and cult initiations is that each gives him a defined status superior to those of his *brothers* who have not as yet undergone them. Whereas during childhood a command-obey relationship had to be fought out, and was usually established on the basis of size and age, now the relationship is culturally determined. An initiated boy has the privilege of derogating all those who are not yet initiated, and he loses no opportunity to do so. Gwiyap, Mey, and Ham were all old enough to be eligible for entry into the age-grade cycle when one of the quinquennial ceremonies took place just before my arrival. The adults told them that they could be initiated if they wished; it was up to them. Gwiyap was willing to undergo having his tongue and penis cut and the other hardships of initiation, whereas neither Mey nor Ham dared do so.[27] Gwiyap, after he had undergone the initiation, did not allow them to forget their cowardice. He frequently referred to them as "children," with the implication that he was in a lofty social position which towered above that of a mere child.

On reaching adolescence a boy gives up trying to gain superiority over his adolescent *brothers* by fighting with them in physical combat. For the most part his relative position has already been established by such means during childhood and by the precedents established by temporal priority in the various initiations. Relative changes in status or circumstantial reversals of position are gained by verbal aggression or by efficiency in the various arts which are culturally defined as giving prestige. A boy can gain a superior position over a hitherto dominant *brother* by becoming a better hunter, a more persistent gardener, or being more adept at gong beating, flute playing, or singing in the cult ceremonies.

Such a struggle for dominance was occurring between Mar and Gwiyap. Mar was older and larger than Gwiyap, and had evidently established dominance during childhood by virtue of his greater physical size. He had also undergone

[27] Gwiyap was physiologically pubescent; Mey and Ham were not.

the initiations before Gwiyap. Mar, however, was a markedly fearful person, whereas Gwiyap was more courageous; Mar had not dared have sexual relations even with his betrothed, whereas Gwiyap had made half a dozen conquests. Mar was clumsy and lazy, whereas Gwiyap was an efficient and hard worker. Mar was, however, still dominant and Gwiyap usually obeyed his commands, although he sometimes refused to do so. Mar did not back up his commands by physical attack when Gwiyap disobeyed him. Gwiyap less frequently commanded Mar and when he did so, the latter sometimes obeyed and sometimes refused to obey him. In particular, Gwiyap gained an advantage over Mar by criticizing the latter when, because of his timidity and awkwardness, he did not measure up to the behavior expected of an adolescent Kwoma. The most noticeable thing about the struggle for dominance between the two boys was that they never resorted to physical violence. Indeed, no case of a fight between adolescent *brothers* came to my attention. Although it cannot be assumed that fights do not occur, it is true that the sanctions against fighting between *brothers* increase as they become physiologically mature. Children, being smaller, are not as likely to injure one another seriously as are adolescents. The sanctions against injury which begin to operate during childhood are increased in respect to adolescents, presumably so that the power of the in-group may be maintained.

The following conflict between Mar and Gwiyap indicates the subtlety of aggression between adolescents as compared to similar behavior between children. One morning Gwiyap was roasting a breadfruit. When it was done, Mar came up and began to help himself. Gwiyap told him that if he wanted something to eat he should cook it for himself. Mar replied that there was plenty for him, too. Gwiyap insisted angrily that Mar eat no more of the breadfruit, but Mar did not heed. Gwiyap then became insulting, and Mar returned the insults. Gwiyap's final response was to get up and leave the fire around which they were squatting and to refuse to eat any more himself. Mar, apparently guilty about what he had done, called to Gwiyap to come back, and promised not to eat any more. Gwiyap refused either to return or to answer and avoided Mar for the rest of the day. He spoke insultingly of Mar when I questioned him about the event.

An adolescent boy continues to behave toward his parents and his *paternal uncles* and *aunts* as he did in childhood. He obeys their commands, lies to them when they accuse him of wrongdoing, and is secretive in doing things that he expects them to punish. If he is aggressive toward them, it usually takes the form of disobedience or grumbling. Occasionally he may talk back to them and sometimes even attack them. Informants reported the case of an adolescent boy who had speared and killed his father a few years before my arrival. He had fled after he had committed this crime and was still living in a neighboring tribe.[28]

The *sisters* of an adolescent boy constitute a sexual temptation to him, since they are the most available sexually mature, unmarried women in the tribe and live in the same hamlet. If he philanders with them, he does so in the face of negative sanctions and of fear of punishment from their *brothers* if he is caught. Even if he dare not have sex relations with them, they nevertheless may evoke in him the desire to do so, and thus produce emotional conflict. To avoid their presence might be the adaptive response under the circumstances, but the necessities of common living and the economic coöperation between *brother* and *sister* militate against this solution. The alternative response of aggression to the frustration which they produce would be dangerous to in-group solidarity and has, furthermore, been strongly punished during childhood. Kwoma culture provides the boy with a solution to this dilemma in the form of a socially permitted joking relationship. This consists of license to exchange insults of a sexual character, mostly mutual accusations of breaking sexual taboos, particularly those of incest.

---

[28] No drastic sanctions are imposed against patricide since the father has no relatives closer than his son to avenge him. Such an act is considered "unnatural," however, and the murderer is shunned. This was probably the reason for the person cited above leaving the tribe.

One day Gwiyap told his *sister*, Kwiya, a girl of about his own age, to copulate with her father. She retorted in an equally bawdy fashion. When I questioned Gwiyap about this behavior, he explained to me that it was customary between *brother* and *sister*. If he had said the same thing to anyone else, however, it would have been a gross insult and would probably have provoked a fight; but, he said, it was a good joke when he talked this way to his *sister*. Kwiya was one of the girls with whom he had had sex relations.

Although a *brother-sister* joking relationship is allowed, physical aggression toward a *sister* under these circumstances is prohibited. The following case illustrates the strength of this prohibition and indicates that by the period of adolescence it has already become internalized. Mar and Awa, his adolescent *sister*, were teasing and insulting one another in accordance with the joking relationship. After the exchange had gone on for some time, Awa told Mar, who had bleached his hair in accordance with the new fashion, that his hair was white because he was an old man and no longer sexually potent. Mar lost his temper at this insult and rushed at Awa, brandishing a stick. She turned and ran. Mar followed her for a few yards and then fell down and remained inert on the ground. When he did not get up, the onlookers went over to discover the trouble. He refused to answer them. Thinking that he was pretending, they began prodding him. He still did not respond, and they finally decided that he must be possessed. Later he explained that his father's ghost had appeared before him and demanded sternly why he was chasing his *sister*.[29]

An adolescent boy is permitted to be physically aggressive toward his *sister* if he catches her philandering, though he may not seriously injure her. Usually a boy's reaction in these cases is to give his *sister* a good scolding. Sometimes he may strike her on her back with his fist, or, if her behavior has been especially flagrant and persistent, he may even beat

[29] Since Mar's behavior in other circumstances showed him to be an unusually fearful person, the above case probably does not represent a normal Kwoma reaction.

her with a stick. He takes care not to cause her serious injury because he has learned that if he did so it would be to his own detriment. He risks losing thereby both her coöperation and the bride-price that he expects to get as a result of her marriage.

An adolescent boy continues the polite and friendly relationship toward those of his kin who live outside the hamlet. As he approaches the status of manhood and its responsibilities, more positive behavior is demanded if he wishes to maintain the relationship unbroken. He must entertain his *maternal uncle*, his *paternal aunt*, and his *maternal aunt* whenever they visit him.[30] He must offer them betel nut to chew or tobacco to smoke whenever he sees them, and give them food if they come to his house at mealtime. Furthermore, if they get into trouble, he must support them in whatever way he can. If someone in his hamlet thinks that one of these relatives is responsible for a sickness in the hamlet, it is his duty to quash such a rumor. Finally, he should be willing to help these relatives if they are undertaking some major economic task, such as building a house, which calls for coöperative activity.

In addition to these rules of behavior which apply to relatives in general outside the hamlet, an adolescent boy has special obligations to fulfill with respect to his *maternal uncle*. He must pay him a fee of a specified amount of shell money at the age-grade ceremony.[31] The boy has used the privilege of taking what he pleases from his *maternal uncle's* garden and sago plot and must make a payment in return. If the boy does not fulfill this obligation, his *uncle* will not only break relationship and thus put an end to the privileges

---

[30] The *mother's sister* is considered to be much less important than either the *mother's brother* or the *father's sister*, and the relationship often lapses from the lack of reciprocal contact. This results from the fact that the relationship between a *brother* and *sister* is maintained after their respective marriages, whereas two *sisters* marrying into different hamlets tend to lose contact with one another.

[31] He obtains this from his father, his *paternal uncles*, his *sisters* if they have married and if the bride-price has been paid for them, and from his *nephews*.

that the boy has hitherto enjoyed, but in addition, since breaking the relationship removes the bars that are erected by kinship ties against aggression, may actually threaten the boy.

An adolescent boy may break his relationship with any adult or adolescent[32] relative. This is the first step that he must take either implicitly or explicitly if he is seriously aggressive toward a relative. After a relationship is broken, all the restraints described in the preceding paragraphs against injuring a relative no longer apply, at least in theory.[33] The two behave toward one another as non-relatives, and the control on aggression between them operates thenceforth as it does between any non-relatives. Sorcery, physical violence, and insult now become both potential dangers and potential weapons. Furthermore all obligations of mutual coöperation are abrogated. To threaten to break a relationship is thus in itself a form of aggression of considerable power. Adolescents learn to use this threat in order to force relatives to fulfill their obligations to them, and as a means of counter-aggression. To use this form of aggression a boy must be courageous, for it lays him open to injury from his opponent.

The following case illustrates the operation of this mechanism in Kwoma society. Gwiyap had for some time availed himself of the privilege of cutting sago from the plot of his *maternal uncle*, Payap. One day War, Gwiyap's *paternal uncle*, learned what Gwiyap was doing and commanded him to stop. War claimed that he was more closely related to Payap than was Gwiyap and proved his point by reference to genealogy. Since a reciprocal economic relationship is only set up between the closest living *mother's brother* and

[32] It is not until adolescence that a person is considered to have enough responsibility to break a relationship. Relationships, however, may be broken for a child by his parents.

[33] The training which a Kwoma receives during his lifetime to inhibit aggression toward a relative cannot at once be dissipated by simply saying, "My relationship with you is broken." The proposition remains relatively true, however.

sister's son (i.e., between those with the fewest intervening relatives), the privilege of cutting sago properly belonged to War and not to Gwiyap. War commanded Gwiyap to stop cutting sago on Payap's plot, and also demanded that he pay for the flour that he had already taken. Gwiyap protested, but War threatened to break their relationship unless the damages were paid. Gwiyap decided that it would be dangerous to have as important a man as War against him, so he paid the fine and broke his relationship with Payap.[34] Had Gwiyap enjoyed a status equal to or higher than that of War,[35] he might have disputed the case with him. Under such circumstances he would have broken with War and maintained relationship with Payap until the matter was settled.

Both the age-grade and adulthood ceremonies bring a boy into "safe"[36] relationships with persons outside the hamlet who are not actually related to him. The person who initiates him into the age-grade cycle becomes his *ceremonial father*, and he becomes his sponsor's *ceremonial son*.[37] Henceforth they behave toward one another just as though they were relatives. Aggression is restricted between them. They may visit one another without fear of sorcery, and they are expected to support one another in disputes. As in the case of relatives, they may break relations with one another, but as long as the relationship remains "safe," it has the distinct advantage of expanding the number and geographic distribution of persons who need not be feared. As with the

[34] This breaking of relationship between Gwiyap and Payap was not an aggressive act, but simply meant that both he and War could not have a relationship with the same *mother's brother*. Gwiyap showed some resentment against Payap for allowing him to make the mistake and thus forcing him to pay damages to War. Actually Gwiyap lost nothing by the transaction because the obligation to pay Payap at the age-grade ceremony was now nullified.

[35] Gwiyap was an adolescent, whereas War was a middle-aged man of high standing in the community.

[36] A safe relationship is the converse of a broken relationship. The Kwoma term for this is *ma kiefi jiju*, literally "man good goes."

[37] *Ceremonial father* and *son* are of different sibs; hence they necessarily live in different hamlets.

ceremonial-father-ceremonial-son relationship, *friends*[38] are "safe" with one another. In addition, their children automatically become *friends*, and the idea that this extension of "safe" relationship is comparable to kinship is so vivid that the sons and daughters of two *friends* may not marry.

As may be inferred from the importance of maintaining "safe" relationships with relatives and even of extending them to persons not included in the kinship proper, a Kwoma adolescent has considerable fear and distrust of non-relatives. As has been shown, the parents engender considerable fear of non-relatives in the boy during childhood, by warning him of the danger of sorcery and attack, so that he has learned to be suspicious of this category of persons and to avoid them. At adolescence, however, he is thrown more in contact with them. He meets them at the various ceremonies, at court meetings, and on the way to and from his garden. His increased size and experience make him less afraid of such persons. Although he still remains on his guard when in their presence, and does not participate intimately with them, he will now gossip with them if he meets them, and even stop at their houses to talk with them. He does his visiting in the afternoon, exchanging betel and tobacco with his hosts, but he does so guardedly and follows meticulously the forms of etiquette. Above all, he is extremely careful not to leave behind him anything which might be used for sorcery, nor to give any intimation that he is interested in stealing sorcery material.

An adolescent boy is ready to become aggressive toward a non-relative at the slightest affront. Two factors operate strongly to produce this pugnacious attitude. In the first place, in his childhood struggles with his *brothers* he has frequently been told by his parents that he should fight for his rights. This social pressure toward aggressiveness increases with age. An adolescent boy who backs down when

---

[38] The sons of a person's father's *friends* are his *friends* as well as those unrelated boys of his own age with whom he wishes to establish this relationship. The formal establishment of such a relationship does not take place until the initiation into adulthood, however.

he is confronted by a non-relative, or who refuses to retaliate when someone has taken advantage of him, is severely criticized by his relatives. The second factor is closely related to the first. A Kwoma man gains prestige by being called *harafa ma malaka* (big older brother man),[39] i.e., one who refuses to be taken advantage of in any way. A man is respected in his own community in proportion as he is feared in others. To become generally known as *harafa ma malaka* is not a wish prompted by idle vanity alone, for with it come specific privileges. Such a person has fulfilled one of the requirements for membership in the highest stage of the yam cult, and thus need not depend on others to plant his garden. His relatives will be eager to help him when he asks for their coöperation in an economic task, although many of them might find that they had more pressing matters to attend to if he were of low status. A man who has either achieved this status or shown promise of achieving it can also expect to find favor with the most attractive women both in philandering and marriage. Finally, his word will carry much weight in any controversy, either at home or at court. Although this position of prestige is not achieved until adulthood, a man starts during childhood to establish the reputation of being hard, and continues the process during adolescence. During childhood his aggression is directed for the most part toward his *brothers;* with adolescence he begins to exhibit his toughness toward non-relatives.

The non-relatives most threatening to an adolescent boy are the relatives of the girls with whom he philanders. He reacts to them, as we have seen, by being secretive, by concealing the behavior for which they will punish him. He does not dare be openly aggressive toward them, for his relatives would be loath to support him, even non-relatives being granted the right to protect their female relatives. A boy does, however, react with verbal aggression behind the backs of such persons. He boasts to his *brothers* that he is not

[39] Cf. aggressiveness of older brothers and submissiveness of younger brothers. See chap. iv, pp. 57–58.

afraid of So-and-so: "His sister likes me, and he cannot stop me from philandering with her. I am a hard man."

The persons who have, or attempt to have, affairs with a boy's *sister* constitute another category of persons who menace him. The danger in this case is not that of physical injury but rather the threat that the value of his *sister* may be depreciated, leaving him less money with which to pay for a wife of his own. A boy is not only supported by his community for reacting aggressively toward his *sister's* lover, he is punished by them if he does not. Custom limits, however, the amount of aggression that he may show. If he oversteps these bounds, he loses the support of his own relatives. The socially expected reaction when a boy discovers that someone has been making free with his *sister* is to retaliate in kind, that is, to philander with a *sister* of his antagonist. He is also expected to shout insults at the latter, to challenge him to a fight (which never eventuates), and to threaten to kill him if he persists. If he catches a lover *in flagrante delicto* with his *sister*, the boy is expected to attack him physically. He may even kill him, but it is wiser not to do so since such an act would certainly precipitate a feud.

Even in courtship, the father and *brothers* of the girl are a source of danger. They stand in judgment over the suitor and his actions. If they do not approve of him, they seriously interfere with his desires. His reaction toward them is a combination of aggression and avoidance. To their face he is alternately friendly and jokingly aggressive; behind their back he may show marked hostility. When Waramus interfered with Mar's courtship of his daughter Aya, Mar accused him behind his back of being a sorcerer and said that he was going to challenge him to a fight. Several times he expressed the intention of "punching Waramus in the nose," and once he told me that he would like to go down and spear the man while he slept. In his face-to-face relations with Waramus, however, Mar was polite to the point of obsequiousness.

Gwiyap's behavior toward the relatives of his betrothed,

Gwimpi, exemplifies Kwoma custom in this respect. One day he told me that Nowel, Gwimpi's brother, had insulted him, and added: "If that Nowel comes around here again, I am going to beat him up. You won't be angry with me if I give him a good licking, will you?" The threatened fight never occurred. Although Gwiyap spoke sneeringly of Nowel several times thereafter when the latter was not present, he was especially friendly to him whenever they were together. A month or so later he began addressing Nowel by the brother-in-law term. The latter would protest at this and deny the relationship. On one occasion Nowel's *paternal uncle* was present, overheard Gwiyap addressing Nowel in this way, and asked him the reason for it. Gwiyap replied: "I am going to marry your niece. Have you anything to say about it? If you don't like it, I will fight you." (Gwiyap was much smaller than the man whom he was challenging.) The uncle laughed indulgently at the threat and jokingly replied, "You are talking pretty big for a child." That evening Gwiyap asked my help in case a fight should result, but nothing came of the matter.

Fear of retaliation prevents a boy from being seriously aggressive toward his future relatives-in-law. They stand as a unit against him, whereas his own relatives will not support him in any unwarranted aggression. If the relatives of the girl do not exceed their rights, a boy is not considered justified in going farther than in the case reported above. Possibly another reason why a boy is inhibited from direct expression of his hostility toward his future in-laws is that the punishment he has received in the past for being aggressive toward his own father and *brothers* has generated anxiety which is generalized to this new situation.[40]

An adolescent boy may be frustrated by the girls whom he flirts with or courts. His sexual wishes or his desire for marriage may be blocked because the girl is not interested in him. He must submit to this frustration, for to express his aggression would evoke retaliation from the girl's relatives.

[40] Mar, directly after Waramus insulted him, had a nightmare in which his father tried to take his soul.

If he dislikes a girl who makes advances to him, he may turn her down, but even this is dangerous, for if he antagonizes her too much, she may claim that he attempted to rape her. If he dislikes a betrothed girl who is already living with him, he may express his aggression by scolding her and by criticizing her behind her back, but if he harms her, he is in jeopardy of retaliation from her relatives.

Foreigners constitute a final category of persons whom an adolescent boy fears. He continues to avoid them as he did during childhood. On the other hand, he is now eligible to go on a head-hunting raid and thus has the opportunity to react aggressively toward them. Since head-hunting is primarily an adult occupation, however, its description, including examples of the reactions of adolescents, will be postponed.

An adolescent girl reacts to pain and danger in a manner frequently similar to, but often different from, that of a boy. Both sexes react similarly to the natural environment. While girls do not participate in hunting, they are not loath to kill a snake or lizard which gets in their way. Toward insects, noxious flora, sorcery,[41] and ghosts, their behavior is also quite comparable. On the other hand, whereas boys are initiated into the cult and thus learn a special type of behavior toward *marsalai*, girls do not undergo such an initiation. In fact, they must avoid the house tamberan during ceremonies, like children, and are supposed to believe that the sounds of gongs and flutes are the voices of the *marsalai*. Nevertheless, adolescent girls have a fairly good idea of what causes the sounds. I once purchased several wooden figures which represented *marsalai*, and was told to hide them carefully, for if a child or a female saw one it would cause their death. One afternoon Kar visited me with his two nieces. Seeing the figures under the bed he pulled them out to examine them, apparently oblivious of the presence of his nieces. The two girls sat watching the proceedings and whispering to one another about the objects.

[41] Girls do not participate directly in anti-sorcery behavior, but they are as vociferous in their verbal aggression against putative sorcerers as are boys, if not more so.

An adolescent girl also resembles a boy in her responses to punishments from persons living in the hamlet. She usually obeys her parents, but is sometimes verbally aggressive toward them and rather frequently grumbles behind their back.[42] She threatens, scolds, and beats her younger siblings as do boys of her age. Toward her adolescent *sisters*, she behaves in a manner comparable to that of a boy toward his adolescent *brothers;* she tries to gain dominance over them so that she may command them and avoid obeying them. On two occasions while I was at Kwoma, an adolescent girl attacked a *sister* with a stick. The relation of a girl to her *brother* is the reciprocal of that described for the boy. She plays her part in the joking relationship, quite adequately holding her own in the insults that pass between them. In regard to sexual behavior which her *brothers* might punish, she either obeys their interdiction or takes care to hide her actions from them.

A girl behaves toward persons outside the hamlet in much the same way as does a boy. She is polite toward relatives who live elsewhere, but has the privilege of breaking relationships with them. She tends to avoid non-relatives except in clandestine love affairs. When she goes to live with her betrothed, however, she has to make a rather difficult adjustment to him and to his relatives. In this situation she has several modes of coping with threats and annoyances from her future in-laws: she may call upon her relatives for help, support, and protection from retaliation; she may submit and become subservient; or she may break the engagement and return to her own home. Girls who are successful in marriage make some compromise between the first two of these modes of adjustment.

Adolescence, in fine, widens the scope of experience of Kwoma boys and girls and brings them into new learning dilemmas. They assume new economic responsibilities and occupy themselves with philandering and courtship. They learn to cope more courageously with the physical environ-

---

[42] Although I have no figures on the matter, it is my impression that girls express verbal aggression toward their parents more freely than do boys.

ment, and, in the case of boys, to be less terrified of the supernatural environment. They discover that sorcery can be combated and that *marsalai* are, in part at least, a fraud. Their social environment expands. The battlefield on which they fight to be respected now extends beyond the hamlet instead of being confined primarily to their siblings as it was during childhood. They learn the value both of maintaining safe relationships and of threatening to break them. Perhaps most important of all, they learn not to let anyone impose upon them.

CHAPTER VI

ADULTHOOD

A KWOMA boy becomes an adult[1] when he receives the keloids which are a symbol of manhood. The scarification ceremony[2] occurs when he has grown to full stature and is ready to marry.[3] This initiation takes place at one of the house tamberans where all the boys of the proper age are operated on at a single ceremony. Each boy, when his turn comes, lies on a sago spathe. While the father of his future wife holds his hands, a special operator incises two semicircular cuts above each nipple and rubs ashes into them to make a raised scar. All boys who are cut on the same spathe become *friends*, a relationship established by the mixture of their blood which it is believed makes them "one blood" like *brothers*.

A girl enters adulthood in a slightly different and less public manner. She also is cut with other girls of her age, to each of whom she becomes a *friend;* but the operation takes place at the dwelling of the operator, instead of the house tamberan, and the design of her keloid is an elaborate circular figure centered about the navel. I do not know who holds her hands during the operation.

By the time a Kwoma man has become adult, he has learned most of the techniques of food getting. Even as an adolescent he has assumed considerable responsibility for producing food. As an adult his economic duties are even more insistently sanctioned. An adolescent need only contribute to the support of his father's family, but an adult must produce

[1] The adults of Rumbima hamlet whose behavior was most closely observed were Wof, Marok, War, Kar, Kis, Yat, Way, Waramus, and Mes. Kar, Kis, Yat, and Mes, since they spoke pidgin English, were my best informants on this period. (See household map and lineage chart in chap. i.)

[2] This ceremony should not be confused with either the age-grade or cult initiation ceremonies which occur during adolescence.

[3] In the majority of cases, a boy marries shortly after the scars are healed, so his wedding also corresponds with his entry into adulthood.

food for himself, his wife, and his children. If he fails to do so, he may be criticized by his relatives, and deserted by his wife.

Gardening is an occupation which involves the coöperative endeavors of several persons.[4] The basic gardening group consists of the members of two or more closely related households, typically a father and his adult sons and their wives and children, or two or more adult brothers and their families. Sometimes a man will make a garden with his paternal uncle. Each adult male in the group has an equal share in the garden set aside for him and his family, the section being marked off with bamboo poles laid end to end on the ground. Each section is subdivided in the same way for every member of each family except the infants. This group coöperates in all phases of gardening. The males and females, children, adolescents, and adults have differing tasks allotted to them, but they work as a coöperative unit under the direction of the boss gardeners, the adult males of the group. A new function for the man is, therefore, to take the responsibility for planning and organizing gardening activities.

Some of the gardening tasks are more effectively performed by a group larger than the gardening group. The Kwoma have a work-bee system to take care of this need. Whenever the boss gardeners decide that they need help on some phase of gardening, either in clearing the site, breaking the ground, or harvesting the crop, they gather together enough food for a feast. They and their families collect a surplus of sago flour and provide meat, preferably a wild pig. If no one has succeeded in spearing a pig, they process a still greater surplus of sago flour, trade it for fish from the river natives, and use this instead of pork. When they have gathered this supply of flour and meat, they announce, both on the house tamberan gongs and by passing the word around, a work bee for the following day and request their

[4] If all the details of the technique of gardening were presented here, the main theme—socialization—would be buried in a welter of detail. Only the major processes of gardening will therefore be presented, leaving the details for another publication.

relatives to help. All the members of the hamlet who do not have pressing work of their own are expected to answer this call and appear the next morning at the place where the work is to be done. The *brothers* of the married women of the households who are giving the bee are also expected to help if they can. While the men work, the women prepare the feast. Then, early in the afternoon, after a long morning's work, the men stop and go to the house of one of the boss gardeners where the feast is to be given. The men form a separate group from the women, eat in a leisurely manner, smoke, chew betel, and indulge in horseplay between courses. After the meal the older men either gossip or nap while the boys tease one another and play. The work is over for the day. The Kwoma are perfectly familiar with the patterned behavior of these work parties, since they have participated in them frequently during childhood and adolescence. When they become adult they have to plan the work bees, direct the gathering of food, and announce the day.

The first task in gardening is to choose a site, a decision which rests with the boss gardeners. They must balance the advantages and disadvantages of cultivating a plot in the hamlet or in an outlying district.[5] If the garden is planted near the dwelling, it has to be enclosed by a fence to prevent domestic pigs from rooting up the crop, but it is near at hand. If a site is cleared in an outlying district, it may take several hours to walk there, but it need not be fenced.

The garden site is usually cleared by means of a number of work bees. Since it takes considerable time and effort to provide food for the feast, the task of clearing a site is normally spread over several weeks, and sometimes months. The first task, which is performed by adolescent boys and men, is to climb the trees and lop off the branches in order to let sun down to the earth below. The old men and children clear the brush and stack it and the cut branches into piles for burning.

After the site has been cleared and the rubbish burned,

[5] Property rights, also, determine the choice. The division and ownership of land will be discussed below.

the boss gardeners normally prepare another bee to break the ground for the yam hills, although the gardening group may do this work alone. If the latter is the case, the women of the group work with the men instead of preparing the feast. Since Kwoma gardens are always on a slope, each hill is made by leveling the ground into a little terrace about a foot square. This is accomplished by means of a spadelike digging stick. When the slope is especially steep, the terraces are buttressed by a retaining wall of sticks laid one on top of the other, held on one side by the pressure of the earth and on the other by pegs stuck in the ground. These miniature retaining walls prevent the hills from being washed out by a heavy rain. The worker, with a final thrust of his digging stick into the middle of each terrace, pries open a hole large enough to receive a seed yam.

The Kwoma consider that the success of the crop depends more upon planting than upon any other part of the gardening process. Only an adult man who has become a member of *Nokwi*, the highest stage of the yam cult, may do this. They believe that if a youth or a woman should put the seed yams in the ground, the yield would be meager, hard, and unpalatable. Normally, one of the boss gardeners has attained the proper status to plant yams. If not, then the nearest patrilineal relative who is a member of *Nokwi* will perform the task in return for a share in the produce of the garden. On the night before a man is to plant yams, he shares with other members of *Nokwi* a ritual soup which is believed to be potent enough to kill a woman or child. From this time on until the yam shoots break the ground, he may not chew betel, scratch himself except with a stick, or smoke except by holding his cigarette with tweezers. If he does not carry out these rituals, it is believed that his yams will not germinate. The planter performs his task by putting the yam into the hole in the hill so that the butt is down and the head (stem) is up, and the axis roughly perpendicular to level ground. He then covers the yam with earth so that the upper end is just below the surface.

Kwoma beliefs about blood appear again to determine a

facet of the yam-planting complex. It is believed that in the process of planting yams a man's blood becomes associated with the seed, and hence contaminates the produce. Thus, if a man should eat his own harvest, it would be equivalent to eating his own blood, and he would sicken and die. If he heeds the warning implied in this belief, he must have yams that are planted by someone else or go without them. Kwoma culture resolves the dilemma as follows: at the time of planting, a section of the garden large enough to produce sufficient yams for the planter's personal needs is set aside. He does not plant this section, but calls on a *brother* to do it for him. This provides a section whose produce will not be contaminated by his blood and which he may therefore eat with impunity. In return he plants a similar section in his *brother's* garden.

After the yams are put in the ground, nothing but weeding need be done until the sprouts appear. The women of the gardening group do this, bending from the waist rather than kneeling, and pulling the weeds with thumb and fingers. They keep the ground clear until the plants have a good start and then allow the weeds to spring up unheeded.

Soon after the yam sprouts have broken the ground, stringers must be provided to support the climbing vines. In preparation for this, men and boys cut lianas from the forest and split them into sections about the diameter of the little finger and about thirty feet long. They tie a loop formed by a half knot on the standing part on one end of each of these ropes and coil them into bundles. The women carry these bundles in their net bags to the garden, where the men hang the lianas by the loops from the branches of the denuded trees. To do this they use a long bamboo pole with a cross stick, lashed a few inches from the top to prevent the loop from sliding down the pole. The free ends of the lianas are pegged to the ground a few inches from each yam hill. Each hill is thus provided with a stringer, one end of which is attached to a branch and the other to a peg in the ground. Once every few days thereafter the men go over the garden and train the yam tendrils on the stringer. The gardener takes care not to place one stringer underneath the other, for this would keep sun and rain from the lower vine.

Once the vines have a firm hold on the stringers, nothing need be done to the garden until the time of harvesting. The gardening group digs the yams with a digging stick. The tubers are then picked up in net bags and carried by the women to the dwelling.

The produce from each section is kept separate so that each member of the gardening group has his or her own yams rather than a lien on a common store. Each person's share is put in a separate bin in the small storehouse, which is built near the dwelling. This storehouse is constructed like a dwelling but has no porch. It is floored with sago spathe to prevent the yams from rotting as a result of contact with the damp earth. The bins are also constructed of sago spathe.

Although yams form the bulk of the crop, the Kwoma utilize the cleared site to produce other vegetables as well. Taro plants are set out, and tobacco and spinach seeds are broadcast between the yam hills. Unlike yams, these latter seeds may be planted by any person—adolescent or adult. There is a belief, however, that if tobacco seeds are sown by women the leaves will be overmild. In order to take full advantage of the cleared site, the boss gardeners set out banana, plantain, and coconut trees which mature after the yams are harvested, but before the towering hardwoods grow up to shut out the sunlight.

In addition to planting a garden, the Kwoma man sets out numerous useful trees around his dwelling. He sets out betel pepper vines from clippings, plants areca-nut palms from sprouted nuts, and puts in seed of a small tree from whose bark thread is made. The orchard also includes two trees whose leaves are used respectively for the inner and outer wrappings for sago briquettes, a large tree which bears an edible berry-like fruit, another which bears a large oblong red fruit, a bush whose leaves are used as greens in soup, as well as a few banana, pawpaw, and breadfruit trees. As many coconut palms as space will allow are also planted.

Pig hunting is an occupation which a Kwoma male does

for the first time as an adult. Women never hunt. A man usually hunts alone, although occasionally he will allow an adolescent boy to accompany him and watch. The bait-and-blind technique is considered the most effective method. For bait the hunter cuts down a sago palm in the swamp wherever pig signs are evident. He erects a blind of fronds alongside this, and on a moonlight night waits for the prey to come to eat the fresh sago pith. The hunter may crouch in the mud for several hours before the sound of sloshing footsteps, punctuated with deep grunts and the breaking of dead sago fronds, heralds the arrival of the game. If he is lucky enough to attract a wild pig to his bait, he edges slowly and soundlessly along the blind to a point opposite his prey and then rises slowly and thrusts his spear into the beast's heart.

The Kwoma also hunt with trained dogs. They walk through the swamp until their dog picks up the fresh trail of a wild pig. If the dog brings his quarry to bay, the hunter dispatches it with a spear. Wild pigs are also trapped. A hole about four feet in diameter and five feet deep is dug in a pig trail and covered lightly with twigs and leaves. The trapper visits this pitfall periodically.

After a pig has been killed it must be transported from the swamp to the hamlet. If the pig is not full grown the hunter lifts it across the back of his neck and carries it as a shepherd does a lamb. If the hog is full grown and fattened on sago pith, however, it is too heavy for a man to carry alone. He therefore, if possible, drags the carcass to a pool and leaves it immersed in water while he goes home to get help from his *brothers*. Kwoma theory believes that the meat keeps better immersed in water than if it is simply left where it falls. At least three men are required to carry a large hog. Two of them lift the burden onto the back of the third man, and he staggers as far as he can before the hog is transferred to the shoulders of another. By taking turns in this way the carcass is finally brought home.

The adult man of the hamlet who is most adept at butchering usually performs this task. The pig is laid on its back on a blanket of leaves and cut up with bamboo knives.[6] The joints are cut with adzes. The mode of butchering differs considerably from the European technique, as the pig is divided in line with the jaws into a ventral and a dorsal half rather than along the backbone into a right and a left half.

A hunter who has killed a pig may eat none of its flesh himself lest he sicken and die. This restriction is parallel to the one placed upon the yam planters. The Kwoma believe that when a man kills a pig his own blood enters the animal; hence to eat its flesh would be to eat his own blood, an act which has the consequence of causing sickness and death. A man therefore uses the pork for one of the following purposes: to provide food for his family and relatives; to discharge a ceremonial obligation to a relative; to give a goodwill feast at his house tamberan to which all members of his cult section (*Yenama* or *Minjama*) are invited; to provide food for one of the regular cult or age-grade ceremonies in order to gain prestige; to give a feast for the members of the sorcery court if a relative is sick; to provide for the second funeral feast for a deceased relative; to provide food for a work bee; or to trade with the river people for shell money. In the event that the pig is to be used for a feast, the whole animal is contributed and a soup is made in several large pots. What is not eaten is distributed to those present at the ceremony. If, however, the animal is to be given to relatives, there are specific rules which govern what part of the animal shall go to each of them. The *maternal uncle* receives the hams; the *paternal aunt* gets the second joints of the fore legs; the *sisters* are given the shoulders and brisket; *paternal uncles* receive the brain case and upper jaw; and the *brothers* get the hind trotters. The remainder—the backbone, hind and fore flanks, and the entrails—is kept by the hunter to provide meat for his immediate family.

This description of the use to which pork is put indicates that a man does not learn to hunt pigs in order to satisfy his

[6] Although the Kwoma now have steel knives, they prefer bamboo ones for butchering.

own hunger directly. Indirectly the amount of pork that is available to him does depend on his hunting activities, for if he never supplies his relatives with pork they tend to utilize the pigs which they kill for ceremonial purposes rather than for distribution among relatives. On the other hand, a man receives his share of pork at ceremonies even though he has never killed a pig himself. Furthermore his negligence in supplying a *brother*, for example, with pork does not mean that this *brother* will not be motivated to distribute a kill to other relatives, in which distribution the man who has never killed a pig automatically gets his share. A man may, therefore, have pork to eat all his life and yet never kill a pig; indeed, this is true of a number of Kwoma men.

Since a man's desire for pork is relevant but not crucial in influencing him to learn to hunt pigs, and since it is an occupation in which men are frequently seriously injured[7] and sometimes killed, other reasons must be sought to explain why so many men do learn the techniques of hunting. One of these motives is that of avoiding the criticism of his friends and relatives, a factor which operates in the following way. If a man does not learn to hunt, but develops some other technical specialty such as wood carving, toolmaking, ceremonial gong beating, dancing, or song leading, then he will not be criticized for not developing the art of pig hunting. If, however, he does not so compensate for this lack, social criticism will be leveled against him. He will be called lazy and scolded by his wife and the other members of the hamlet for not doing his share of productive work.

There are positive gains which motivate a man to learn to hunt. If he uses the pork as the chief food of a work bee, his hunting activity is rewarded by getting his work accomplished more quickly, for more people are likely to answer his call for help if they know there will be pork. If he uses it to provide a feast for a sorcery court and his relative recov-

---

[7] During my stay at Kwoma, two men were seriously injured. One of them had his leg badly lacerated and escaped death by climbing a tree; the other's hand was badly chewed and he was saved by another hunter who happened to be in the vicinity.

ers, he feels that his hunting has not been in vain. If he uses the pig as part payment of the bride-price, hunting helps to put an end to the snooping, interference, and threats of his relatives-in-law. If he trades the pig with the river people, his reward is in shell money. If the pig is used for a funeral feast, he may thereafter eat the food which he has denied himself ever since the death of his relative many months before. If he contributes the pig to a cult or good-will feast, he is rewarded by a gain in prestige. More particularly, he will command greater respect at court meetings, he will have more supporters to come to his aid on the event of a sorcery charge being leveled against him, and his relatives will be less apt to have important work of their own to do when he announces a work bee. Indeed a good pig hunter is a *harafa ma malaka*. All these factors combine to force a Kwoma man to learn to hunt pigs despite the danger and effort involved.

Although pigs are the most-prized game, Kwoma hunters kill other animals as well. Cassowaries come next in importance both in giving prestige to the hunter and in providing food. These large birds are hunted by dogs in the same way as wild pigs, and are likewise dispatched by a spear. Bait-and-blind hunting is not employed, but a hen is sometimes speared while she is on her nest. All smaller birds are killed by means of bow and bird dart. Since most of the wild fowl perch at the top of the jungle trees some sixty to eighty feet from the ground—a very difficult shot even with a rifle—this form of hunting is not highly developed. A native will attempt a shot only when he is within a few feet of the game, when birds alight on the shrubbery near the house. Bow and bird dart are also employed in the hunting of gouria pigeons. These large birds often feed on the windfall under wild fruit trees. A native hunter sometimes makes a blind under such a tree and shoots the pigeons if they are attracted by the fallen fruit.

Men spend little time hunting small game, leaving such activities to children. They sometimes kill rats, snakes, and lizards. The usual method is simply to beat them with any handy stick. Some of the smaller lizards are caught and strangled by hand or are snared by means of a running noose tied to the end of a stick. A man sometimes constructs a small deadfall trap in the granary or dwelling to catch stray rats, but more frequently he sets a hunting dog on these pests.

If a man does not use a bow and dart or spear to kill small animals, the belief about his blood does not strictly apply. He may eat them without harm. Many Kwoma, however, do not take the chance of eating something which has been killed even in this way, and give the meat to some other member of their family.

Opossums and birds of paradise are exceptions to the lack of interest in small game. A man may expend considerable effort hunting these, not because of their food value, but because they yield homicidal insignia. A man who has taken the head of an enemy is permitted to wear a band of opossum fur on his forehead and bird of paradise plumes in his comb. Hence a man who already has the privilege of wearing such insignia eagerly seeks them, and one who does not yet have the privilege seeks them to use in the future or to give to a *brother* or *uncle*.

Processing sago is a continual chore for Kwoma adults of both sexes. The technique which they master during adolescence has been described in the preceding chapter. The only change which occurs at adulthood is that the work group is composed of a man and his wife rather than of a brother and his sister. The habits of processing sago are maintained by the family's need for an everyday supply of sago flour, for a surplus to be traded with the river people for fish, and for contributions to necessary work bees and ceremonial feasts.

An adult woman continues to fish as she did during her adolescence and childhood. Since marriage is patrilocal, she fishes in a new locale with the women of her husband's hamlet. The main fish supply comes from trade; consequently fishing is only a supplementary occupation in an economic sense and is engaged in primarily for recreation.

A woman supplements the larder with edible produce from the forest. She collects the leaves of certain wild trees for use as greens; she searches in the dead butts of sago palms for

Adulthood

the grubs, which are considered a delicacy roasted; and she picks up the windfalls from edible varieties of wild fruit trees. These are subsidiary economic tasks for the woman, but, if she neglects them, her husband will criticize her. Her own wish for these additions to her diet also provides a motive for this work.

A woman continues during adulthood to perform many of the tasks that she learned during childhood and adolescence. She is responsible for keeping the household supplied with firewood and water until she has daughters old enough to take over this work. It is her duty to build the fire in her hearth, to plan and prepare the midday meal, and to keep on hand a supply of sago briquettes. Her husband sees to it that she performs these wifely duties, criticizing and even beating her if she is unduly lazy or negligent.

The men and women of a family share the responsibility of caring for the domesticated animals. It is the man who captures wild pigs whenever he spears a sow with a litter. After he brings them home, he tethers them to stakes near the house, where his wife and children feed them sago pulp mash until they are habituated to the dwelling; then he allows them to go free and forage for themselves. The wife has the responsibility of feeding them whenever they return to the dwelling or calling them to be fed if they stay away for more than a day. Special care is taken of a pregnant sow. Husband and wife coöperate in watching her so that they can catch and tame the offspring before they run wild. The man castrates all male pigs because it is believed that boars cannot be domesticated. The litters born to domesticated sows are therefore sired by wild boars. A domesticated pig is speared and butchered and its flesh used in the same manner as wild pigs, and the same taboo against eating its flesh applies to the man who kills it.

One or more dogs are attached to every Kwoma family. Each dog is individually owned, and is fed and cared for by his master or mistress. Some dogs are trained for hunting. To do this a man must teach the dog to follow pig tracks in the forest but not in the hamlet, for if a man's dog chases and injures the domestic pig of one of his neighbors, he must pay an indemnity. It is not an easy task to teach dogs to make this discrimination, and for this reason a good hunting dog is highly valued. Dogs are also used as food, but no one will eat the flesh of a dog owned by a member of his family. To do so, they believe, would be almost equivalent to cannibalism, since dogs are referred to as the son or daughter of the owner and by kin terms appropriate to this relationship by other members of the family. Dog meat is therefore used only for ceremonial and trading purposes. If a dog dies a natural death, the women of the household may wail and watch over the body as though it were human. The corpse is formally disposed of by suspending it in a net bag from the limb of a tree in the forest.

Adults are responsible for making the tools and utensils which are indispensable in the production of food. The adz[8] is the Kwoma tool of all work, and is essential in gardening, the production of sago flour, and butchering, as well as in the manufacture of many of the special tools used in the various economic pursuits. It is made and used only by men. The technique of adz construction need not concern us here, except to say that there is little variation in the haft, or handle, and that there are two types of lashing, plain and fancy. Only a few men learn to do the fancy lashing, and they can readily trade an adz lashed in this manner for shell money. The celt for an adz was formerly of ground stone; today plane irons obtained from the whites are used exclusively.

The large net bag of the women is as essential in economic activities as is the adz. It is used to carry seeds and tools to the garden, to bring back the harvest, to transport sago flour from the swamp, to carry a pig after it has been butchered, and to bring firewood to the dwelling. This container is used only by women and is netted by them. Since these bags must be replaced frequently, a woman spends much of her spare time manufacturing them.[9]

[8] The adz is also essential in activities not directly associated with hunger, such as housebuilding and gong making.
[9] As was stated in the previous chapter, a girl learns this technique during adolescence.

Adulthood

A variety of tools are required for special purposes in various aspects of the Kwoma economics. Spears,[10] sago scrapers, dippers, gruel mixers, bamboo water containers, and digging sticks are made by men and kept for repeated use. The sago washing outfit is assembled by the man from the materials at hand in the swamp and abandoned when the site is moved. A man constructs the pole used to hang up yam stringers from a bamboo section marker and replaces it when he is through. The men make, decorate, and harden by fire the clay pots used for cooking. All these tools and utensils are necessary to the economic activities in which they are used so that the functions and sanctions which pertain to these activities also apply indirectly to the manufacture of the tools. In addition to this, a man who does not make the necessary tools is directly criticized for his negligence by his relatives. Furthermore, a good toolmaker not only gains prestige for his dexterity, but is also able to trade any surplus of neatly made permanent tools for goods or services.

Fish is the only food product which the Kwoma obtain primarily by trade from other tribes.[11] The river natives catch a surplus of fish, whereas the Kwoma produce a surplus of sago flour. On the other hand, the river tribes do not control large enough sago swamps for their needs, nor have the Kwoma developed adequate fishing techniques.[12] A regular exchange of these products therefore takes place between the Kwoma and the river people, particularly those from the villages of Yambon, Malu, and Avatip. The women of both groups do the trading, the men going to the market only for the purpose of gossiping and in the hope of making a tryst.[13] A Kwoma girl may attend these trading meetings during childhood; she participates in them during adolescence; as

[10] The pig spear used for hunting is somewhat heavier and constructed somewhat differently from the spear used in war.

[11] Shell money, tools, and pigs are sometimes exchanged between the Kwoma and adjacent tribes. Men carry on this type of trade.

[12] Canoes are employed by the river natives for fishing. The Kwoma had only one canoe, which was so badly constructed that it could scarcely be used. Very few of the natives knew how to paddle it.

[13] In the days before the tribes were brought under control, each market was attended by armed men to prevent a possible head-hunting assault.

an adult she takes the responsibility for seeing that a surplus of flour is produced and for arranging the day for the next market.

By the time a Kwoma has reached adulthood, he has learned the system of property rights of his culture. He knows that garden produce belongs to the person on whose section it was grown, that sago flour belongs to the persons who process it, fish to the women who catch or buy them, a pig to the person who owns or kills it, pork to the person who receives it from the original owner, and tools to the person who makes or buys them. He also knows what liens his various relatives have upon his property and what liens he has upon the property of his relatives. He has learned that if he disregards the property rights of others he may expect them to punish him if they catch him, but he has also learned during childhood that one may often thieve without being caught, and few Kwoma adults are above stealing if they are sure they will not be discovered.

It is not until adulthood that a Kwoma man is expected to defend property rights in land. This duty falls upon him, his adult male relatives, the men of the subtribe, and the men of the tribe as a whole; women and children have no direct concern in the matter. A man's duties in the defense of property rights depend upon who transgresses them and under what circumstances such transgression takes place, and upon his membership in the tribe, subtribe, hamlet, lineage, and family line.

The Peilunga Range and the adjacent swamps are owned by the Kwoma tribe as a whole, and as a member of this tribe a man is expected to defend this territory against conquest by another tribe. Such conflict rarely occurs, but a struggle over land in which all the subtribes of Kwoma banded together to annihilate and drive from the Peilunga Mountains a tribe who at one time shared the territory with them occurred during the lifetime of the grandfathers of the present generation. Minor disputes over boundaries with the tribes contiguous to Kwoma do not, however, concern the tribe as a whole, but at most the subtribe and usually only the hamlet whose territory is under dispute.

If a dispute involving a considerable amount of sago swamp or gardening land arises between the members of two subtribes, all the adult men of each subtribe may eventually become involved. Such a dispute normally arises when someone extracts sago flour or plants a garden near or beyond the territorial boundary of his subtribe. Those of the other subtribe who control the land contiguous to the boundary normally claim trespass, destroy any tools which they may find, seize the produce, and even threaten personal harm. Unless the affair is settled quickly by the withdrawal of one or other of the parties concerned, each may call relatives to his support until the dispute finally becomes the concern of both subtribes. When such a situation arises, the disputed land is normally left unused by both parties until the affair has been settled by an intertribal court meeting.[14]

A man has certain duties with respect to the defense of all lands claimed by the members of his hamlet. These duties apply only when the transgressor of property rights is a member of some other hamlet. Again minor disputes may be settled by the parties concerned, but, if they are not, they are settled by a meeting of the domestic court which a man must attend in order to defend his *brothers*. In a similar way property disputes between members of different lineages in the same hamlet and between families in the same lineage are finally settled by a court meeting attended by the men of the largest group involved.

The rights and duties with respect to land are thus determined by a man's membership in the various groups described above. Since membership in family line, lineage, and hamlet follows patrilineal descent, inheritance may likewise be considered as patrilineal. The Kwoma do not, however, distinguish inheritance of land from descent. Hence the rules which determine to what family line, lineage, and hamlet a

[14] An intertribal court meeting will be described below with reference to payment of wergild after head-hunting raids.

man belongs govern where he has the right to build his house, plant his garden, and gather sago flour. In order to clarify this principle it is necessary to show the relation between these descent groups and land.

Each family line has control of a not too clearly delimited district near the house tamberan of the hamlet on which its male members build their houses. The exact site is decided by the builder with the consent of the other men of the family line. The districts of each family line are clustered with respect to their lineage affiliations. The gardening land which immediately surrounds the hamlet is divided into large sections belonging to the various lineages of the hamlet, and each of these is subdivided into districts controlled by the various family lines. Similarly, each lineage controls one or more sections of gardening land in the outlying districts of the subtribe and several sections of the sago swamp. Each of these plots is subdivided into subplots administered by the family line. If a man wishes to plant a garden or extract sago flour, he must choose a site on one of these subplots and must obtain the consent of the other members of his family line.

The number of persons in a family line is kept relatively constant through adoption. Those lines who have few or no sons adopt boys from more numerous family lines. By this process the relationship between men and land is kept relatively constant in a society where land may be neither bought, sold, nor willed to a particular heir.

The responsibility for defending property rights in land, produce, and tools falls more fully on the shoulders of a man during adulthood than during the earlier periods of his life. He not only must defend his own property against theft and trespass, but must assume most of the responsibility for preventing property violations against members of his immediate family and for helping his relatives to defend their rights against outsiders.[15] In order to prevent trespass or theft

[15] Theft and trespass are considered to be aggressive acts by the Kwoma, and sanctions and retaliation with respect to them are discussed in detail below.

from the house when the entire family leaves it to go to the garden, the sago spathe door to the inner room of the dwelling is closed and barred in a particular manner so that the head of the house will know if anyone tampers with it. To prevent persons from pilfering his garden, a man casts a magical spell so that anyone who enters the garden will break out in boils.

If the owner of property catches a thief in the act of stealing, he may attack him physically or may threaten to do so. If, however, the owner notices that some of his property has been stolen or disturbed, but is not sure of the identity of the culprit, he may publicly accuse the person whom he suspects, stating his reasons for suspicion and threatening aggressive action unless adjustment is made. If the evidence is so clear that the accused cannot deny the charge, he will normally pay the accuser damages in order to maintain "safe" relations. If, however, the accused is not guilty or if the case is not clear, the matter will be settled by a court meeting.[16] A court meeting may also be called to discover the identity of the culprit if the thief or trespasser is unknown.

A few examples of theft and trespass will illustrate this formal structure. Yat, a young man of Hayamakwo sib and Rumbima hamlet, built a pig blind on the edge of one of his sago patches. He visited it one day and found that it had been destroyed, and that a taboo fence[17] had been erected across his path to the blind. He suspected Dowar, also a Hayamakwo but a member of Sumwe Sumwe hamlet,[18] who owned the property next to his. On returning home he told his wives about the matter and went to the Rumbima house tamberan that evening to announce his anger. Those present agreed with his suspicions, and the evening was spent discussing the evil ways of the people of Sumwe Sumwe. The

[16] The procedure at a court meeting for property disputes is identical to that at the sorcery court described below.

[17] A taboo fence consists of the branch of a tree or a sago frond placed across a path. The implication of such a fence is that "anyone who goes down this path does so at his own risk and in the face of my threat."

[18] The Sumwe Sumwe split off from the Rumbima several years before as a result of a quarrel.

next day Yat sent a message to Sumwe Sumwe, announcing that he had discovered that his pig blind had been destroyed and that if they trespassed on his land again there would be trouble. The Sumwe Sumwe returned an equally aggressive message to the effect that Yat had built his blind on their property and that he had better not try to rebuild it. Angry and insulting messages flew back and forth most of the day. A few days later Yat again visited his pig blind, and on the way he met Dowar. Both of them were carrying their pig spears. After an angry exchange of insults, according to Yat, he challenged Dowar to a spear duel, but the latter threw down his spear and ran. Yat picked up the discarded spear and broke it against a tree. Then he returned home and boasted of his prowess at the house tamberan that evening. The topic for gossip was again that the Sumwe Sumwe were a bad lot and, in addition, were cowards. Many tales were recounted of their sexual depravity. Yat felt that Dowar had learned his lesson and would not interfere again. He said that if the offense were repeated, he would take the case to the patrol officer.[19]

Another case involved theft within the house-tamberan group. Kafa, Yat's wife, began shouting angrily one afternoon at Mar's betrothed, Yawa, accusing her of stealing sago grubs from a tree on her husband's plot. Yawa, being a rather cowardly and unaggressive girl, made a feeble denial, but Mar's mother and *aunt* immediately took over her defense and shouted invective in reply. Yat's other wife then joined in the argument, and for almost an hour the four women kept up a stream of insult, accusation, and threat. Now and again other women of the neighborhood would make a point on one side or the other, but none of the men joined in the argument. I asked Mar what he was going to do about it. He replied that it was a woman's argument and no affair of his. He was not very fond of his betrothed, and felt that she was a lazy good-for-nothing who had been foisted on him. He commented proudly on his mother's sharp

[19] If the dispute had continued it probably would have actually been settled at a meeting of the subtribal court.

tongue, however, and told me that most of the women of the hamlet were afraid of her. Finally the shouting subsided, and that evening Yat and Wof, Mar's *uncle* and foster father, discussed the affair calmly, decided that Yawa was guilty of stealing the grubs, and arranged for Kafa and Yat to be repaid in kind with grubs taken from one of Mar's plots. When Wof returned home, he lectured Yawa severely for her offense and threatened to beat her if she did it again.

A Kwoma weds soon after he becomes adult. Adolescent courtship, culminating in the trial marriage in which the girl comes to live with the boy's parents, is finally terminated, if all goes well, by a special ceremony which makes the couple man and wife. The boy's mother determines when this ceremony shall take place. If she is satisfied with the girl and knows that her son is also, she tells her to cook the food for the afternoon meal. Hitherto the betrothed has cooked food only for herself, and the boy's food has been prepared by his mother or sisters. The mother chooses an occasion when the boy is away from the house, so that, when he returns, he begins eating his soup unsuspectingly. When he has nearly finished his first bowl, his mother informs him that it was his betrothed who cooked the meal and that he is now married. At this announcement, it is expected that the boy will rush from the house and exclaim as he spits out the soup: "Faugh! It tastes bad! It is cooked terribly."

After the wedding ceremony, the couple live together as man and wife, and the customs which regulate marital sexual behavior apply to them. They never sleep in the same bed but lie alone on separate bark slabs, joining only for copulation, which is performed with a minimum of embracing and foreplay. All informants insisted that a husband and wife should not sleep together. When I asked Gwiyap if he might not sleep with his wife on cold nights, he replied, "No, I would be ashamed to." I asked why and he replied, "It is a bad thing to do. The big men like my uncle War would be cross. It is his duty to take care of me and see that I do nothing wrong."[20]

[20] *Homba,* "shame" or "guilt" is the same word which Kwoma use to

A woman supposedly takes the initiative in sexual intercourse even after marriage. It is the wife who visits her husband's bed. Informants admitted that the husband sometimes takes the lead, but that much more frequently the woman does so. The Kwoma men spoke of this custom as being related to that of the woman taking the initiative in clandestine love affairs and courting.

A man may not have sexual intercourse with his wife when she is menstruating, lest his penis be damaged by menstrual blood; nor when she is obviously pregnant, lest he damage the foetus; nor when she has an infant still at the breast, lest she have a second child and thus be forced to neglect the first one;[21] nor when he has just returned from a cult ceremony, lest his recent contact with the cult spirits harm the woman. This last restriction lasts from one to three nights, depending on the degree of sacredness of the ceremony. In any case he must wash himself carefully before lying with his wife to remove the dangerous spirit "infection." Finally, a husband and wife take care not to copulate while their children are still awake.

A Kwoma man's sexual behavior is not restricted to intercourse with his wife. He continues to have affairs with other women in a manner similar to that described for adolescents. He carries on his affairs secretly at carefully arranged trysts. He must be very careful not to stare at another man's wife, lest it cause suspicion, and must wait for the woman to take the initiative, lest she bring upon him the wrath of her

describe their feeling about brother-sister incest. In this context the effect may be derived from the punishments which a child receives during the weaning period for trying to sit in the lap of, sleep next to, and otherwise gain physical contact with, his mother. It is possible that if a man should sleep in contact with his wife, this earlier situation would be to some extent recreated and he would have feelings which he describes as *homba* as a result. The fact that Gwiyap referred this feeling to fear of the big men of the hamlet suggests that it may be related to the Oedipus situation. It should be remembered that at the same time that the mother no longer permits her infant to sleep next to her, the taboo on sexual intercourse which applied during the infancy of her offspring is lifted and the father, when he visits the mother at night, literally takes the place vacated by the child.

[21] Polygyny and philandering lessen the frustration of all these restrictions.

protectors. With regard to these affairs the Kwoma take the attitude that they are discreditable only if discovered. Every man knows that his wife is probably unfaithful to him, but unless he is extremely jealous he does not spy on her and punishes her only if she is indiscreet enough to be conspicuous.

There are two occasions of ceremonial sexual license. One occurs during the yam-cult ceremonies. As described in the previous chapter, the yam cult is divided into two sections, *Yenama* and *Minjama*, and every Kwoma male is initiated into one or the other of these sections at pubescence. When the cult holds a ceremony, the *Yenama* dance on the first day and night, and the *Minjama* on the second. On the afternoon of the first day, the married women of the tribe dance in the clearing on one side of the house tamberan. They bring with them net bags which are decorated on one side only. These they hold above their heads as they dance with the decoration either toward them or away from them, depending on whether their husband belongs to *Yenama* or *Minjama*, and the men note the information thus given. Taking advantage of the fact that all the *Yenama* men will be at the house tamberan that night, the *Minjama* visit their wives. The *Yenama* have a chance to retaliate on the following night when the *Minjama* men are dancing. The second occasion for ceremonial sexual license occurs during one of the nights of the age-grade initiation ceremonies when the men and women dance together at the house tamberan. During the dance, the women slip tokens to the men of their choice as a sign that they are willing to have intercourse with them, and the couples unobtrusively drop out of the dance and repair to the bush. For several days before and after these occasions of license, salacious jokes and sly boasting are rife. The taboo on sexual relations between relatives operates with respect to all extramarital affairs.

When a man has children, daughters appear as a new interdicted category of women. The following myth represents the Kwoma horror of such a relationship and the intensity of guilt associated with breaking this incest taboo.

"Once upon a time, long, long ago, a man came home one night after dark and lay with a woman, thinking that she was his wife. Later he discovered that she was his grown daughter. He was very ashamed. He decorated himself in all his finery, painted his face black, and went to the house tamberan to sleep. Early in the morning he arose, cut a bamboo, and sharpened an edge on it. He went down to the lake, embarked in a canoe, and paddled out into deep water. Here he cut off his penis with the bamboo, jumped into the water, and drowned himself. Since then it has been taboo for a man to have sexual intercourse with his daughter."[22]

The frequency of philandering with *sisters* decreases when they marry and leave the hamlet, because the factor of proximity no longer operates. They are replaced by the wives of a man's *brothers* who live conveniently near to him. They are classed as relatives, designated by the term *brother*, and are sexually taboo. The belief that a man will become ill if he eats food cooked by anyone except his wife serves to prevent philandering with a *brother's* wife. If a man deviates from this custom and has sexual relations with her, it may lead to an embarrassing situation. He frequently eats at his *brother's* house, particularly when he is helping in some coöperative economic task, and he must either risk becoming sick by eating the food offered him or publicize his illicit behavior by refusing to do so. If a man suspects his *brother* of such adultery, he may threaten to beat or sorcerize him. The accused usually denies the fact, and establishes an alibi if he can. Such accusations and denials are not infrequent in Kwoma life. If the husband's suspicions are not allayed by his *brother's* denials, they may actually come to blows, and, if the offense be too flagrant and the husband powerful enough, the culprit may be forced to flee the community or be killed.[23]

[22] It is interesting to note that the man kills himself; no one else holds him responsible for the crime. The native explanation for this is that he committed suicide because he was "ashamed." The term for this feeling is *homba*, the same word used for the feeling about brother-sister incest and about sleeping with one's wife.
[23] Takawur had fled from the tribe and was living with one of the river

The rules of sexual etiquette regulating staring and indecorous postures hold in adulthood. The aged, however, need not be so careful in this respect. In particular, an aged man or woman may embrace when greeting a person of the opposite sex, behavior denied them since infancy.

The levirate operates when a woman's husband dies. Although not absolutely bound by this custom, the widow normally marries the oldest man of her husband's lineage and generation. If she chooses to marry someone else, the man whom she marries must pay a bride-price to her levirate inheritor.

When a woman dies, the following rules govern the behavior of her husband and relatives. If she dies shortly after she has married and before the bride-price has been paid, her husband need not pay for her. If he has already paid the bride-price, her relatives are obliged to return it in full or in part or else to provide another wife from their lineage. If her death was due to her husband's negligence, however, he must pay the bride-price and cannot demand compensation from her relatives. When a woman dies after she has borne children, her husband or her sons must pay a small amount of shell money to her brothers in order to maintain the mother's-brother-sister's-son relationship, a payment completely distinct from the bride-price transactions. If this payment is not made, the two kinship groups behave toward one another thenceforth as non-relatives.

A man may marry as many women as he can win and pay for. While I was at Kwoma, out of a population of approximately 375, one man had four wives, and two had three. The rest of the adult males had either two or one in about equal numbers; only the aged and recently widowed had none.

Soon after a man marries he must build a house of his own, as custom no longer permits him to escape wind and rain by living in his father's house. To do this he must first gather food for a work-bee feast, and then call on his relatives to help him. Since a feast must be prepared for each day's work,

tribes because War's wife had accused him of attempting to rape her. Had he stayed, War might have killed him.

and since it is difficult to get helpers to leave their own work for more than one day at a time, housebuilding is usually slow. A year or more often elapses between setting the central post and lashing the final shingle in place. A young married man chooses a level plot near his father's house for a site. Sometimes two brothers will build a house together and share it, but more often each builds one of his own. Since the thatched houses at Kwoma do not last indefinitely, a man usually has to build several during the course of his lifetime. Old men live in their houses until these become too dilapidated to give adequate shelter, and then move in with one of their sons.

Toward dangers from the natural environment, the Kwoma adult behaves in much the same way as he did during adolescence. He is somewhat more bold in coping with dangerous animals, particularly wild pigs, for he now begins to hunt them. He still respects supernatural dangers and heeds the warnings issued during the previous periods of his life concerning *marsalai*, ghosts, and sorcery.

As an adult, a man may come in closer contact with *marsalai* by joining the second stage of the yam cult. If he gains enough prestige by aggressively defending his rights, if he shows himself to be a good worker, if he becomes adept at one of the ceremonial accomplishments such as singing, gong beating, flute playing, or dancing, if, in fine, he shows promise of becoming a "big older brother man," he will be asked to join the other section of the yam cult.[24] If he does so, the initiation ceremony is less formal than was his first entry into the house tamberan at adolescence. He learns definitely at this time that the opposite section is similar to his own, differing only in minor variations in ritual and paraphernalia. Thenceforth he has the privilege of attending either or both of the ceremonies, a gain in prestige, in rapport with the *marsalai*, and in opportunities for singing, dancing, and feasting.

[24] The yam cult, it will be remembered, is in two sections, *Yenama* and *Minjama*. Every male is elected into one or another of these sections during adolescence. If a boy enters *Yenama* during adolescence, the next step is to become a member of *Minjama*, and vice versa.

A man who has attained high prestige in the community and, in addition, has taken the head of an enemy, is asked to join *Nokwi*, the highest stage of the yam cult, and he thereby receives the greatest honor that a Kwoma man can attain. If he is able to achieve this mark of status, the final mystery of the *marsalai* is unfolded to him. He is told that the booming rhythm that he has always heard at the *Nokwi* ceremony is not the footsteps of the great female *marsalai* in whose honor the ceremony is held, but is a sound made by a huge water drum.[25] A man plants yams for the first time on the occasion of his initiation into *Nokwi* and learns from the cult members how to solicit the aid and coöperation of the *marsalai*, which are believed necessary for a successful yam crop.

The yam cult, in addition to being a mode of ranking men in accordance with their attainments and of providing a means of gaining the support of the *marsalai*, is the primary institution for artistic expression. It has been shown how the child secretly learns to play the gongs, to sing, and to dance, and how during adolescence he is formally taught these skills, first in the bush house and later at the house tamberan. During adulthood men vie with one another in demonstrating their accomplishments in these artistic techniques. A man who is superior in one or more of them gains high praise from the community; people speak of him as a *harafa ma malaka*. At the beginning of each ritual the participants examine the carved wooden figures on the altar and comment on their excellence, those who have made them standing by to receive the praise. Men who are adept at carving may expend considerable time and effort fashioning and painting the formalized wooden heads and figures which are supposed to represent the *marsalai* of the cult, in order to have them so displayed.

Men who show a talent for gong beating have the opportunity during the cult ceremonies to play the most sophisticated rhythms in the orchestra, and those who excel in com-

[25] The water drum is a hollowed log shaped like a canoe, truncated at both ends, suspended in water so that the lips are submerged, and beaten by a pole wielded by two men.

posing rhythms become the orchestra leaders and may hum out a new arrangement to be interpreted under their directions by the gong-players. "Let's try this one—'gading gadong, gading gadong, kura kura, kura kura',"[26] he will say, and each player must know which part his gong should take and should be able to translate the words of the leader into the proper blows on the lips of the gong at the proper moment. Usually the leader merely suggests that a named rhythm be played, if the ritual permits such a choice, or, if not, simply directs the players. Good players are permitted to play only when the gong rhythms are the central part of the ritual, and the dubs and novices take their turn when the gongs are being used primarily to accompany the dancers, so that every member of the cult has an opportunity to perform on the gongs at some time during the ceremony. While those who play well are praised, those who are clumsy and inept are teased, criticized, and ridiculed.

Dancing during the cult ceremonies also provides an opportunity for a man to gain status. He may be applauded either for being a tireless, or for being a spectacular, performer. The man who can dance an entire night without ever sitting down to rest and smoke is spoken of as having "dry bones" and being "hard too much." Similarly, anyone who can join the dance with fervor when it is lagging and put new spirit into the performance is highly regarded. Once at a *Nokwi* ceremony, when a dance which had been going on for several hours had begun to lag, a man who had just arrived, adorned with particularly striking face paint and decorations, rushed into the circle balancing a spear over his head, stamping his feet on the ground, and shouting. The other dancers quickly caught his enthusiasm, the tempo increased, and loiterers joined in. Spectators shook their heads, smacked their lips, and allowed that he was indeed a man of parts.

Singing provides another means of self-expression during the ceremonies of the yam cult. The men blend their voices

[26] This is actually a formalized gong rhythm known as "the cassowary" and supposed to represent a hen cassowary and her chicks.

in shouted choruses while they dance. The men of prestige sing the verses. One man will sing as many verses as he can either remember or compose and then announce that he is through by repeating the chorus, when another man continues. When no one can think of any more verses, the group dances silently until someone starts a new song. The man who can remember the most verses or who is most adept at improvising them gains considerable prestige.

Novices are not permitted to play the flutes during a ceremony, as this requires considerable skill. A pair of those who have learned one of these complicated melodies as a result of long, guided practice at the bush house are called upon to play the flutes when the ceremony calls for them. They stand facing one another each with a flute cradled over the left arm. One plays the big "male" flute, a large bamboo about seven feet long, and the other plays a "female" flute, slightly shorter and of smaller diameter.[27] Since these instruments have no stops and are therefore capable of producing only a few notes, the melodies are arranged so that the two flutes are played in series, thus permitting double the range of variation that would be possible if they were played in unison. This necessitates close coöperation between the two players, which apparently requires a great deal of practice to accomplish, and those who master it are rewarded with high praise.

The man of Rumbima hamlet who had gained most renown in the cult ceremonies was War. He could dance tirelessly though not brilliantly, he could lead a gong chorus, he was a skilled wood carver, and he could compete with anyone in the subtribe in remembering the verses of songs. The other men of Rumbima did not vie much with War, but put him forward as their champion against the high-ranking men of other hamlets. When a ceremony was given at Rumbima, it would be War who would arrange and direct it.

Even after a man has experienced the whole gamut of initiation rites, he still avoids the dwelling places of *marsalai*

---

[27] The "male" flute is about three inches in diameter; the "female," about two.

just as he did as a child. He still believes that rain and wind storms, thunder and lightning, earthquakes, and rainbows are caused by angry *marsalai*.[28] Although he takes care not to walk near the dwelling places of these supernatural beings, he reacts aggressively toward them after they have brought about the annoying natural event. If a storm is brewing, a Kwoma man will customarily repeat an imprecation: "Cursed *marsalai* who is causing this storm to come, may you be killed. May you be bound hand and foot so that you cannot move. May you be stuffed in the bottom of a hollow tree so that you may no longer annoy us with rain and wind."[29] At the end of each line of the imprecation, the cursing man spits toward the oncoming storm.

Many Kwoma men learn to abstract the unseen sago needles which *marsalai* sometimes shoot into the feet of those who disturb them. The method employed consists of rubbing the painful spot with a leaf and of repeating a malediction which supposedly causes the needle to come near to the surface. The operator then sucks the painful spot, extracts the needle, and spits it on a coconut leaf, which is wrapped up, immersed in water for a time, and then thrown away.

When the clouds of mosquitoes are thicker and hungrier than usual, it is believed to be the work of *marsalai*. A huge supernatural crocodile is supposed to live somewhere in the great swamp below the range on which the Kwoma dwell. Mosquitoes make their home in the belly of this monster and swarm out to pester the Kwoma when he opens his mouth. When this occurs, or rather when the mosquitoes are so thick that it is believed to have occurred, the men of one or another of the Kwoma hamlets will beat a special rhythm on the house tamberan gongs, a message to this *marsalai*, angrily commanding him to shut his mouth. The men of other ham-

[28] Earthquakes are believed to be caused by a huge *marsalai* when he thrusts his digging stick into the ground as he plants yams. If anyone should approach his swamp dwelling, the Kwoma fear that mountains would be leveled by the terrible quake that would ensue. Rainbows are thought to be caused by another *marsalai* when he spits betel juice through the sky.

[29] The curse is repeated for all the *marsalai* who are suspected in the particular instance.

lets, when they hear this rhythm, rush to their own house tamberans and repeat the rhythm on their gongs. The *marsalai* must tremble, it is said, when he hears the thunderous command issuing successively from each house tamberan in each of the Kwoma subtribes. Doubtless he hastily shuts his mouth.

A Kwoma male must submit to the hazing of age-grade initiation even after he has reached adulthood. There are four occasions on which he attends this ceremony as an initiate, and, since it takes place only once every five years, there are normally three rites during adulthood when he must permit his *ceremonial father* to slash his tongue and penis. Thus it is not until a man is over thirty that he ceases to be an initiate. On each occasion he advances a degree in prestige and is permitted to wear a certain hair ornament that those of lower grades may not wear. Just as the newly initiated adolescent derogated the uninitiated children, so the adult derogates those in stages below him and struts about wearing his newly acquired headgear.

After a man has passed through the initiation cycle, he takes his turn as an initiator. He adopts a *ceremonial son* whom he sponsors through the cycle. Finally, at the age of fifty or more, after twenty years as an initiate and twenty years as an initiator, he attends the age-grade ceremonies merely as a spectator.

The attitude of an adult man toward ghosts differs little from that of a child. He still reacts to them with a mixture of aggression and avoidance. Kwoma men are quite loath to walk very far from their dwellings after dark, and if they do so they either carry a torch or wear a dagger made from a human thigh bone, both of which are supposed to frighten ghosts and make them keep their distance. In spite of these precautions, men not infrequently encounter what they believe to be ghosts. One evening I heard frightened shouting, then the patter of feet rushing by the house, and finally angry shouts and imprecations from the house tamberan. The next morning I learned that Kar and Marok had stayed late on a visit to another hamlet and had been forced to return after dark. They had almost reached home when they heard a rustling in the path by their side which they knew to be a ghost. At first they froze in their tracks and then shouted out their predicament, hoping that there would be someone in the house tamberan to come to their aid. Wof and War heard the shouting and told them to run. They did. When they reached the house tamberan safely, they and the other men present shouted angrily at the ghost to go back to the land of the dead and to stop annoying them.

A Kwoma adult may be possessed by ghosts under the same circumstances and for the same reasons as adolescents. The only new rôle which he must play at this time is that of exorcist. Any adult may try his or her hand at questioning the ghost through the medium of the possessed person, but those who show the most aptitude for discovering the cause of the ghost's anger gain reputations as exorcists and are usually called upon. Marok and Chinuwa were considered to be the best exorcists at Rumbima.

The Kwoma have certain techniques for curing minor ills, most of which have already been described. Although children can depend on others to perform these techniques, adults must learn to treat both themselves and their sick relatives. An adult must know when and how to practice phlebotomy, how to lance and care for a boil, and when to rub a person with nettle-like leaves in order to revive him. He must also learn some of the spells which are thought to be effective under various circumstances.

The Kwoma believe that all serious sickness is caused by sorcery. The list of maladies which are thought to result from sorcery includes not only common illnesses, such as malaria, filariasis, and tuberculosis, but also injuries which result from accident. When, for example, a boy from a neighboring hamlet fell from a tree and fractured his skull, the fall was believed to have been caused by the machinations of a sorcerer. Sorcery is even suspected to be the cause of minor ills, such as ulcers, headaches, and upset stomachs whenever they are unusually protracted or resistant to cure. All but the mildest ailments are thus believed to be caused by personal agents. This belief gives the Kwoma something to do when sickness occurs: they can attack the sorcerer and prevent him from continuing his operations. If a person believes that he has stopped the sorcery, his fear of continued illness or death is reduced; and since the Kwoma have developed no "realistic" modes of curing these diseases, the belief in sorcery is psychologically adaptive.

Whenever it is believed that a person is suffering from the results of sorcery, the men of his hamlet immediately launch an anti-sorcery campaign. The first step is to make an announcement on the house tamberan gongs, "So-and-so, our relative, is sick from sorcery. Anyone who is guilty of sorcerizing this person must answer for it. If anyone is sorcerizing an unknown person, stop at once. It may be our relative." After this command is issued, all the men of the subtribe, if they wish to be free of suspicion, visit the house of the sick person, pay their respects, and drink water. Since a sorcerer cannot work his evil magic if he drinks water during the process, this is taken as proof of innocence. If the sick person is a close relative of a man of high prestige, there will be many visitors, but if he is not there will be few. If the sick man does not show signs of recovery, some of his relatives will visit around the subtribe, going to the houses of those whom they suspect of sorcery and asking them to drink. The relatives may resort to another expedient in the anti-sorcery campaign by calling a "sorcery court," in which an attempt is made to discover the guilty person.[30]

The Kwoma are in a constant state of anxiety about sorcery. Hardly a week passed during the seven months of my stay at Kwoma that the command to stop all sorcery did not boom out from the gongs of one or another of the house tamberans. Whenever the sorcery message was spelled out, everyone would stop what they were doing, listen intently, shake their heads seriously, and make some such statement as: "Somebody is sorcerizing Sowinambi's wife. What is the matter with people anyway? Why do they have to go about

[30] The procedure at the sorcery court is described below.

sorcerizing people? This place is no good." Then there would follow speculations as to who the guilty party could be. Comments like this were frequently made: "There were some children from Tug sib wandering about the hamlet this afternoon. The Tug train their children to steal sorcery material. We had better be careful with our food leavings." Or, "Yat asked me for my cigarette butt to get a light this afternoon. I do not remember that he gave it back. I'll bet that he kept it for sorcery material. He had better not try anything or I'll show him. If I get sick I'll know who is the cause of it."

The Kwoma preoccupation with sorcery is so marked that they are notorious for it. The river people look upon them as "man bilong poison." My Yambon houseboy was extremely nervous about being stationed at Kwoma and was constantly warning me of the danger of sorcery. He finally became ill and, being sure that some Kwoma who wished him ill was causing it, fled home despite my protestations. Gwiyap once told me that he wished I would take him to America, where, I had told him, there was no sorcery. Some of the young men who have recently returned from working for European enterprises talked of banding together to put an end to sorcery.

It is not surprising that a person suspected of sorcery has a difficult time at Kwoma. Anyone caught stealing sorcery material may be killed on the spot, and his close relatives will receive little support in any plan for retaliation. If the relatives of a sorcery victim succeed in fastening on someone the responsibility for the victim's sickness, the sorcerer is in danger of his life unless he nullifies the magic and the sick man recovers.[31] To sorcerize a relative is a particularly heinous crime, and, if it were proved that a man had done such a thing, he would be ostracized from the community. Kwoma society permits a man to use sorcery only against someone who has committed a capital crime[32] against him or one of his relatives.

[31] This does not apply to sorcerers who work their magic for pay. The person who hires the sorcerer is held responsible for the crime. The professional sorcerer usually does not know the identity of the victim, but he is hated, feared, and if possible avoided.
[32] Rape, murder, arson, or sorcery.

Adulthood

A person is seldom, if ever, convicted of sorcery. I am reasonably certain that there were many fewer occasions on which sorcery was actually practiced than there were cases of sickness and death attributed to this cause. I was unable to discover anyone who would admit to having practiced sorcery, and the Kwoma themselves were unable to convict any sorcerer during my stay, despite their constant efforts to do so. This evidence should not, of course, be taken as proof that men never practice sorcery, but as indicating the probability that they rarely do so.

Mar's nervous breakdown illustrates how sorcery works from the point of view of the person sorcerized and how it may be used as an explanation for neurotic anxiety. One evening shortly after Mar began his courtship of Aya we heard him exchanging shouts with someone down the mountainside. Later he came to my house and told me that he had been arguing with Waramus. The latter had discovered that Mar wanted to marry Aya and had shouted: "You stay away from my daughter; you are nothing but an excrement eater. Do you think that I am going to let her marry a lazy person like you, and one who is her relative, too?" When Mar had told me this, he asked plaintively, "Do you think that I am an excrement eater?" I reassured him. He then bit his underlip, raised his hand, and shook it as though he were balancing a spear, "That damned Waramus! I am going to fight him tomorrow and break his nose." I asked, "Why don't you do it now, Mar?" and he replied, "It is too dark, but I'll do it tomorrow."

Mar did not carry out his threat, nor did he make any move to see Aya for the next few days. A week later he went with several of his *brothers* and *sisters* and his betrothed to work on their garden. Three days later Fit came running back from the garden and told us that Mar was dying. He said that Mar had had a nightmare the previous night and that his father's ghost had appeared and tried to take his soul away. We took some medicine and went back to the garden with Fit and Wof, who had also been told of Mar's sickness. When we arrived at Mar's bush house, he was moaning on his bark slab bed. He seemed unable to talk and could only groan inarticulately. We took his temperature and found that it was normal. When we asked him where the pain was, he shook his head, refusing to answer. Wof then diagnosed the sickness as the result of sorcery and said, "Well, if he dies, he dies, that's all." This elicited a groan from Mar. We told him that we had some very strong medicine which would counteract sorcery, at which he lifted his head and looked at us with a doglike expression and then took the Eno's salts which we gave him. We suggested that he go home, for the bush house was damp and lonely, but he groaned and shook his head at this suggestion, indicating that he could not make it. Wof then gathered some nettle leaves, formed them into a cone, into which he muttered a prayer, and then rubbed them over Mar's chest and belly. This made Mar gasp and come out of his lethargy enough to mumble that he believed Waramus was sorcerizing him for courting Aya. We finally raised him to his feet. Leaning heavily on us, he swayed and staggered but was able to walk. As the trip progressed, he seemed to become stronger and for the last part of the journey walked unaided, but when we arrived at his home he fell groaning on his bed, where he stayed for two days without speaking. Wof meanwhile approached Waramus, who denied that he had sorcerized Mar, but said that he still did not want him to court his daughter.

Mar did not leave his house for over a week, gradually recovering his voice and his strength. He believed that Waramus had sorcerized him but had stopped after being accused by Wof, and that this had saved his life. Waramus denied Wof's accusation, and as far as I was able to determine his denial was truthful. The case would have progressed in much the same way, however, whether he had done so or not. Thus it is evident that sorcery functions as an explanation for sickness and that accusations are made against persons who are feared, and finally that the actual performance of black magic is not pertinent.[33]

[33] The fact that Mar had a nightmare in which his father's ghost attempted to take his soul suggests that his sickness may have been due to

Adulthood

When a man does resort to sorcery, he is reputed to use the following technique. First he either steals or gets someone to steal sorcery material[34] from the person whom he wishes to injure. Then he either gives it to a noted sorcerer[35] to whom he pays a fee or, if he is confident in his own powers, proceeds himself. The sorcerer puts the sorcery material in a special, narrow-necked clay pot and places it on the fire. When the pot and its contents are very hot, he pours a small quantity of cold water into it. If the sorcery material completely disappears in the burst of steam which ensues, the victim will die; if some fragments remain when the pot cools, he will merely become very sick. The operator may not drink water during the process or the sorcery will not be effective. Another type of sorcery consists of inserting in the victim's food a white powder purported to be poisonous. Whether this powder is actually harmful I was unable to discover.

All deaths are believed to result from sorcery. Death repeatedly proves to the Kwoma the efficacy of this type of magic and increases everyone's fear of and anger against sorcerers. This is particularly true in the case of close relatives of the deceased. When a person dies, one of his relatives tolls the house tamberan gong in a slow, measured beat to announce the event to the tribe. I was on a hunting expedition with Sof, a young man who had recently returned from working on a white plantation, when the gongs of Sombundura house tamberan began to toll. He stopped in his tracks, and his jaws began to work. He said nothing for a minute and then in a very emotional voice spoke of the evils of sorcery. "This is a bad place. All anyone can think of is sorcery. That is all the old men think of. We young men who have worked for the whites are going to rebel against it. We are going to round up all the old men who practice sorcery and

sexual anxiety which was rooted in the Oedipus situation and which was evoked at this time by his courtship with Aya and the threats of Waramus.

[34] The Kwoma believe that food leavings, blood, sperm, and the feces of infants are effective materials for sorcery.

[35] No one ever publicly admits that he is a sorcerer, for to do so might mean death or ostracism. Many persons are believed to be powerful sorcerers and privately admit it, if it is to their advantage to do so.

take them to the white court at Ambunti. The police officer will put them all in the calaboose for it." At the funeral the next day, most of the talk was of sorcery. The reaction was hysterical. A group of young men talked in loud excited voices, expressing sentiments similar to those of Sof. They asked me to help them bring the culprit to justice at the white court. During the night following the death and for several days thereafter the anti-sorcery gong messages were sounded at intervals from the house tamberan of the deceased. His relatives redoubled their efforts to discover the sorcerer and to force him to end his machinations, for they feared that they might be the next to be affected by it.[36] The people of Rumbima hamlet were still worrying because they had not yet discovered who had killed Gwiyap's father two years before. They suspected someone from Wanyi sib because Gwiyap's father had prevented some of the young men of this sib from philandering with his sister.

The death of a relative not only increases a Kwoma's fear of sorcery, it also means the loss of one who has hitherto contributed to his support and defense or, if the deceased is a child, one who promises to do so. Hence relatives of the deceased react with real as well as with formalized sorrow. The wailing of the women is the most dramatic of these formal expressions of grief. As soon as the tolling of the gong announces the death, they gather in the house where the corpse lies and start to cry in a long-drawn-out wail punctuated by short sobs on a lower note. A dozen or more women, each wailing in a slightly different key and sobbing at different intervals, produce a strange and moving sound. The women wail continuously until the following morning, when the deceased is placed on the burial platform. The male relatives show their sorrow by breaking their lime gourds on the shield which is used as a bier, and by pouring the contents over the corpse and their own heads. Close relatives, both male and female, smear their faces and sometimes their bodies with

---

[36] Kwoma believe that one magical performance may kill not only the person from whom the food is stolen, but his close relatives as well, for they may also have had intimate contact with the sorcery material.

clay or mud, and give up some preferred article in their diet during the interval between the first and second funeral ceremonies. Whether a person makes such manifestations of sorrow depends more on how close a bond of friendship or dependence he has established with the deceased than upon formal kinship ties.

Beliefs about ghosts, as well as fear of sorcery and the feeling of bereavement, determine Kwoma death customs. It is thought that the ghosts of the relatives of the deceased come to escort his soul to the land of the dead. It is further believed that they are attracted by the corpse and hover near the body both while it is in the house and when it is on the funeral platform, and do not leave until the bleached bones are finally buried. If a Kwoma does not express sufficient sorrow for the death of a relative, the ghost of the deceased is likely to become angry and either frighten or possess the unappreciative man or woman. Thus those who are not motivated by personal feelings for the deceased may still mourn to avoid antagonizing his ghost.

A corpse is allowed to lie in the house until a burial platform is built. Early in the morning of the day following the death, the relatives erect near the house of the deceased a covered platform set on stilts about ten feet from the ground. When it is finished, the corpse is placed upon a wooden shield carried by several of the male relatives and lifted to the platform with the aid of a ladder. The body is then washed, and three of the spears of the deceased are placed across the neck, abdomen, and legs and lashed to the floor of the platform to prevent the corpse from falling. The points of the spears are broken so that they will not be stolen. These rites are performed by any old man who is willing to play the rôle of undertaker. All who have had contact with the body wash themselves immediately as a prophylactic against the sickness which they believe would otherwise result.

A corpse is allowed to stay on the burial platform for several months. During this time the relatives who have chosen to go into mourning continue to fast and to daub themselves with clay. At the end of this time a second funeral is held, and the bones, which are by this time dried and bleached by the weather, are taken from the platform and distributed to *friends* of the deceased. The best *friend* gets the mandible, the second best receives the clavicle, and the third best one of the arm bones. The oldest son inherits the femurs, which he may fashion into daggers. The remaining bones are buried under the floor of the house in which the deceased has lived. After the bones have been distributed, everyone who attends the funeral[37] joins in a big feast, which is a joyous occasion. Those who have fasted eat the food which they have denied themselves, and those who have worn clay wash. There is a great deal of joking and merriment, and when the meal is finished the men go to the nearest house tamberan, where they beat rhythms on the gongs, play the sacred flutes, dance, and sing. Only those males who have received their keloids are allowed to attend.[38]

A Kwoma adult lives in an environment of people who may cause him pain to an even greater extent than the natural and supernatural environments. They beat, insult, scold, punish, sorcerize, and even threaten to kill him. He has already had a long apprenticeship in learning to anticipate these pains. By adulthood, a Kwoma has learned to differentiate the various categories of relatives, non-relatives, and foreigners. Toward threats from each of these categories of persons he responds with acts which his culture defines as appropriate. If he does not do so, he may expect pain from another source, from those members of his society who sanction custom.

A man's parents and *paternal uncles* and *aunts* still command and punish him as they did when he was a child. Now the punishments take the form of scolding and criticism, as

[37] Everyone in the subtribe is usually invited.

[38] A young man from a neighboring tribe who was not yet scarified was severely beaten and almost killed for entering the house tamberan at such a time. This man had killed his wife with an adz in a fit of rage and had fled from his own tribe to escape the wrath of his wife's relatives, taking refuge with his mother's relatives at Hongwam. The Kwoma all considered him crazy, and indeed he did exhibit some psychotic symptoms. It is probable that these circumstances were in part responsible for the beating he received.

he is too big to be spanked or beaten. The habit of obeying their commands has been so firmly implanted that, for the most part, he continues to do so even though the parent may not have the strength to punish disobedience physically. More often than when he was an adolescent, however, he ignores the commands of his aged parents. He is seldom physically aggressive toward them, though he not infrequently attacks them verbally. Kwoma informants could remember no case of an adult son wounding or killing a parent. Since there is no relative closer than the son to retaliate for the crime, there is no direct control of patricide. Its rare occurrence is explained in part by the punishments received during childhood for aggression toward the parents, and in part by the active negative sanction that would be applied by the whole community. Members of the hamlet would consider the deed unnatural and would avoid the murderer.

A grown man is more frequently aggressive toward his *brothers* than he was during adolescence. As already noted, his *brothers'* wives take the place of his *sisters* as persons in the hamlet with whom, although they are sexually taboo, he frequently has clandestine affairs. If such behavior is suspected or discovered, it usually leads to blows or at least to an exchange of threats and insults between the *brothers* concerned. In order to avoid suspicion, a man takes great care not to look at his *brother's* wife or to be in any other way intimate with her when he is likely to be observed. This is the nearest approach to an avoidance relationship—in public, at least—that is found in Kwoma culture.

The following cases illustrate conflicts between adult *brothers* which spring from sexual jealousy. Yat accused Kar of having an affair with his wife and threatened him. Kar denied the accusation and said that it was a bad state of affairs when one was falsely accused by his *brother*. He intimated that he might break relations with Yat. They remained hostile for about a week and then apparently forgot the matter, for their relations became friendly again. A more serious case occurred between Wof and War. The latter planned to leave the hamlet for several days and asked Wof if he would take care of his wife, Mbora, during his absence. Wof agreed, and Mbora came to stay with him. When War returned, someone gossiped to him that Wof had taken advantage of the situation and had had sexual relations with Mbora. War accused Wof of adulterous behavior and threatened to spear him. Wof ran away, but his wife stood her ground and counterattacked War with an adz, wounding him in the arm. In still another instance War's wife complained that while gathering firewood she had been sexually attacked by his *brother*, Takawur. War set out with a spear after Takawur, and would have killed him had he not fled from the tribe. He still lives in exile.

Fighting between *brothers* sometimes results from economic conflicts. The responsibility for maintaining his property against theft and trespass, which a man assumes as an adult, sometimes generates enough antagonism between *brothers* to overcome communal disapproval and their early training against fighting one another. The following case illustrates such a conflict. Kwal and Daw, two brothers in their early thirties, lived in adjoining houses. One day, while Kwal was away working, Daw climbed an areca palm which they owned in common and began to gather the nuts. Kwal's wife told Daw to stop, as the nuts were not yet ripe, and, when he paid no attention, began to insult him. Daw, stung by her insults, climbed down the tree and beat her with the handle of a spear. When Kwal returned home and was told by his wife how Daw had treated her, he set upon his brother with a stave, and the two battled until Daw received a severe blow on his head.

The reaction of the community indicates the sanction on fraternal aggression. Daw and Kwal shouted angrily at one another during the fight, and when the former received the blow on his head he cried out as though he were mortally wounded. As soon as the sounds of the fracas were heard, nearly everyone in the hamlet rushed to the scene. When I arrived, the battle was over and several persons were standing by each contestant. Mes was supporting Daw, who stood trembling with blood flowing down his cheek from a cut in his scalp. Most of the spectators formed a neutral group between Kwal and Daw. When they had discovered what had happened, they began to discuss the merits of the case and were divided in their opinion as to which brother was right. Since Kwal and Daw were real brothers, the only persons who could take sides, being more nearly related to one principal than to the other, were their wives and children. The children were not grown up, and their reaction was one of fear, but the respective wives stood, eyes blazing, with digging sticks in hand ready to join in the fray. When I asked the spectators their opinion of the affair, they said that after all it was Kwal's and Daw's business to fight if they wanted to, but that they were stupid to injure one another since brothers should stand together against trouble from an outsider rather than quarrel among themselves. This opinion represents the communal sanction which is imposed on fighting between brothers. As can be seen, the direct social control of fraternal aggression is minimal. From this it might be expected that fights between brothers would occur frequently. This case, however, was the only one in which brothers actually came to blows during a period of seven months. This indicates that the disadvantages of in-group aggression and the advantages of fraternal coöperation have been well learned during the socialization process.

When a fight occurs between *brothers* who are not closely related by blood, their relatives rally in support of them. If the dispute is not serious, it usually ceases after an exchange of invective. If the affair cannot be settled in this way, members of the hamlet who are not emotionally involved try to discover the blame and suggest a settlement. The discussion usually takes place by shouting from house to house, but sometimes the men will gather at the house tamberan and hold court. If even these measures fail to settle the dispute, a permanent rift may result, and the minority group may withdraw from the hamlet.

The division of a hamlet as a result of a dispute between its members is not uncommon in Kwoma society. Such a split had occurred in the not-too-distant past in each of the three sibs of the subtribe in which I lived. Rumbima, for example, had at one time been the only hamlet of Hayamakwo. A number of years before my arrival a small group had seceded as a result of a quarrel which started when someone defecated in the house tamberan. Accusations and counteraccusations led to the formation of two groups who would not compromise. The smaller group left and moved to another locality to make a hamlet and house tamberan of their own. Some years later, the Australian Government, in a punitive expedition against the tribe, killed seventeen members of the two hamlets and burnt both house tamberans. During the process of rehabilitation, the two groups decided to recombine to build a single new house tamberan. In deciding the site for the new building, however, a new dissension arose, and a new fission resulted. The larger group built the house tamberan and the surrounding dwellings of the present Rumbima hamlet. There were not enough men in the other group to build a house tamberan, so they lived in a hamlet without one, and were therefore called *sumwe sumwe*, "without." Such fissions as these lead to deprivations which the Kwoma well appreciate. They weaken the defensive power of the in-group, and make large coöperative endeavors such as building a house tamberan more difficult. They even interfere with the coöperative work of building dwellings and clearing garden sites, easy tasks for a large number of men, but arduous for a few. The importance of these factors in controlling in-group aggression should not be underestimated. Parents continually stress their value.

A Kwoma man sometimes reacts to annoyances from his wife by scolding or beating her; sometimes he submits to them. Although he has more practice in physical combat than she, knows how to use a spear, and is living among his own kin, who are pledged to support him, she too has some very effective weapons. She has access to his food leavings and other sorcery material, which she may take to a sorcerer if she becomes sufficiently angry. Of course, she does this in the face of the negative sanction against sorcery. The husband may even kill her if he discovers the crime. Nevertheless, she

Adulthood

has plenty of opportunity to take material without being discovered, and the fear that she will do so is a strong deterrent to his aggression. In addition to this weapon, she has the support of her own relatives if he maltreats her, particularly before he has paid the bride-price. Finally, she is free to leave him, an act which lowers him in the eyes of the community and is an economic and sexual loss.

Disputes between husband and wife arise for a variety of reasons. A wife may fail to do her share in the economic duties of the household, she may be openly unfaithful, or she may be annoying in a variety of minor ways. The following cases illustrate conflicts between husband and wife. One evening, when the mosquitoes were more plentiful than usual, Kaya began to complain about them. Wof, her husband, became annoyed at her carping and told her to stop. This started an argument which ended by his pounding her on the back with his fist. Kaya began to wail, and Wof left the house.

War on one occasion became angered at one of his wives and thrust a spear through her leg. Mey, who reported the case to me, said that he took care to thrust it into her leg rather than into a vital spot, because by killing her he would lose both a wife and the money he had paid for her. He also reported that before this event she had been very disobedient to War, but that afterwards she was a dutiful wife. Cases of men beating their wives as a result of the suspicion or knowledge that they were unfaithful are numerous. A man does not always react to frustrations imposed by his wife with aggression; he often submits to them. A homely example of such a reaction occurred one night when I was sitting by a fire in front of my house with a group of men. While we were talking, a gong sounded from down the mountainside. One of the men sighed, picked up his net bag, and trudged off. The gong had been a message from his wife telling him to return home immediately.

Since the way in which a child behaves toward his parents as he grows from infancy to adulthood has been described in detail, much of how parents behave toward their children has already been told. The status of father and mother is important enough to summarize here, however, even at the risk of repetition. By the time a Kwoma couple marry, they are well aware of the assets of a large family. They know that a son will help with gardening, housebuilding, and the other economic tasks, that, when he grows up, he will stand by them in the struggle against sorcery and in disputes over property, that he will increase the prestige of the family in the community, and finally that he will support them when they grow old. The young couple know that a daughter is also an asset. She will help with economic tasks until she marries and she will also bring prestige to them. Furthermore, her brideprice will bring in shell money which the sons will need to pay for their wives. For these reasons a man and woman set out to produce children as quickly as possible and are gravely disappointed if they cannot do so. Indeed, a barren marriage often leads to divorce.[39]

The Kwoma believe that a fetus is formed from the mixture of the woman's blood and the man's sperm and that repeated insemination is necessary to cause fertilization. They know that the cessation of menstruation is a sign of pregnancy, but do not cease their sexual relations until the woman is big with child. A woman observes certain food taboos during pregnancy. She does not eat certain kinds of fish, flying fox, or cassowary in order to insure a normal and healthy child, and she may not eat birds lest the child grow feathers in place of hair.

When the expectant mother goes into labor, her husband must leave the house, and he and all other men must stay away until the child is delivered. Her own mother is called to attend her, and the adult women of the household or nearby households assist. These women take charge of the baby when it is born, cut the umbilical cord, and bury the placenta under the floor of the house to prevent it from coming into

[39] I am not certain whether barrenness constitutes formal grounds for divorce. The fact that there were several couples still married, who had no children except by adoption, suggests that it is not. In two of the four cases of divorce on which I have detailed information, barrenness was given as one of the reasons for the separation.

Adulthood 151

the hands of a sorcerer. As soon as the mother is able, she takes care of the baby and nurses it.[40] Both parents show special concern for the child until his fontanel closes,[41] as they believe that he is particularly susceptible to sorcery during this time. For this reason the mother stays at home and does not receive visitors. The father, in order to insure the child's safety during this period, does not chew betel, or scratch himself except with a stick, and he holds his cigarettes between tweezers.[42]

Under certain circumstances, when the parents do not wish to bring up an infant, they may either offer it for adoption or kill it. If a woman gives birth to a monstrosity, she disposes of it as soon as it is born. She treats one of twins in the same way. Parents may decide not to bring up a normal child when there are already several children of one sex in the family and the new baby is of the same sex. If the children are all girls, for example, there will be no one to inherit the land nor to protect and care for the parents in their old age, so the mother may offer for adoption or kill a new girl infant in order to free herself more quickly to produce another child with the hope that it be a boy. Similarly, a boy infant may be killed or offered for adoption if the previous children are all male, since it will be very difficult to obtain sufficient shell money to pay for their wives if they have no sisters. The optimal family, therefore, is one in which boys and girls are equally balanced. Infanticide and adoption are employed to approximate this ratio.

The mother has full responsibility for the immediate physical care of her offspring during infancy. For the first few months she permits no one else to handle the infant, but after this she allows her co-wife to give her short respites. She may permit the father, uncle, or aunt to hold the infant for a few moments for their amusement, but she rarely intrusts it to

---

[40] The above information was obtained from male informants and hence is incomplete and not necessarily reliable.

[41] Informants described this as "when the baby's heart stops beating on the top of his head."

[42] A man observes these same taboos when he plants yams.

an older sibling and then only under her direct supervision. The father's duty with respect to the well-being of his infant is primarily to take special precautions against sorcery and to be ready to issue a strong anti-sorcery protest the moment the infant becomes ill. Unless he has a second wife or daughter old enough to work, he may have to cook his own meals, process sago flour alone, and make some reciprocal arrangements with the wife or daughter of a brother to supply his household with wood or water. The mother may not indulge in sexual intercourse during the infancy of her offspring lest she be forced to wean it while it is, according to Kwoma standards, too young. Thus the birth of an infant necessitates considerable changes in the habits of both its father and its mother and is a burden to them as well as a promised asset. Despite this, Kwoma parents may not express annoyance at these frustrations by hurting the infant in any way; they may not even punish it except very mildly and only under the circumstances which have been described. This prohibition seems to be effected more by the fact that it is incompatible with the strong wish for children than by any direct sanctions.

It is not necessary to repeat here the details of the behavior of Kwoma parents toward their child as he passes through the various stages from infancy to adulthood, since these facts may be inferred from previous chapters. It may simply be stated, however, that the parents take the final responsibility for their child's well-being and for teaching him to behave in the way that the culture dictates as right and proper. Parents who neglect their children are censured by other members of the hamlet. Takawur, for example, had to flee from the tribe after he attempted to rape War's wife. He left his young son, Gwamp, behind him at Kwoma. Way, Takawur's brother, took care of Gwamp. Although the event had occurred several years before, Takawur is still criticized for not providing for his son, whereas the rape is now no longer held against him.

Although a *brother* is separated from his *sister* when the latter marries and moves away from the hamlet, they continue to maintain a very friendly relationship. The opportunity for clandestine affairs between the two is decreased and they seldom occur, but the joking relationship continues. They frequently visit one another either for purely social or for economic reasons. A *brother* participates in many of the work bees called by his *sister's* husband, and a *sister* often helps her *brother's* wife in gardening.[43] The warm feeling a man has toward his *sister* generalizes to her children. He is especially kind to them and gives them whatever they wish; he treats them, indeed, as a "good father." He is repaid for his kindness by a gift of shell money from the children at the time of the age-grade ceremony. The kinship system arranges relatives in such a way that a man's father's *sister's* child falls in the same relationship to him as does his own *sister's* child. When his father dies, therefore, a man inherits the responsibility of playing the "good father" to his paternal cross cousins.

A man continues during adulthood the special relationship toward his mother's brother, the reciprocal of the one described above. He is still privileged to help himself from his gardens and sago plots and in return is obligated to pay him the specified amount of shell money. When his mother's *brother* dies, he carries on the relationship with the mother's *brother's* son, whom he addresses by the same term, *maternal uncle*.

A man does not have a very close relationship with his *mother's sister*. She neither lives in his hamlet nor in his mother's hamlet, but with her husband.[44] For this reason he does not come in contact with her either at home, or when he visits his *mother's brother*. Thus a man's behavior toward the *sisters* of his mother approximates that toward a nonrelative.

[43] If a man is injured while helping his *sister* or her husband, he receives compensation in the form of shell money. No compensation is paid if a man is injured while helping his *brother,* however, since it is believed that they are working with a common purpose. A *sister* is probably similarly compensated if she is hurt while helping a *brother,* although I do not have specific information on this point.

[44] If, by chance, she marries into the hamlet, she becomes his *paternal uncle's* wife and he treats her as such.

A man calls his mother's *brother's* daughter by the *mother* term. Her behavior toward him is supposed to be "motherly." She cooks for him if he visits the hamlet in which she lives, and behaves as kindly as she can toward him. All the persons whom I observed in this reciprocal relationship were warm and friendly, but contacts were not frequent.

A man has but little contact with his *father's sister*, since she marries out of his hamlet. When they do meet, however, the man theoretically behaves toward her as he does toward his *father*. Actually, the relationship is friendly.

A Kwoma's *friends* are of considerable importance to him. It will be remembered that this pseudo-kin relationship is established with the young men whose blood is mixed with his at the time of initiation into adulthood. A man's *friends*, usually three in number, are always members of another sib and unrelated to him by any true kinship ties, but after he has established blood bonds with them he treats them as though they were real relatives. He may eat at their house or invite them to eat at his, without fear that they will steal sorcery material from him. He supports them at court meetings, and in return they stand by him against those who threaten or accuse him; they may even take his side if he has a dispute with their own relatives.[45] He is supposed to steal sorcery materials from members of his own hamlet if he is requested to do so by a *friend*, and he may ask the same favor in return. A man calls his *friends'* parents *father* and *mother*, their sisters *sister*, and their children *children* and behaves toward them as he does toward such relatives; incest taboos apply to their close female relatives. When he dies, various of his bones are inherited by his friends or their heirs to symbolize the close bond between them. No economic cooperation is expected between these blood brothers; the relationship functions primarily in the defensive-aggressive sphere and is closely integrated with the sorcery complex.

Every Kwoma has two other pseudo-kin relatives, a *cere-*

---

[45] A man is theoretically supposed to support his *friend* in preference to anyone outside his immediate family. I am not sure whether he does this in practice.

monial father and a *ceremonial son*. The first of these relationships is established during adolescence, when he enters the age-grade cycle, while the second is instituted approximately twenty-five years later, when he starts playing the rôle of initiator in these ceremonies. Although the primary function of these relationships is carried out in the ceremonies themselves, the *ceremonial father* and the *ceremonial son* also stand as pseudo-kin in everyday life. A man is normally less intimate with them than with a *friend*, and he usually will not support them so strongly. Nevertheless, he is "safe" to visit and entertain them. Thus both the *friend-friend* and the *ceremonial-father-ceremonial-son* relationships bind the members of the subtribe together with ties like those of kinship, and are a consolidating force that is highly functional in a tribe with no king, chief, or council of elders, and no central political organization except a loosely organized court.

Affinal relationships are not so friendly as consanguineal ones. Until a man has paid the bride-price, he is frequently antagonized by his wife's relatives. They are continually dunning him to pay and criticizing him for his treatment of his wife. Furthermore, a man may be frustrated by his sister's husband, for, as long as the latter does not pay the bride-price, he has no money to obtain a wife of his own. Also he must be continually ready to protect his sister against maltreatment. As a result, brothers-in-law are frequently aggressive toward one another. For the most part such aggression is expressed verbally in the form of insult and threat. Fear of retaliation and the disadvantages of open conflict within the subtribe are the limiting factors. The following is a typical case of such antagonism. Sof beat his wife for being indiscreetly adulterous, and she ran to the house of one of her older brothers, but he was not at home. Sof followed her and dragged her back. When her brother returned and learned what had happened, he shouted up the mountainside to Sof:

"You had better stop beating my sister."

"I will beat her all I want, if she continues to behave so badly."

"You talk as if you had already paid the bride-price for her."

"Well, if you don't like my beating her, what are you going to do about it?"

"I am not afraid of your threats. You are just a child anyway."

"Just because you have been away working for the whites, you think you are pretty tough. Come to the house tamberan and you'll see whether I'm a child or not."

The shouting continued for about two hours and then subsided. Nothing further came of the affair.

When the bride-price has been paid, an affinal relationship becomes friendly. The woman's relatives no longer have to look after her, and they have the money to use to their own advantage. The husband need no longer fear their interference in his behavior toward his wife. He may visit and eat with them without fear of sorcery, and he coöperates with them economically.

Thus toward all relatives, except affines before the bride-price is paid, a man maintains relationships which are for the most part friendly. He is safe from sorcery danger from them as long as the kinship bond remains unbroken, and is supported by them in disputes and helped by them in many economic tasks. He, in return, is obligated to support and help them in the same ways. Aggression is theoretically prohibited, but it nevertheless not infrequently occurs. If it is at all serious, the kin tie is broken, and the two act toward one another as non-relatives.

The greatest contrast between the experiences of an adult man and an adult woman results from the custom of patrilocal marriage. A man's relationship with his affines is attenuated by the fact that he does not live in close contact with them, but this is not the case with the woman. Her adjustment to her affines-to-be has already been described. After marriage her position in her husband's hamlet is somewhat firmer, although it is not until his parents die and his sisters marry out of the hamlet that her position becomes relatively dominant. By this time the other adult women of the hamlet also belong to it by marriage, and her status is thus at least as high as theirs. There is considerable rivalry and dissension between the wives of *brothers*, arising both from sexual jealousy and from economic disputes. Aggression between a woman and her husband's *brother's* wife is usually on the verbal level, but in this sphere she is considerably more expressive than her husband. In any dispute between two households, the voices of the women usually rise above those of the men. On the other hand, a woman depends on the wives of her husband's *brothers* for much of her intimate social participation. In the afternoons and particularly in the evenings, these women visit one another and gossip of the day's events.

An important social relationship which a woman experiences but a man does not is that between a woman and her co-wife. Although the culture rules that they should not fight one another, but live together amicably and coöperate in the household duties, there is considerable antagonism between them. A woman seldom expresses her anger directly toward her co-wife, for to do so would bring punishment from her husband. If his wives fight he stands ready to beat the one who was responsible or both of them if he cannot decide who is to blame. Sexual jealousy and the difficulty of fairly allocating the economic tasks of the household create a strong pressure in opposition to this sanction. The following case demonstrates one of the techniques which a Kwoma woman uses to express her aggression toward a co-wife. Wof, a middle-aged man, had one wife, Kaya. Shortly after I arrived he inherited his deceased brother's wife, Chinuwa, by the rules of levirate marriage. Kaya was not pleased with the prospect of having another woman share her husband and protested vigorously to Wof. On the eve of the wedding she argued vociferously with her husband and, when she could not dissuade him, wailed bitterly. After Chinuwa came to live in the household, the two wives seldom spoke to one another, and when they did, they were coldly polite. Instead of being openly aggressive toward Chinuwa, Kaya disparaged her behind her back and finally, a month or so after the marriage, accused her of stealing sorcery material. Wof's store of sago flour had been tampered with. Kaya told her husband that she had seen Chinuwa in the vicinity of the food store that morning. When Chinuwa returned to the house, Wof confronted her with Kaya's charge, but Chinuwa hotly denied it and threatened to leave Wof if he believed any more malicious gossip about her. Although Chinuwa may have taken a bit of sago flour to hold as sorcery material over Wof's head, it is much more probable that Kaya engineered the scheme to make Wof angry and suspicious of his new wife. Despite such conflicts, Kwoma co-wives are usually quite amicable. Each has her separate fire and does her own cooking. Each is allotted a special part of the garden to care for. If a dispute arises concerning their coöperative activity, the husband acts as arbiter.

A woman's relationship to other relatives need only be briefly sketched. She acts in a motherly way toward the children of her co-wife, and toward the children of her husband's *brothers*. She calls her father's *sister's* children *son* or *daughter* and mothers them even though they may be older than she. She is kindly toward the children of her *brother*, calling them niece and nephew. She rarely sees her *sisters*, since they are not permitted to marry into the same hamlet.

Thus a Kwoma man lives in a hamlet surrounded by relatives with whom he is comparatively safe, who coöperate with him and support him, and who share with him common interests and goals. He is bound to the other hamlets of his sib by patrilineal ties and to the hamlets of other sibs of the subtribe through ties with his *sisters*, his *maternal uncles*, his *paternal aunts*, his wife's relatives, his *friends*, and his ceremonial *father* and *son*. Each of these bonds implies reciprocal obligations, some of which are economic but all of which are protective and friendly. A woman lives with her children among her affines. She maintains throughout her life a close tie with the hamlet of her birth through the strong bond that she has with her parents and her *brothers*, and she also has havens of safety and friendship in other hamlets with her *maternal uncle,* her *paternal aunt,* her *sisters,* and her *friends.*

Despite the ties which a man has with various kinsmen, the great majority of the members of the other sibs of the subtribe are not related to him. Nevertheless, he is united to them by common interests and participates with them in common enterprises, not so frequently nor so intimately as with relatives but still enough to weld the subtribe into an integrated unit. Cult, age-grade, and initiation ceremonies are the concern of the whole subtribe, not of a hamlet or even of a sib. Head-hunting raids, intertribal and intratribal court meetings, and the building of a house tamberan all entail the coöperative endeavors of non-relatives[46] as well as relatives. Finally, the members of a subtribe call themselves by a common name, and a Hongwam will support a Hongwam against members of the other Kwoma subtribes.

Despite the bonds which unite the unrelated members of a subtribe, considerable antagonism and suspicion is the rule between non-relatives. Fear of sorcery is ever present between them. They do not eat with one another, and when they visit or meet they do so guardedly, exercising great care not to leave anything behind which could be used for sorcery. Whenever anyone becomes ill it is usually a non-relative who is first suspected.

A man must be aggressive if he is threatened by a non-relative, lest he be criticized by his own relatives, but he may not be overaggressive lest he give the non-relative good cause for serious counteraggression. I personally felt the application of the sanction against not being aggressive enough. Shortly before the end of my field work, a young man from one of the other sibs pilfered my last tin of tobacco. I complained about it to Gwiyap and Mar. They had no sympathy for me. They said that it was all my fault for letting people from other hamlets wander around my house. Shortly afterwards, War came in and I told him what had happened. He gave me a sound scolding: "You are a little baby. Don't

[46] The term "non-relative" is used here to apply to all persons in the subtribe not addressed by a kinship term.

you know enough to keep non-relatives out of your house? No one is going to keep these people from stealing from you if you are afraid to protect your own rights."

Although a man must be aggressive when he is threatened by a non-relative, he must not be disproportionately so. In general, the amount of aggression he may show is determined by the kind and amount of threat that he has endured. If he catches a non-relative in the act of stealing or trespassing, he may beat him on the spot or threaten him with a spear, but may not kill him. If he discovers the crime after it is done, he may threaten physical violence unless reparations are made. If the thief or trespasser refuses to comply with these demands, a court session is held in which the principals meet with their relatives and discuss the matter until an equitable settlement is made. If a man detects a non-relative stealing sorcery material, or raping a wife or sister, he may kill him on the spot. If he discovers that a non-relative is having an affair with his wife or sister, he may threaten or beat him but may not kill him. Following this he may retaliate by seducing a sister or wife of the man whom he has discovered. If a man suspects a non-relative of sorcery, he may openly accuse him and turn public opinion against him in order to make him stop. If it is well established that a non-relative has been guilty of sorcery, the victim or his relative is not condemned for retaliating in kind.

A man is inhibited from being disproportionately aggressive toward a non-relative by a complex of sanctions. In any controversy between two unrelated members of the tribe, three groups appear: the relatives of the aggressor, the relatives of the victim, and those who are related to neither. If the behavior of the aggressor is deemed appropriate, he will be supported in his action by his own relatives and by the group related to neither principal. Furthermore, although his relatives will support the victim and will verbally threaten and insult the aggressor and his relatives, they will take no physical step toward counteraggression. Then, too, there are always persons among the relatives of the victim who are related to someone in the aggressor group, and who therefore do not wish the controversy to continue to such a point that they will be forced to break these relationships. These persons, if the aggression has adhered to custom, will point out that the victim received what he deserved and will suggest that the matter be closed. If the aggressor demands compensation, it is these persons who bring pressure to bear upon the victim to pay it. If, however, the aggressor's behavior has been disproportionate, if his reaction to some minor threat imposed by a non-relative has exceeded the bounds of custom, then the situation is reversed. Public opinion swings in favor of the victim: If the aggressor has been exceedingly disproportionate in his aggression, his own relatives may even withdraw their support from him, and he is then forced to leave the tribe to escape retaliation from the victim and his relatives.

The Kwoma court system provides a formalized mode of settling disputes between non-relatives.[47] The court may meet to settle any disagreement, whether it be over property, sex, or sorcery. Only adult males attend the meetings, which are held at a house tamberan, usually a neutral one. The men convene in the morning carrying spears and wearing bone daggers. When everyone has arrived, the most important man of the hamlet in which the meeting is being held stands and states the purpose of the meeting and his view of the case. When he has finished speaking, someone else will stand and state his opinion. Then another presents his views. Thus the meeting progresses. A man's speech usually starts with an exoneration of himself and his relatives and ends with an accusation of someone else. While making a speech a man stamps his feet on the ground, brandishes a spear or dagger, and speaks loudly, often raising his voice to a shout. Sometimes, when someone has made a particularly pointed accusation, the accused will rise and stand facing his accuser. Each may draw his dagger, stand close to his opponent, reach over the other's shoulder and make jabbing movements at his back, shouting insults and threats. It is particularly im-

---

[47] Disputes which only concern relatives are settled at similar but less formal meetings at the local house tamberan.

portant for a man not to flinch in these circumstances, for to do so would not only mean a great loss in personal prestige, but would also be taken as an admission of guilt. The men, therefore, slowly back away from one another as the heat of the discussion cools down, or one of them will make a particularly telling remark and turn contemptuously on his heel and sit down. Their place is then taken by another speaker. Men sometimes make short comments without standing. Courts to settle a dispute usually come to a successful conclusion after everyone has aired his opinion and those less closely involved begin to discuss the matter more rationally. A meeting to discover sorcery guilt goes on endlessly, however, reconvening day after day. The Kwoma themselves admit that it is "talk nothing," but they attend, nevertheless. It gives them an opportunity to vent their hostilities, even though they seldom convict anyone.[48]

Although a Kwoma is suspicious of all foreigners, he nevertheless distinguishes between them in accordance with whether they belong to a tribe which is friendly with his subtribe or not. There is considerable trading between Kwoma subtribes and their neighbors. The Hongwam not only exchange sago flour for fish with the river tribes, but they are a link in the chain which passes shell money from the sea up the Sepik and into the interior. These shells are exchanged for pigs, tools, and carved wooden figures, and since they are difficult for the interior tribes to obtain, the Kwoma can make a profit as middlemen. Both of these forms of exchange entail visits between members of the various tribes. Furthermore, there is some intermarriage between neighboring tribes, and visiting takes place between the woman and her relatives, and Kwoma men sometimes attend ceremonies which are being held at a near-by tribe, or entertain foreigners at their own cult ceremonies. For these reasons it is advantageous for neighboring tribes to maintain sufficiently friendly relations so that these visits may take place safely. Under normal cir-

[48] Another reason for attending court is that to be absent raises suspicions of guilt.

cumstances this is the case, but a dispute over property, the abduction or rape of a woman, or a head-hunting murder may break off these safe relations. Visiting then takes place only at the risk of one's life, until the matter can be settled. Finally a foreigner may sometimes steal, trespass, or encroach upon Kwoma land.

Safe relations with another tribe are reëstablished after a dispute by means of an intertribal court. After the heat of a dispute has cooled,[49] the adult males of the two tribes arrange by gongs to meet at an appointed place on neutral territory. They all carry daggers and spears to be prepared for treachery and to give force to their arguments. The two groups face one another, and a spokesman advances from each in turn to present the case of his tribe. Each spokesman accentuates his speech by slapping a flat board on the ground. Often the two representatives stand close to each other, chests out and eyes flashing, and jab bone daggers over one another's shoulder. Just as in the intratribal court, it is important not to flinch, so only the most courageous of the tribesmen act as spokesmen. Such courts are most commonly held to settle territorial disputes, to arrange the payment of a bride-price for an abducted girl, or to decide on a wergild for a head-hunting murder.

Open warfare between New Guinea tribes is infrequent, and the Kwoma are no exception. A war was waged in the time of the grandfathers of living informants. It began with a territorial dispute with the people who inhabited part of the area that the Kwoma now occupy. After a prolonged series of raids and counterraids, the Kwoma exterminated all but a small remnant of the enemy, who fled to another location. During the war, the Kwoma captured the leader of the enemy. They dragged him to one of their house tamberans and trussed him to the center pole. Then they held a dance around him, jabbed spears into him, spat at him, and otherwise tortured him. Finally they killed him, cut him up like a

[49] Informants said that it was of no advantage to hold a court when "bellies were hot with anger," as it would probably end in a fight.

pig, and made soup of him. Only the adult males were allowed to eat the soup,[50] and it was believed that they were thus made such brave fighters that they were able to conquer their enemies.

The head-hunting raid provides the most frequently employed means of expressing aggression toward a foreigner. Such a raid is planned in advance, and allies are often recruited from friendly neighboring tribes. A careful itinerary is drawn up, and an unsuspecting and weak hamlet is chosen for attack. The men meet before setting out on the raid to eat a ceremonial soup. They travel under cover of darkness, arranging to arrive at their destination just before dawn. Then the men quietly surround an outlying dwelling and stand with spears poised while two of the boldest of the attackers creep toward the house. When they reach the entrance they let out a blood-curdling scream and kick the door down. The other attackers join in the shouting and in spearing the dazed occupants as they rush from the dwelling. When the attackers have killed the whole household, they rush to other houses in the hamlet, hoping to catch and kill some inhabitants who have not awakened at the outcry and fled. Then they return and behead the corpses with a bamboo knife. They carry the heads home. When they near their own tribe, they set up a victorious shout and dance into their hamlet, holding their trophies by the ear in their teeth. Then follows a victory dance which lasts for several days and nights.

A man is impelled to go on a head-hunting raid to gain prestige, as well as to avenge himself on a foreigner. No man is eligible to join *Nokwi*, the highest grade of the yam cult, until he has taken a head. Until he belongs to *Nokwi* he cannot plant yams, nor is he considered to be a man of importance in the community. It is the *Nokwi* members who have the greatest weight at the court sessions. Furthermore, a man

[50] This is the only occasion in the memory of informants that the Kwoma had practiced cannibalism. They showed disgust and contempt for those tribes who ate human flesh and betrayed some shame in reporting the above incident.

who has not taken a head is held in contempt by his wife. Yat explained to me why he went on a raid. "I was angry with my wife one day and began to beat her. She taunted me. She said, 'You are very brave when it comes to beating women, but fighting a man is quite different. If you had taken a head, I would not complain when you beat me. It makes me ashamed to be married to a man who dares beat only his wife.' My belly became hot with anger at this taunt, so I went down to the house tamberan and called together my friends. We planned a raid and carried it out. I came back with a head between my teeth and showed it to my wife. Since then she has not complained when I beat her. Many of us Kwoma go on raids because we are taunted in this way by our wives."

In addition to the motives of vengeance and prestige, a head-hunting raid is a means of expressing aggression in displaced form. Much of the aggression generated in the ingroup is inhibited from direct expression by the sanctions against aggression toward members of one's hamlet, relatives, and certain non-relatives. There are no sanctions, however, against killing a foreigner on a head-hunting raid, so that in this way a man can express much of the aggression which he has had to inhibit.

The following case concerns the genesis of a head-hunting raid which took place during my stay in Kwoma. It illustrates, in particular, how a raid may be a means of expressing aggression in a displaced form. War, a man of considerable prestige in the community, owned and operated a garden in common with his two younger brothers, Kar and Kis. One day War and Kar were working on this garden with their wives. War returned to the hamlet in the afternoon, leaving Kar and the two wives to spend the night in the bush house. He gave his own wife orders to weed a certain portion of the garden before he returned the next afternoon. When he returned he found the work not yet done. He asked his wife for an explanation, and she said that she had been possessed by a ghost the night before and that this had upset her so that she had been unable to work. Kar's wife said that this was not the explanation at all. The real reason why the work was undone, she said, was that the woman had spent the morning in the bushes with Kar. War became furious at this, knocked his wife down with his fist, and threatened to spear his brother Kar. Kar denied the accusation indignantly, saying that his wife had merely invented the story to get him in trouble, whereupon he, in turn, clouted his own wife. War was still suspicious, but did not proceed further against Kar. War's wife, however, returned in a fury to the hamlet, packed her things, took her young daughter by the hand,[51] and left before War returned. Kar, who had arrived before she left, tried to dissuade her, but did not succeed. When War returned that evening and found his wife gone, he was even more angry than before. He painted his face with clay and swore that he would not take it off until he had brought her back or killed the man to whom she had fled. The next day he traced her to Yelagu, a neighboring tribe consisting of only six families. He took three spears and set out alone to bring back his runaway wife. Someone warned the Yelagu that he was coming, so that when he arrived there was only a cripple left in the village. War demanded where his wife had gone, but the cripple either could not or would not tell him and offered him a dog and some shell money if War would spare his life. War demanded more money, took it and the dog, and returned home.

The next evening War called his friends and relatives together. He distributed the dog meat among them, told them what had happened, and suggested that they go on a head-hunting raid against the Yelagu. He argued that it was a very small tribe and that they were all cowards. He said that it would be a good opportunity for some of the young men who had not yet taken a head to do so. He admitted that he was interested in getting his wife back and teaching her a lesson, and in punishing the man who had harbored her. Most of those present thought that it was a good idea, but several objected on the grounds that Yelagu was too near

---

[51] Theoretically she should have left her daughter with her husband, since children belong to their father's hamlet.

Adulthood

Ambunti, the government post. Some of the men present had seen six river natives hanged by the white government for head-hunting and did not relish the idea of being caught themselves. They said that it would be much safer to attack Sowal, a tribe far in the swamp which the whites had not yet visited. Wof, a *brother* of War, voiced another objection to the raid. He pointed out that his gardens adjoined Yelagu territory, and since they would be sure to retaliate, it would not be safe for him to work in his garden if the raid were carried out. The group disbanded, excited but undecided.

For two weeks there was a great deal of discussion among the men of the tribe. War and Wof argued with particular vehemence, War presenting over and again the reasons why it was a good idea to raid the Yelagu, and Wof countering with his objections. The two even broke relationship for a time because of the dispute. Neither visited the other's house, and they passed one another guardedly without speaking. The other men of the tribe, meanwhile, had been swayed by the argument that there was considerable danger of punishment from the whites if Yelagu were attacked, whereas Sowal involved much less danger. It was also reported that high water had driven the Sowal out of their central village, and that they were living on knolls in small isolated groups that would be particularly vulnerable. The pressure of these arguments finally forced War to give up his idea of attacking Yelagu, and he threw his weight into planning for the Sowal raid. He and Wof reëstablished their relationship.

War and some of the older men of the hamlet began to incite the young men to go on the raid. He told them that this was their chance to become big men. In particular he played upon the emotions of Mes, because he, as my shoot boy, could use a gun. The effect of these incendiary talks put Mar in a strong conflict. One evening he came to talk to me about it. He told me that he had decided not to go on the raid. He was afraid that the raiders would get in trouble with the whites, and he was not going to have anything to do with it. Then he began talking about what he would lose by not going and started to weep. He sobbed: "Never mind. I'll never be a man but never mind. I'll just be a woman all my life until I die. I am afraid of being hanged, that's all. I am not going."

Finally, all the men of the subtribe and some from neighboring tribes met one night at the house tamberan near War's house. Those who had already taken a head were dressed with homicidal insignia. Their faces were blackened with soot, bands of opossum fur were fastened around their foreheads, and bird of paradise plumes attached to combs bobbed from the backs of their heads. When all had arrived, a ceremonial soup was served, the special ingredients of which were supposed to make men bold and powerful fighters. It is so strong, the Kwoma believe, that a woman or child would die if they eat it. After eating, they broke up in small groups to plan the itinerary. It was decided to send a scout ahead to discover the lay of the land. After the scout had left, the men had nothing to do but wait until he returned the next day. Some went home, but many stayed and began to play ball. The game soon turned into a spontaneous rehearsal of the raid, as the men lined up in sides and threw the ball to each other, shouting and stamping their feet at the same time.

The next day the scout returned to say that the road to Sowal was impassable. The water was so high that it was impossible to walk there, but it was not high enough to go with a canoe. The raid was therefore called off. I think that if it had not been for many who, like Mar, feared punishment from the whites,[52] a way would have been found and the raid carried out.

[52] Not a few of the men opposed going on the raid because they feared that I would report them.

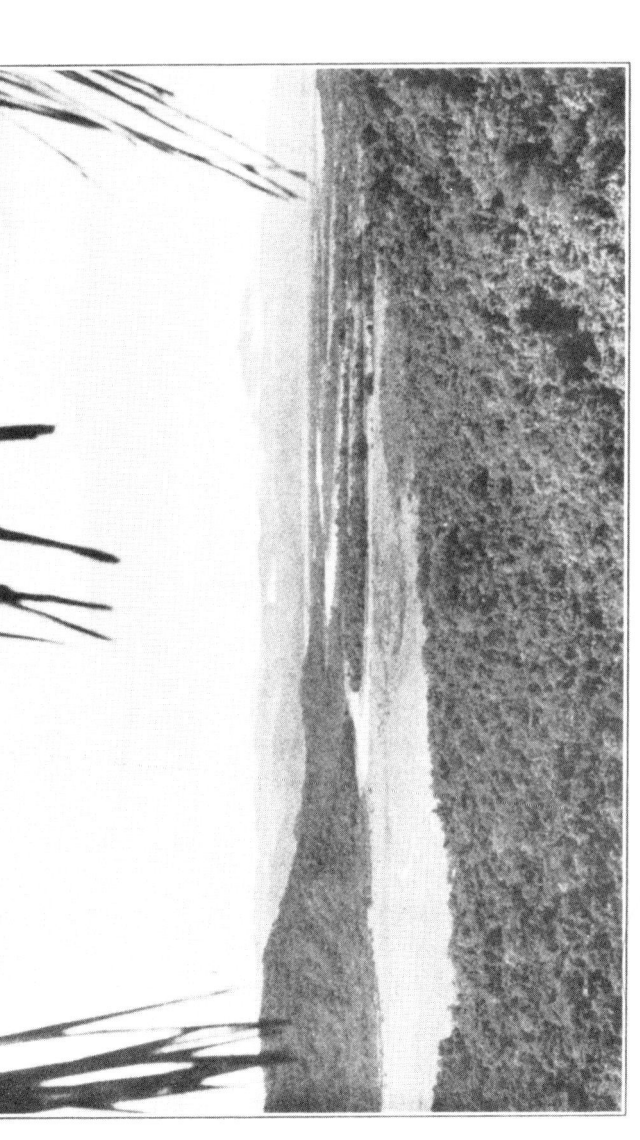

View of the Sepik River taken from near Rumbima house tamberan. The forested slopes of the Peilungua range upon which the Kwoma dwell may be seen in the right foreground and left center. The sago swamp at the base of this range extends from the left foreground to the right center. The light section which is partially surrounded by this swamp is a mat of grass floating on the lake, the unchoked part of which may be seen beyond. Above and to the right of the lake may be seen glimpses of the Sepik as it winds its way around the spur at the left toward Ambunti. See Chapter I, page 3.

Coöperative work group constructing the house of the ethnographers. The roofing material is split limbom palm spathes. The construction is that used by the Kwoma in making bush houses, permanent dwellings having an enclosed room and sewn shingles. See Chapter VI, pages 129–130.

Work bee dragging a log from the forest where it was cut to the Rumbima house tamberan. The log was later hollowed into a slit gong which Yat contributed to the community. The workers are those of Yat's relatives who answered his call for help. In return he will provide them with a feast. See Chapter VII, pages 198–199.

The market at which Kwoma women are trading their surplus of sago flour for fish brought by the river natives. The woman in the foreground is Marok's sister, Uka, holding a lump of sago flour in each hand. See Chapter VI, pages 119–120. The scars on her chest and around her navel are those she received as a mark of adulthood. See Chapter VI, page 106.

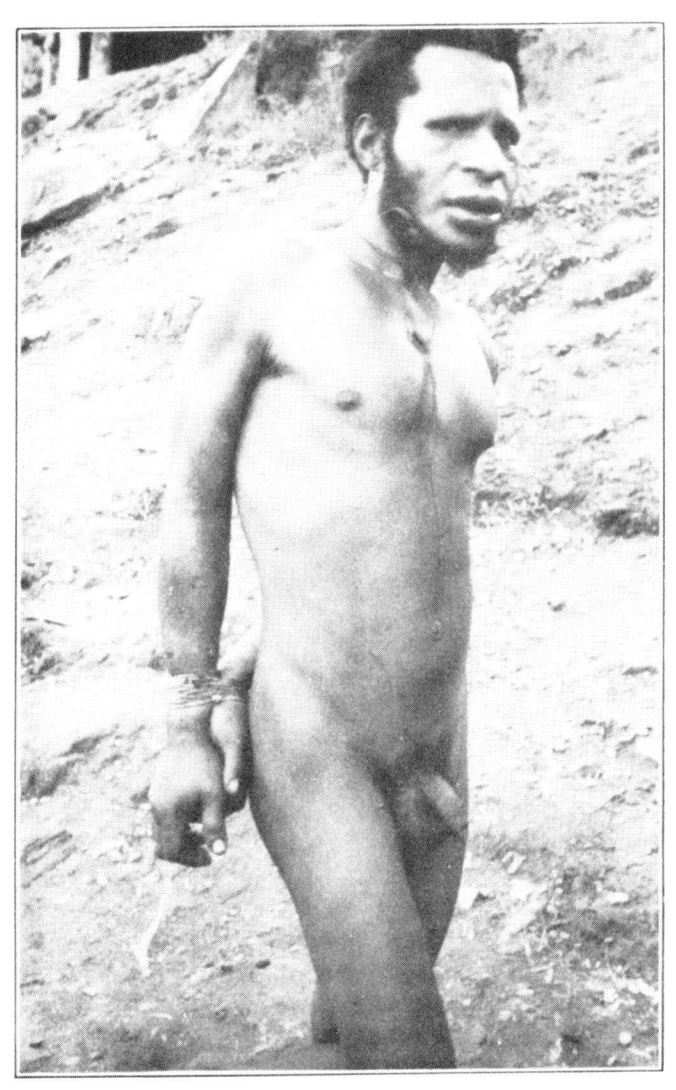

Mundik just after he had fled to our house for sanctuary after having been beaten and bound for attending the cult meeting associated with the second funeral feast. This ceremony is restricted to those who have received their keloids of manhood. Mundik, being a Yelagu, had not received these. A further reason for his being beaten was that he had killed his wife in a fit of rage and fled to Kwoma, his mother's former home, to escape being killed by his wife's relatives. The Kwoma shunned him and used his breach of cult rules as an excuse for expressing their feelings toward a person they believed to be a homicidal maniac. Had he not loosened the bonds on his ankles and escaped from the house in which he was imprisoned, he may well have been killed before the ceremony ended. See Chapter VI, page 144, and Chapter VIII, page 213.

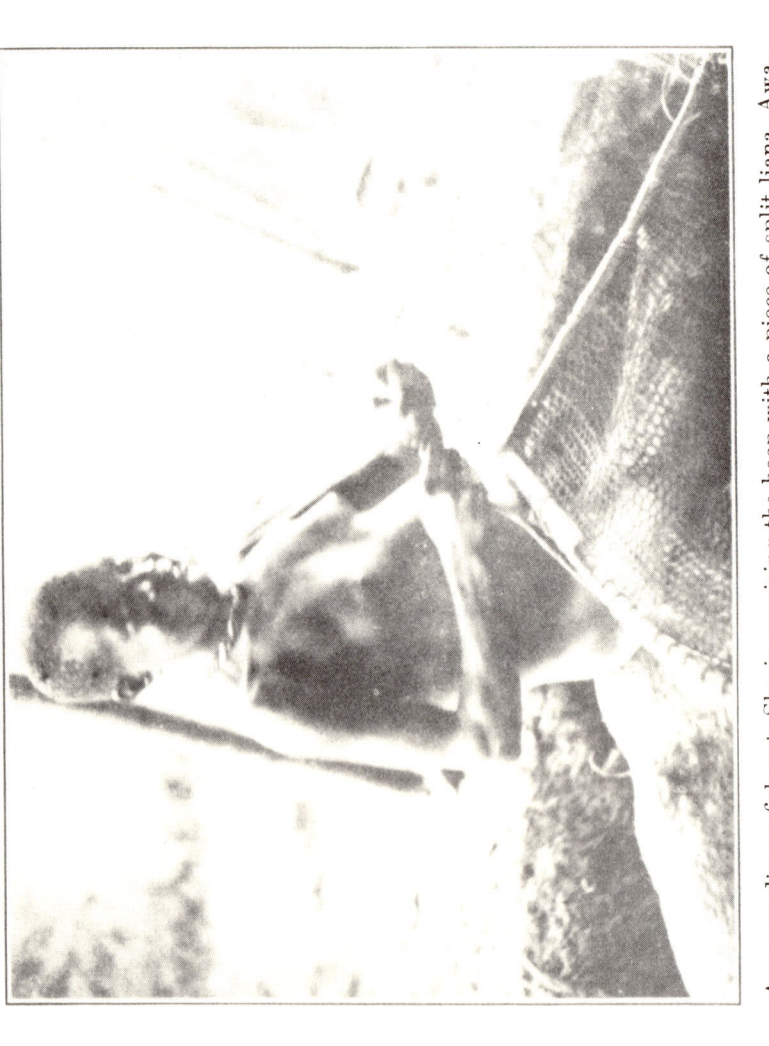

Awa mending a fish net. She is repairing the hoop with a piece of split liana. Awa, Mar's real sister, was one of the adolescent girls of Rumbima hamlet. See Chapter V.

Kum, the chief character of the weaning period. See Chapter III.

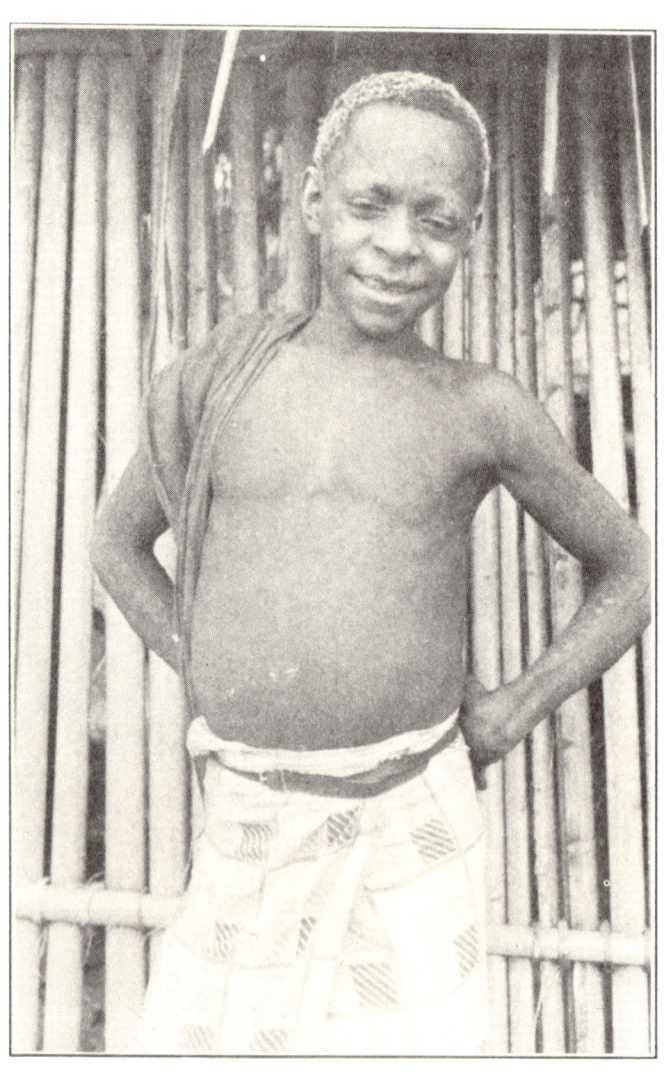

Gwiyap, our best informant, wearing a laplap which he had earned working for us as a house boy. See Chapter V.

PART TWO

CHAPTER VII

THE PROCESS OF SOCIALIZATION

THE previous chapters have stressed the particular customs which Kwoma society chooses to transmit to its children, the categories of persons who teach them, and the stage in the life cycle of the individual to which these customs apply. The purpose has been to present the data on these aspects of Kwoma life so that they might be useful for comparative or historical purposes.

The present chapter is devoted primarily to an inquiry into the nature of the transmission of culture and to a psychological analysis of the manner in which this transmission takes place. Although Kwoma data are employed in this analysis and the statements are made in terms of these data, the purpose is to develop hypotheses concerning the process of socialization which have significance not alone for the Kwoma but for all cultures. It is obvious that such hypotheses, validated by only a single society, cannot be considered more than tentative. Since the data with which to test these hypotheses in other societies have not yet been reported in the anthropological literature, they are presented in this form, primarily in the hope that they may be sufficiently suggestive to be tested by those future fieldworkers who become interested in a theory of the transmission of culture.

Were the transmission of culture a genetic process, it would be expedient to turn to the biologist for a basic theory of socialization. Anthropologists have demonstrated, however, that the behavior of peoples in various societies is not instinctive but cultural; it is a matter of habits. Since a habit is something which is learned, it is evident that a theory of learning must form the basis for an understanding of the process of socialization.

The theory of learning developed by psychologists has been demonstrated to apply both to animals and to men in Western society. It may be assumed that this theory also applies to the behavior of the members of other human societies. Such an assumption follows from the more general hypothesis of the basic psychological unity of mankind, an hypothesis which has been supported by anthropological evidence. Although it may be assumed that the basic mechanisms of learning apply to the Kwoma, it remains to be demonstrated how the Kwoma take advantage of these mechanisms to indoctrinate and train the oncoming generation; from this evidence some hypotheses concerning socialization may be developed.

Learning does not take place in a vacuum, but only when certain necessary conditions are present. In social learning these conditions are determined by the society, the culture, and the natural environment, whereas in the laboratory the conditions have been determined by the experimenters who have artificially and systematically varied them. Psychologists have built mazes of different shapes, decided where and when to provide food or electric shock, and carefully controlled the degree of hunger of the experimental animal by withholding food from it. With human subjects they have similarly varied the conditions. They have used fear of authority and the wish for approval as motives and employed praise or money as rewards whenever the problem investigated demanded it. It has been expedient for the psychologists to control the conditions in this way, for by so doing they have been able to discover many of the dynamics of learning. From the point of view of the social scientist concerned with the problem of socialization, however, psychologists have accomplished only part of the task, for the conditions under which social learning takes place are determined by the necessities of social living and by the regulations of the existing culture. The conditions of social learning are for the social scientist to study, not to manipulate.

Before examining the social and cultural conditions of learning, it will be helpful to present a summary of the findings of the psychologists which are most relevant to the present problem. Reinforcement, the most basic of learning principles, can best be presented in the following paradigm. This

Process of Socialization

statement of the essential conditions for habit formation has been adapted from the theories of Pavlov, Thorndike, and Hull by Miller and Dollard.[1] Since this adaptation has been developed for use in the field of social learning, it precisely fulfills the requirements of this chapter. In order to learn, an animal must be motivated, he must act, he must perceive the cues that are present during his action, and he must gain satisfaction. In outline form the Miller-Dollard paradigm may be presented thus: There must be a

A. *Drive* or drives of sufficient intensity to produce a
B. *Response* or series of responses made in the presence of
C. *Cues* which stimulate the animal's receptors until a[2]
D. *Reward* reduces the intensity of the drive.

Whenever the above conditions occur, the bond which connects the drives and cues to the response is strengthened. That is, when the organism again experiences the same drive and the same cues, it will have a greater tendency to make the same response. In the early stages of learning the increment in the strength of the habit is large, but after the conditions represented in the paradigm have been frequently repeated, and the habit well established, the increments become progressively smaller. Each time the conditions expressed in the paradigm are repeated and the habit thereby strengthened, reinforcement may be said to have occurred.[3]

The drives which are of greatest importance in the process of socialization are: hunger, thirst, sex, colon distention, bladder distention, heat, cold, fatigue, and pain.[4] Each of these drives may vary in intensity, and this variation is a function of the interaction between the organism and the environment.

[1] See N. E. Miller and John Dollard, *Social Learning and Imitation* (New Haven, 1941), chap. ii.

[2] Cues are also present during and after the reward, but these are not relevant to the formation of the habit in question.

[3] See N. E. Miller and John Dollard, *Social Learning and Imitation* (New Haven, 1941), chap. ii; E. R. Hilgard and D. G. Marquis, *Conditioning and Learning* (New York, 1940), chap. 4; C. L. Hull, "Outline of a Systematic Theory of Learning," *Educational Psychology Yearbook* (in press).

[4] For a recent statement of socially relevant drives see H. A. Murray, *Explorations in Personality* (New York, 1938), pp. 67-89.

The intensity of the hunger drive depends both upon metabolic processes within the organism and upon the amount and kind of food provided by the environment. The hunger becomes more intense as the number of hours of food deprivation increases. It becomes strong more quickly when the expenditure of energy increases the rate of metabolism. Its intensity is an inverse function of the amount of food previously ingested and depends in a complex manner upon the physiological needs of the organism and how adequately they have been satisfied by the types of food available. In a similar way the other drives vary in intensity according to processes which take place within the organism and according to factors in the external environment which need not be detailed here.[5]

Acquired drives, as well as the above-listed basic ones, motivate behavior and belong in category A of the Miller-Dollard paradigm. Although these acquired drives are most frequently found to be the immediate impelling force for social habits, their intensity and even their very existence depend upon a continued relationship with basic drives.[6] It is not necessary here to describe the manner in which acquired drives come into being, but simply to state that whereas basic drives depend upon the relationship between the organism and the environment, acquired drives depend, in addition, upon the past experience of the organism. In other words, acquired drives must themselves be learned. Fear,[7] anger,[8] the wish for prestige, the desire for money, the

[5] The best evidence for the factors which govern the intensity of drives has been adduced by the physiologists; for hunger see W. B. Cannon, *The Wisdom of the Body* (New York, 1932); for a general statement see C. P. Richter, "Animal Behavior and Internal Drives," *The Quarterly Review of Biology*, II (1927), no. 3, pp. 307–343; for experimental evidence on drives see P. T. Young, *Motivation in Behavior* (New York, 1936).

[6] For a detailed account of acquired drives see N. E. Miller and John Dollard, *Social Learning and Imitation* (New Haven, 1941), chap. iv.

[7] See S. Freud, *The Problem of Anxiety* (New York, 1936); E. Zinn, "Anxiety, Clinically Viewed," and O. H. Mowrer, "Anxiety, Some Social and Psychological Implications," *Papers Presented before the Monday Night Group* (1939–40), pp. 116–144, Institute of Human Relations, Yale University.

[8] See John Dollard, et al., *Frustration and Aggression* (New Haven,

wish for words of praise, the craving for affection, and the various conditioned disgusts and appetites are examples of acquired drives.

The second essential of learning is that a response shall be made. Responses may be gross muscular, such as walking, running, throwing a spear; glandular, such as the secretion of gastric juices; verbal, such as issuing a command; or ideational, such as thinking, fantasying, or planning. In fact, any activity of the organism falls in the category of a response.

Cues, the third essential for learning, are those stimuli which act as guides in the performance of any response. They tell the organism when, where, and how to act. They may originate from objects outside the organism, such as patterns of light, sound, smell, taste, and touch, or they may arise within the organism, as in the case of feelings of hunger, thirst, bladder and colon distentions, stomach cramps, and stimuli arising from the movement of muscles.[9] A cue is thus any stimulus which is appreciated by an organism and which acts as a guide in the learning or performance of a habit.

Reward, the final essential condition for the formation of a habit, may be defined as an event which reduces the intensity of a drive. The ingestion of food reduces the hunger drive; drinking reduces thirst; sexual orgasm reduces the sex drive; defecation and urination reduce colon and bladder distentions; escape from heat, cold, fatigue, and pain effect the reduction of the heat, cold, fatigue, and pain drives.[10]

Since there are acquired drives, there are also corresponding acquired rewards. In so far as one is motivated to strive for social goals, he gains satisfaction from achieving them. Safety, high status, the destruction of enemies, the gaining

1939); N. E. Miller and John Dollard, *Social Learning and Imitation* (New Haven, 1941), chap. iv.

[9] Both drives and cues are stimuli. When the intensity of a stimulus is its most important function, it may be spoken of as a drive, when it functions primarily as a guide, it may be referred to as a cue.

[10] The response which is most closely correlated in time with a reward is called a goal response.

of money, hearing words of praise, receiving affection, avoiding disgusting objects, and satisfying appetites are some of the common acquired rewards which are present in our society.

The Miller-Dollard paradigm may be illustrated from the Kwoma data presented in the previous chapters. An example will be taken more or less at random from each period in the life cycle in order to elucidate the terms of the paradigm. Kwoma infants when they are hungry turn toward their mother's breast and suckle. In this case the drive is hunger; the response is turning toward the mother's breast and suckling; the cues are the sight of the mother and her breast, and the feeling of contact with her; and the reward is the ingestion of milk. From many repetitions of this sequence an infant learns the habit of turning toward the mother's breast and suckling when he is hungry in the presence of the mother. During the weaning period a Kwoma child learns not to cling to his mother.[11] In this case the drive is pain from being pushed away and the fear of being scolded, the response is staying away from the mother, the cues are the presence of the mother, and the reward is escape from pain and reduction of fear.

During childhood a Kwoma boy learns to avoid the house tamberan while ceremonies are being held. The drive in this case is anxiety (he is warned that he would die if he did so); the response is avoiding the house tamberan; the cues are the sound of the gong rhythms, the statements of others that a ceremony is being held, the sight of his father, *uncles*, and older *brothers* decorating themselves; the reward is escape from anxiety. In adolescence a boy learns to carry on secret love affairs with adolescent girls. The drives are sex, sex appetite, and anxiety (sex impells him to seek girls, sex appetite leads him to choose a girl culturally defined as attractive, and anxiety impells him to do so secretly); the response is the complex of behavior which leads to and includes sexual intercourse in the bush; the cues are the sight of an attrac-

[11] Not to cling to his mother should be thought of as a habit of avoidance involving active responses, rather than as the absence of a habit.

tive girl, verbal permission from her, the environmental scene which has both public and secluded spots, etc.; the reward is sexual orgasm, satisfaction of sex appetite, and anxiety reduction. The adult habit of beating gongs against sorcery when a relative becomes ill may be used as a final illustration of the paradigm. The man's drives in this case are fear that he, too, may become ill unless the sorcery is stopped, fear that his relatives may die, and anger at the sorcerer; the response is going to the house tamberan and beating the gongs in a particular way; the cues are those which indicate that a relative is sick; and the reward is a reduction in fear and anger. Thus, although the habits become more and more complex[12] as the individual matures, the four essentials of learning and performance pertain to the behavior of individuals of all ages.

A Kwoma child learns but a small part of his cultural habits by free trial and error, that is, without some member of his society guiding and directing him.[13] Were he to do so, he would learn those habits which were most rewarding to him and to him alone.[14] This, however, is not what actually happens. He is forced to learn, not the habits which might be most rewarding to him alone, but the habits which are specified in the culture as being best. For generations before his birth his forbears have tried various ways of dealing with one another and with their environment. Those habits which were successful have persisted in the form of customs, while those which have failed have either suffered extinction or passed out of existence with the untimely death of those who

[12] It is not the particular purpose of this chapter to detail how complex habits are learned, although this is a crucial problem. Hull has suggested a very important mechanism as a partial explanation in his theory of the assembly of behavior segments. This theory, together with the integration of habits on a cultural level, should go far toward the solution of the problem. See C. L. Hull, "The Mechanism of the Assembly of Behavior Segments in Novel Combinations Suitable for Problem Solution," *Psychol. Rev.*, XLII (1935), 219–245.

[13] Limited trial and error operate in nearly all learning situations. The concept of free trial and error is used here to mean learning which takes place without the guidance or interference of any other person.

[14] See C. L. Hull, "The Concept of the Habit-Family Hierarchy and Maze Learning," *Psychol. Rev.*, XLI (1934), 33–54, 134–152.

tried them.[15] For various reasons this accumulation of adaptive habits is passed on to the child. He does not simply learn to get along in the world; he is socialized. Thus an essential set of conditions for social learning is the behavior of the socializing agents. The remainder of this chapter will be devoted to an analysis of these conditions and their relation to social learning.

Before the analysis of teaching techniques is undertaken, several terms which are to be used should be defined. The terms "teacher" and "pupil" will be employed in a special sense, the former to mean anyone who attempts to change the habit structure of another person, the latter, any person whose habit structure is being so changed. Although Kwoma parents most frequently play the rôle of teacher, with their children as pupils, the teacher-pupil relation is not by any means restricted to them. Co-mothers, siblings, *paternal uncles* and *aunts*, and other relatives frequently play the rôle of teacher as well. The concept of teacher will also be extended in this context even to an adult who tries to influence the behavior of another adult. Although such behavior may be considered an act of aggression or coöperation, as the case may be, it is also a teacher-pupil relationship if a habit of the pupil is thereby strengthened or weakened.

A second set of terms will be used for responses, which will be characterized as "right," "not right," "wrong," and "not wrong." A right response is a specific act which the teacher wishes the pupil to make, whereas not right responses are all those acts which are incompatible with the right response under the given conditions. Similarly, a wrong response is a specific act which the teacher wishes the pupil not to make, and not wrong responses are all those acts which are incompatible with the wrong response under the given circumstances. These concepts may be illustrated from the cases which will be reported in detail below. When Wof punished Buka for failing to gather firewood, "getting firewood" was the right response, while playing, sleeping, eating, gossiping,

[15] See A. G. Keller, *Societal Evolution* (New York, 1929); W. G. Sumner, *Folkways* (Boston, 1906), chap. v.

or any other response which Buka might make when she should be getting firewood can be described as not right responses. When Mes warned Kwos not to play with a cartridge, "playing with the cartridge" was the wrong response, while doing anything else would be the not wrong responses. Teachers normally describe the specific act, whether it be right or wrong, and refer to the not right or not wrong responses as the negative of the specific act. Sometimes they exemplify the not right or not wrong, by stating a specific act in the negative category. For example, in the above cases Wof may have specified playing as one of the not right acts which Buka did, or Mes might have specified joining the play group as a not wrong response. Teachers normally try to make their pupils learn to make a right response or to make a not wrong response. The other two categories, not right and wrong, denote behavior which the teacher wishes to prevent, but which he can prevent only by teaching the pupil an incompatible habit, i.e., right or not wrong, respectively. This will be illustrated in the cases to be analyzed below.

In socializing their pupils, Kwoma teachers use various techniques, all of which make practical use of the paradigm of learning presented above.[16] Some of these techniques stress motivation, some the response, some the cues, and some the rewards, but the whole process is implicit in all of them. Kwoma teachers use different techniques for different situations; the kind of habit to be taught, the age and maturity of the pupil, and the kin relationship between teacher and pupil are some of the factors that determine which technique shall be used. The following presentation does not purport to be a complete list of the methods of teaching employed at Kwoma nor a full account of the situations in which they are used, but is rather an analysis and description of the more important ones observed.[17]

[16] Since pupils in our society learn by the same mechanisms as do Kwoma pupils, it is not surprising that many of the techniques of teaching in the two societies are similar. In fact, the following techniques will seem quite obvious to anyone who has been either a parent or a teacher.

[17] The following theory of teaching techniques was not worked out before the data were gathered. For this reason the cases analyzed below were not

Unless the essentials for learning are already provided by the interaction of the environment and the pupil, they must be supplied by the teacher. In other words, when such conditions are not already present, the teacher, in order to change the habit structure of the pupil in the desired manner, must provide *motivation, guidance,* and *reward.* Each of the various teaching techniques employed at Kwoma may be classed under one or another of these three categories. The following table presents this classification:

1. Providing motivation
   a. punishing
   b. scolding
   c. threatening
   d. warning
   e. inciting
2. Providing guidance
   a. leading
   b. instructing
   c. demonstrating
3. Providing reward
   a. giving
   b. helping
   c. praising

A Kwoma teacher must often provide motivation in order to make his pupils learn the habits which he wishes to teach them. He employs five techniques for doing so: punishing, scolding, threatening, warning, and inciting.

Punishment is not infrequently employed by a Kwoma teacher when other methods fail to correct the behavior of a pupil or when his behavior is particularly annoying to the teacher. A teacher punishes a child after he has made a wrong, or a not right response. The mode of punishment is usually either a blow on the back with the fist or a blow on the legs with a stick. The following cases will serve to illustrate its use.

Wof left early one morning with his second wife, Chinuwa, to work in his garden. Since his first wife, Kaya, had previ-

carefully followed up, and observations with which to test the predictions arising from the analysis were frequently not made. The rather complete record of daily events which was kept did, however, provide data to check some of them.

ously sprained her ankle and was incapacitated, he told his adopted daughter, Buka, to replenish the supply of firewood, which was very low. When he returned late that afternoon, he discovered that Buka had not obeyed his command and that there was not even enough wood to cook the afternoon meal. He, therefore, called to Buka and, telling her that she was lazy and disobedient for not getting the wood, struck her several times on the back. Buka cowered and ran away crying. Wof continued for some time to scold her in a loud and angry voice. Since I observed her a few days thereafter going by my house with her net bag filled with firewood, the punishment was presumably effective.

In order not to make the error of taking the effect of punishment on the habit structure of a pupil for granted, it is expedient to analyze the above case in detail in accordance with the paradigm of learning. It can be seen from such an analysis that the drive was that of pain from a blow on the back; the responses were running away, and crying; the cues were the sight of Wof, his words of criticism for not having obeyed his command to get firewood, and the memory of his command; the reward was escape from the pain of the blow. From this analysis it is evident that the habit which was reinforced was that of running away and crying when the cues described above were present. Wof, presumably, did not wish to teach her this habit but rather that of getting the firewood when he told her to. Although the punishment evidently did have this effect, it has not yet been shown how this came about. It is necessary to introduce the principle of anticipation to explain it.

By the principle of anticipation[18] any response which is attached by reward to the last of a temporal series of cues tends to occur earlier in the series. Thus when Wof again commands Buka to get firewood she will have a tendency to run away, to cry, and to make various visceral responses induced by pain. In other words she will have anxiety.[19] If she

[18] C. L. Hull, "Goal Attraction and Directing Ideas Conceived as Habit Phenomena," *Psychol. Rev.*, XXXVIII (1931), 487–506.

[19] Freud defines anxiety as the anticipation of pain. See S. Freud, *The*

were to run away or cry under these circumstances, she would be doing something other than getting firewood. In other words she would be making not right responses as implied by Wof's statement of the reason for the punishment at the time of its occurrence. To run away and cry would therefore tend to raise her anxiety rather than to reduce it. Similarly, if she played, went to sleep, ate, or made any response other than getting firewood, her anxiety would not be reduced, for all such acts have been implicitly defined by her father as "not getting firewood responses." The only way in which she can reduce her anxiety is to get the firewood. When she does this and only when she does this, the real effect of punishment as a teaching technique becomes clear. The drive is anxiety; the response is getting firewood; the cue is her father's command; and the reward is the reduction of anxiety. It is thus that Wof's punishment was not in vain and did accomplish the effect that he desired.

The following case also illustrates the use of punishment by a Kwoma teacher. One afternoon, when several Rumbima children and adolescents were playing in front of my house, the ball which they were kicking bounded into the bushes. Gwiyap, an adolescent, commanded Ham, a child, to fetch it, and when he refused kicked him in the buttocks. Ham ran away crying. Several days later the situation was repeated, and this time Ham ran away as soon as Gwiyap issued the command. Weeks later I observed Ham obediently fetch the ball, at first only after he was ordered to and later on his own initiative.

In the above case the drive was the pain from Gwiyap's kick; the response was running away and crying; the cues were the ball in the bushes, the sight of Gwiyap, and the sound of his commands; the reward was escape from the pain

Problem of Anxiety (New York, 1936). O. H. Mowrer has developed this thesis and urged that anxiety is a learned response based upon an anticipatory response to pain. See O. H. Mowrer, "A Stimulus Response Analysis of Anxiety," *Psychol. Rev.*, XLVI (1939), 553–565. Miller has shown that the acquired drive value of anxiety is based upon the response-produced stimuli of an antedating pain reaction. See N. E. Miller and John Dollard, *Social Learning and Imitation* (New Haven, 1941), chap. iv.

of being kicked. From the principle of reinforcement it could be predicted that Ham would learn to run away when these cues were again present. Observation bore this out. It could further be predicted that he was also reinforced on this occasion, the reward being escape from anxiety. However, just as Wof presumably did not wish to teach Buka to run away, so Gwiyap wanted to teach Ham to fetch the ball for him rather than to escape. That he was successful in doing so remains to be explained. It has been shown in a previous chapter that Kwoma children spend most of their time playing with other children, an activity which is apparently rewarding to them and hence one which comes to have the value of an acquired reward. Exclusion from playing with one's fellows should thus have an acquired drive value. There is no evidence that Ham was exceptional in these respects. Therefore each time that he ran away, although by so doing he achieved the reward of the reduction of pain or anxiety, he was thrown into another situation of discomfort. The acquired drive to play with his fellows was aroused. This placed him in a conflict situation:[20] to play aroused the fear of being kicked; not to play aroused the discomfort arising from being excluded from the game. Ham finally solved this dilemma by obeying Gwiyap's command. On this occasion, if the above analysis is correct, the drives were the fear of being kicked and the wish to play with his fellows; the response was fetching the ball; the cues were the ball in the bushes and Gwiyap's command; and the rewards were escape from being kicked and joining in the ball game. Thus Gwiyap's kick finally did have the desired effect, but only after time had elapsed and after a rather complicated series of psychological events had occurred to Ham.

This analysis suggests that another factor may have been operating in the case of Wof and Buka. She might have learned not only to run away from Wof, but to stay away from him. Unless some relative were willing to care for her,

[20] For a discussion of the factors governing conflict see N. E. Miller and J. S. Brown, "Conflict, an Analysis of Approach and Avoidance" (in preparation).

however, she would be in the same dilemma as the one in which Ham was placed, the negative side being much more serious, since it would be impossible for a girl of Buka's age to live alone in the Kwoma environment. Thus it is apparent that the primary effect of physical punishment is to make a pupil run away,[21] but that the strong acquired reward value which teachers have for the pupil, as a result of his dependence on them, and the fear of being alone, bind him to the teacher until he learns the habit which the teacher has wished to instill in him.

In the cases analyzed above the teacher was bigger than the pupil. When teacher and pupil are of the same size or when the pupil is bigger than the teacher, the response to punishment is often counterattack rather than running away.[22] The case of Fit and Mey illustrates this. Fit struck Mey for teasing him, and Mey grabbed a burning brand from the fire and began belaboring Fit with it. In this case Mey's drives were pain from Fit's blow, anger at Fit,[23] and the fear of being hit again; the response was attacking him with a firebrand; the cues were the sight of someone his own size and the feeling of the blow; and the rewards were reduction of the pain from Fit's blow, the reduction of the fear of being hit again, and the reduction of anger. Thus Mey was

[21] In the middle and upper classes of American society, pupils are not usually permitted to run away from punishment. They are either held by the parent or punished more severely if they attempt to escape. The usual response which is reinforced is the promise "I won't do it again." Furthermore, doing wrong in secret is more severely punished in the United States than at Kwoma. The American technique should be more effective in teaching the correct response, but, at the same time, it should produce more anxiety in the pupil than does the Kwoma technique. A correlation of the extent to which parents in various societies permit children to escape punishment and do wrong in secret, and the degree to which the society produces neurotic adults might be fruitful.

[22] When such a situation arises between adults, it is normally the reputation of the teacher and the pupil as fighters and the size of the group which supports each of them, rather than their physical size, which determines whether the pupil counterattacks or runs away.

[23] The conditions at Kwoma are such that anger as a response to pain is frequently reinforced, particularly with respect to younger siblings. See chap. iv, pp. 57–62.

rewarded for aggression, instead of learning to stop teasing as his would-be teacher wished.

A Kwoma teacher scolds his pupils even more frequently than he punishes them, and uses this technique under similar circumstances. In fact, in all the cases that I observed of a teacher inflicting physical pain on pupils, he also scolded them. Scolding, like physical punishment, is employed by the teacher after the pupil has made a wrong or a not right response, and it can be presumed to operate psychologically in the same manner, except that the drive employed is acquired rather than basic.

Scolding acquires its motivational power in the following way. One of the most common phrases used by a Kwoma teacher in scolding a pupil is *kafwa sek otato*, "you have behaved badly." *Kafwa sek* is a modifier which is applied to rotten meat, to feces, to food "poisoned" by sorcery, as well as to bad behavior. Thus these words are associated with things which are disgusting or dangerous—things which all children have learned to avoid because of the pain which is inherent in such objects, because they have been punished for touching or eating them, or both. Furthermore, since a pupil is always scolded while he is being punished, these words come to symbolize a beating as well, and thus gain the power to evoke feelings of fear.

A second phrase frequently used by Kwoma teachers in scolding a pupil is *karaganda yikafa*, "little child" or "infant." This phrase implies that the pupil is behaving like an infant. It is the antonym of *harafa ma malaka*, "big older brother man," which is used for praise. Like *kafwa sek*, this phrase is used during physical punishment frequently enough so that it gains a strong fear potential. In addition, it is used in many contexts in which children are barred from doing what they would like to do. Thus the phrase comes to mean the denial of privileges. The fact that Kwoma children will mutilate their penises and willingly undergo scarification in order not to be classified as *karaganda yikafa* indicates the motivational power of this concept.

The following case illustrates the manner in which scolding is used by Kwoma teachers. One morning Kum defecated in the path near his house. His co-mother, Kaya, found out what he had done and began to scold him for it: "You little baby (*karaganda yikafa*), you know better than to defecate in the path. I should beat you for it. Come and clean it up." Kum, instead of heeding her, ran away and hid in the bushes. After she had repeatedly called for him to return, she sent Gwiyap and Mey to search for him, but they could not find him. He waited until the hue and cry had subsided and then returned to the house. By this time the mess had been cleaned up and Kaya was so worried that he might be lost that she said no more about his misdemeanor (in my presence, at least). For the remainder of my stay at Kwoma, Kum did not defecate again in the path, but properly went to the latrine.

It can be seen from the above case that scolding apparently operates in a manner very similar to that of punishment. The motivation was the acquired drive of fear evoked by scolding; the response was running away; the cue was the memory of having defecated in the path, Kaya's presence, and her words; the reward was a reduction in fear. As with the cases of physical punishment, the primary habit learned was running away, and the right habit of defecating in the latrine was only subsequently reinforced by the reduction in the fear of being scolded.

The above case is not typical, in that Kum's response was to run away from scolding. Since running away takes some effort and since it is more difficult to get out of earshot than out of reach, this response is not as strongly reinforced as a reaction to scolding as it is to physical punishment, and Kwoma children normally learn by trial and error the more adaptive habit of waiting until the teacher stops scolding them. They also learn not to talk back, for this tends to lengthen the duration of the scolding and sometimes even leads to a beating. The following case will illustrate this type of response to scolding.

One afternoon when Kaya was sitting by her fire making

Process of Socialization

sago briquettes, she asked Mey to pass her the two sticks which Kwoma housewives use to stir and ladle the thick gruel. Mey brought her two old sticks which she had long since discarded rather than the desired ones. She made Mey take the wrong ones back and get the right ones and began scolding him for his inattention and stupidity. Mey stood looking sullen and sheepish, and heard out her tirade. In this case the drive was anxiety evoked by the scolding; the response was looking sullen and sheepish and listening; the cues included being told to get stirring sticks and the memory of having brought his mother the wrong ones; the reward was reduction of fear (after she stopped scolding him). Thus listening and not talking back, rather than running away, was the response reinforced in this case.[24] The right response, of paying attention when spoken to, would be learned by Mey when on the next occasion he was asked to do something by his mother, did it correctly, and was not scolded for it.

Threatening is the third technique of motivating pupils employed by Kwoma teachers. A threat, like scolding, activates the acquired drive of fear in the pupil, but it differs from scolding in that it precedes the wrong or not right response. A threat is an "if . . . then" statement—"if you do such and such, then I will scold or beat you." Threats are used by Kwoma teachers in situations where they foresee that the pupil is likely to make a wrong response, either because the pupil is beginning to make such a response or because the teacher's knowledge of the pupil's habits suggests that he may do so. Kwoma teachers employ the technique of threatening as widely as scolding although perhaps not as frequently, since it is usually more difficult to predict a wrong response than it is to observe one.

Threats, like scolding, depend for their motivational power upon the acquired drive of fear. The phrase most commonly employed by the Kwoma teacher when threatening a pupil is *anafa fiju*, "I will beat you." *Fiju* is the term employed for all types of physical violence and injury. It has

---
[24] Unfortunately I observed no case of a child being specifically scolded or punished for talking back, but informants stated that this did occur.

the meaning of fighting, beating, spearing, and killing. *Fiju* was the word used to denote the fight between Daw and Kwal in which the latter received a bad scalp wound; to denote Mey's action when he struck Fit on the back with a burning firebrand; by hunters when they successfully spear and kill a pig; and to killing someone in a head-hunting raid and to in-group murder. From these contexts, many of which have been directly experienced and all of which are known to Kwoma pupils, it is evident that the threat *anafa fiju* should arouse anxiety. Furthermore, teachers usually carry out their threat by beating the pupil if he does not heed. From these two sources, therefore, a threat gains the power to evoke fear in the pupil.

The following case will serve to illustrate threatening as a technique of teaching. Kum, while playing under the porch at Mar's house one afternoon, picked up a broom and started carrying it outside. Kwiya and Awa, his older *sisters*, both noticed him and told him to put it down. Kum did not heed at first, but when Kwiya threatened to beat him unless he did so at once, he quickly dropped the broom. In this case the drive was the fear of being beaten; the response was dropping the broom, the cues were the instructions to drop the broom given by Kwiya and Awa, the sight of objects and people under the porch, the feeling of the broom in his hand, etc.; the reward was the reduction of the fear of being beaten. It can be seen that the effect of a threat on learning is somewhat different from the effect of punishment and scolding. In the first place, the right response is made immediately rather than on a subsequent occasion, and, in the second, the motivation is stronger, since a fear-evoking person is present when the pupil makes the right response and the reinforcement is consequently greater.[25]

Social control is largely effected by means of threats. In Kwoma the threat of breaking relationship is one of the more important techniques by which an adult can control the be-

[25] The amount of reinforcement is probably a positive function of the strength of the drive. See C. L. Hull, "Outline of a Systematic Theory of Learning," sec. v, *Educational Psychology Yearbook* (in press).

Process of Socialization

havior of a relative. The case of War and Gwiyap will serve to illustrate how this technique operates. Gwiyap had for some time been taking sago flour from the plot of his *maternal uncle*, Payap. War, Gwiyap's *paternal uncle*, discovered this and told him to stop. He explained that he was more closely related to Payap than was Gwiyap. Gwiyap chose to argue this point and tried to maintain his claim, whereupon War threatened to break relations with him. In response to this threat Gwiyap turned over the privilege to War and paid him for the sago he had already taken.

In the above case the drive was fear of a broken relationship with War;[26] the response was giving up the privilege, paying War, and getting sago from another plot; the cues were War's words and the knowledge of having taken sago from Payap's plot; the reward was reduction of the fear of a broken relationship. Thus Gwiyap learned to behave correctly with respect to his kinship privileges and to heed the threats of his relatives. The fear of sorcery and of other retaliatory measures tends similarly to maintain correct social behavior. Theft, trespass, and breaking sex mores or rules inhibiting aggression, result in threats from those who suffer from these deviations from custom, whereas right behavior is continually reinforced by the reduction of fear implied by these threats.[27]

The fourth technique which teachers may use to motivate their pupils is to warn them. A warning is similar to a threat except that the source of the specified pain is some person or some event in the natural environment other than the teacher. A warning normally consists of two elements: a specification of the danger and its source, and instructions for escape from or avoidance of the danger. If the danger is imminent, the teacher normally introduces a warning by a sharp ejaculation—either *e ye!* (no!) or *sa!*, an expletive to call attention.

[26] As previously noted, a broken relationship involves removing the taboo which is implied by a safe kin relationship, and the loss of coöperation and support.

[27] A much more elaborate analysis of the relationship between threats and social control might be profitably made, but it is not within the scope of this chapter to do so.

Warnings are extensively used by Kwoma teachers. A Kwoma pupil in the course of his life is normally warned about all the dangers which inhere in the natural and social environment.

The following case exemplifies how a child is taught to avoid danger by means of the technique of warning. I had removed the shot from some twelve-gauge cartridges which had spoiled and lit the powder in them for the amusement of the natives. The powder exploded with a harmless puff. Kwos, seeing me do this, decided to try it himself. Mes, his older brother, saw him and warned him not to. He said that cartridges were dangerous and could kill people. Not heeding the warning, Kwos tried to light one. The cartridge did not explode at first so Kwos looked into it to see what the matter was. At that moment the powder exploded directly into his face, burning it so badly as to close one of his eyes. In this case the drive was pain from the explosion and burn; the response was withdrawal from the cartridge, and a visceral pain response; the cues were the cartridge and the words of warning which Mes issued; the reward was reduction in the pain of the explosion.[28]

It should be noted that stopping playing with the cartridge accorded with the instructions in Mes' warning. The effect of this experience on Kwos should have been to reinforce both heeding a warning and not playing with cartridges. There is evidence that exactly this did occur. Kwos did not play with cartridges again, and he heeded a warning not to walk around alone. Although he could barely see out of one eye, he came from his house to mine to get salve. His father came later and warned him not to return home alone lest he get lost. Kwos, heeding this warning, waited until his sister came and led him home.

Kwos' teachers were not satisfied with the lesson he learned from the explosion but scolded him in addition. Waramus, his father, told me in the presence of Kwos, "He will go

---

[28] The pain of the burn persisted much longer and reinforced whatever successful attempts were made to ease it, asking me for salve and applying it to his face being one of them.

blind; he will never be able to see again; but it serves him right for not heeding his brother's warning." Kis, one of his *paternal uncles*, said to him, "You little feces-eater, that's what you get for not heeding your brother." The habit of heeding a warning thereby gained additional reinforcement as a result of the application of the technique of scolding.

The following case is one in which the warning concerned pain from another person rather than from an event in the natural environment, and in which the warning had been issued some time before the pain was experienced. Ham had been warned by his parents not to walk around in other people's houses. He had been told that, when visiting, he should sit down and remain seated, and that, if he did not do so, the owner of the house would be very cross with him. One day Ham started wandering about the porch of Wof's house. Wof shouted at him to sit down and then scolded him severely.[29] He accused the boy of trying to steal sorcery material and implied that only thieves walk around in other people's houses.

In this case the drive was fear aroused by Wof's scolding; the response was sitting down; the cues were the memory of the warning and the sight of another person's house; and the reward was the reduction of fear. Since the response reinforced in the parental warning corresponded with the instructions issued, that is, sitting down and not walking around, it would be expected that Ham's tendency to heed a warning was increased by this experience. Unfortunately, since I have no record of a warning issued to Ham after this experience, this prediction cannot be tested. About an hour after the experience, however, Ham obeyed with alacrity a command from his mother to pass sago fritters to his father. His alacrity may have been in part due to his recent experience, since both a warning and a command have the common element of instructions.

The only technique of motivating pupils used by Kwoma

[29] Wof was, of course, also a teacher in this case, and he used the technique of scolding. For the present purposes, Ham's parents will be taken as the teachers, using warning as a technique.

teachers which does not depend upon pain or fear is that of inciting. This consists of presenting to the pupil the verbal symbols which have been associated with reward along with instructions as to how to achieve such reward. The following case will serve as an illustration. At a coöperative work feast given by Nambomai, my Yambon houseboy, one of the foods prepared was stewed apricots. Gwiyap took it upon himself to teach some of the adults present to eat this food, which was hitherto unknown to them. To do this he said: "It is good. It tastes like ripe bananas." Afolawanj, an old man who was somewhat of a clown, was thus tempted to try some, but he had no sooner taken a mouthful than he spit it out, and refused to eat any more.

In the above case the drive was the appetite evoked by Gwiyap's statement that the stewed fruit tasted like ripe bananas; the response was eating; the cues were Gwiyap's instructions to eat and the sight, smell, and taste of the fruit; the reward was absent. Since there was no reward in this sequence it could be predicted that learning would not take place. The fact that Afolawanj did not again try the fruit is evidence that this was indeed the case. It could also be predicted that Afolawanj would have a decreased tendency to follow Gwiyap's instructions,[30] but I do not know whether or not this was true.

War's attempt to incite Mes and Mar provides a more dramatic instance of the use of this technique. When the Hongwam were planning a head-hunting raid on the Sowal, War, who was the prime mover in the affair, spent a whole evening at the house tamberan inciting Mar and Mes to go on the raid. He described to them all the advantages that they would gain from taking a head—that all the girls would want to marry them, that they could become members of *Nokwi*, that they would gain high prestige so that their words would be listened to at the court meetings, that their

---

[30] This follows from the principle of extinction. When a response is not followed by a reward, the connection between this response and the preceding cues is reduced in strength. See E. R. Hilgard and D. G. Marquis, *Conditioning and Learning* (New York, 1940), chap. v; N. E. Miller and John Dollard, *Social Learning and Imitation* (New Haven, 1941), chap. iii.

relatives would be eager to help them in coöperative tasks, etc. He suggested to Mes that he take my shotgun along (he was acting as my shoot boy at the time) because with it he could be certain to kill someone and take his head. Mes asked me for the gun and was very disappointed when I refused. Mar, on the other hand, had seen several river natives hanged for participating in a head-hunting raid and had been so moved by the sight that he was afraid to go. He reacted to War's incitement by weeping and telling me that he guessed he could never be a man. Since traveling conditions prevented the raid from taking place, the correct response could not be made. A few days later a recruiter came to the tribe, and both Mar and Mes "signed on" for a three-year contract to work on a plantation.

Although the reaction of Mes and Mar indicates that War's incitement successfully induced motivation by evoking a complex of acquired drives and appetites based upon sex, hunger, fatigue, and prestige, his teaching was blocked because the correct response could not be made. Since both Mar and Mes said that they were going to work for the whites in order to gain prestige, so as to win an attractive wife, and in order to earn money to buy many wives, "signing on" may have been, in part at least, a substitute for going on the raid.[31]

Kwoma teachers do not always have to motivate their pupils in order to inculcate right responses, for this is frequently done for them either by others or by the natural environment. In such cases their task is to guide the pupil so that he makes the right response and to provide the proper cues.[32] Furthermore, even when the teacher himself motivates the pupil, the problem of guiding him still remains, and Kwoma teachers seldom simply motivate a pupil and

[31] Although it happens that the aim of the teacher was accomplished in neither of the above cases, this does not imply that the technique of inciting is not an effective means of teaching.

[32] Since responses and cues are so closely attached to one another in a habit, it has been deemed expedient to treat these two aspects of learning under a single heading, even though teachers may at times stress the cues and at times the responses.

permit him to discover the reward by free trial and error. There are three techniques of guidance: leading, instructing, and demonstrating.

The most primitive technique by which a teacher can make his pupil perform the correct response is by leading. To do this the teacher physically limits the random responses of the pupil so that he makes the right response more quickly, or so that he is prevented from making wrong responses. Such guidance is used by the Kwoma primarily when the pupil has not yet learned to talk and therefore cannot follow instructions. The following case illustrates the use of leading. Njan, while lying in his mother's lap one afternoon, began to cry and struggle. His mother lifted him up to her breast, and, holding his head with one hand, directed her nipple into his mouth with the other. Njan began to nurse. Had his mother not directed his head, he would probably eventually have found her nipple as the result of random movements and satisfied his hunger. The mother, by holding his head, prevented him from making errors and thus forced him to make the right response more quickly. Informants stated that mothers taught their children to defecate in the latrine by leading them there and holding them in the proper position. These are the only situations observed in which Kwoma teachers employ the technique of leading, though there may well be others.

Verbal guidance or instruction is probably the most widely used of all teaching techniques. As indicated in the preceding analysis of punishment, scolding, threats, warnings, and inciting, instructions normally form a part of these techniques. In other words, teachers usually motivate and guide at the same time. On rare occasions, however, when the pupil is already motivated by some other agency, a teacher need simply help the pupil to make the right response, or not to make the wrong response, by instructing him.

The following case illustrates the use of instructions as a teaching technique. Fit was trying to light the fire in my cook house one afternoon. A strong wind was blowing, and the matches kept going out. Mar, who was watching him,

Process of Socialization

told him to try lighting the fire on the leeward side. Fit followed the suggestion and was successful. Fit was already motivated to light the fire and was striving to do so. If left to himself he would probably eventually have succeeded, perhaps by hitting upon the response which Mar suggested, perhaps by discovering some other solution to the problem. Mar entered the situation as teacher by giving instructions which, when Fit followed them, achieved the desired goal.

Although the above analysis indicates the function of instruction as a teaching technique and the way in which it operates in a gross way, it does not explain why a pupil follows instructions. In other words, how did Fit know how to react to Mar's words, and why did he react at all? The answer to the first question depends upon verbal symbols and how a pupil learns their meanings. Although this is a most important part of the process of socialization, it lies beyond the scope of this inquiry. An answer to the second question—why does the pupil react to instructions at all?—can, however, be suggested. As has been observed above, instructions normally form a part of each of the teaching techniques which stress motivation. Therefore, since most teaching techniques result eventually in the learning of a rewarding habit, following instructions becomes a strongly reinforced habit. Words of instruction thereby come to have an acquired drive value.

Just as instructing depends upon the pupil's knowledge of language, so demonstrating, the third technique of guiding, depends upon the ability of the pupil to imitate. Miller and Dollard[33] have shown that conditions in our society are such that a child is more frequently rewarded and less frequently suffers pain if he behaves like certain people with whom he comes in contact, particularly his parents and older siblings, than if he makes responses which differ from theirs, and that therefore, by the principle of reinforcement, children learn to imitate. These investigators have also assumed that the conditions which lead children in our society to learn

[33] See N. E. Miller and John Dollard, *Social Learning and Imitation* (New Haven, 1941).

to imitate are present in all societies, and in a chapter on diffusion have presented evidence which supports this assumption. The Kwoma are no exception to this rule. Most of the right and not wrong responses in Kwoma culture apply to all persons, and with respect to these responses a child will be rewarded for imitating anyone. Furthermore, although those responses which are right for only certain categories of persons—particularly those which depend upon the sex, age, or prestige position of the pupil—are both punished and not rewarded if the pupil imitates a person in another category than himself, he is rewarded if he imitates a person in his own category. Thus in the majority of cases a Kwoma is rewarded, and in only a minority of cases is he punished or not rewarded, for imitating. Since Miller and Dollard have presented imitation as a process of socialization in detail, it will not be further discussed here. It stands with teaching as one of the most important mechanisms by which culture is transmitted.

A Kwoma teacher takes advantage of the fact that his pupils have all learned to imitate, when he employs demonstrating as a technique of guidance. In using this technique the teacher gets the attention of the pupil, performs the right response, and then the pupil imitates him. Afok and Fokotay employed this technique when they were teaching Mes and Mar to play the sacred flutes. The two teachers would first play a piece while the pupils watched and listened. Then the two pupils would take the flutes and attempt to imitate them. The teachers would repeat their performance, and the pupils would try again.[34] This example reveals that this technique is similar to instruction, the difference being that the cues are the correct responses made by the teacher rather than his verbal representation of them.

Commanding, as a teaching technique, may be classed either as primarily motivating or as primarily guiding. A command consists of an implicit threat and explicit instruc-

[34] Afok and Fokotay did not depend entirely upon imitation but issued many instructions, scolded the pupils after errors and praised them after a correct performance.

tions. Since both threats and instructions have been analyzed, it is not necessary to discuss commanding in detail, but it should be stated that it is an extremely important method of teaching.

Providing rewards, the third general category of teaching techniques, is also employed by the Kwoma. It consists of providing a reward after a pupil has made a right response. A teacher may use this technique after he has motivated and guided the pupil, or he may use it when either the motivation or the guidance or both have been supplied by some other agency. The general category of rewarding may be subdivided into helping, giving, and praising.

Kwoma teachers take advantage of the fact that a pupil can satisfy but few of his drives, either basic or acquired, without the aid of another person or persons.[35] Being helped is thus in many cases the *sine qua non* for achieving a reward. Teachers may, therefore, employ helping as a means of rewarding the right response of a pupil. They use this technique primarily to teach the pupil coöperative habits. In other words, teachers most frequently help a pupil after the pupil has helped them. The technique of helping is thus one of the important methods of transmitting that part of the culture which makes for in-group solidarity and reciprocity.[36]

Giving is closely allied to helping as a technique of reward, being used in the same coöperative context. If a teacher gives a pupil something, it is significant as a reward because the teacher has done the work of producing or otherwise obtaining the gift, and thus relieves the pupil of the necessity of doing the same himself. Gifts in Kwoma are of food, tools, or shell money. Barter and exchange are a form of reciprocal

[35] Malinowski has shown that all cultural habits are an integral part of institutions which imply the coöperative efforts of an organized group of persons for the satisfaction of a need. See B. Malinowski, "The Group and the Individual in Functional Analysis," *The American Journal of Sociology*, XLIV (1939), no. 6, pp. 952–54.

[36] Hull has suggested a psychological basis for this in the principle of reciprocal reinforcement. C. L. Hull, "Outline of a Systematic Theory of Learning," sec. ix, *Educational Psychology Yearbook* (in press).

gift giving in which both parties in the transaction play simultaneously the rôles of teacher and pupil.

The work bee is a good example of how both helping and giving reinforce coöperative habits. Yat gave a bee to get a log, from which he intended to make a slit gong, dragged from his garden to the house tamberan. He and his wife gathered a surplus of sago, traded some of it for fish, and then announced that they wanted help. Wof, War, Marok, Mar, Gwiyap, Mes, and Mey, as well as several of Yat's affinal relatives, answered the call, and this group spent the morning dragging the log to the house tamberan clearing. When the task was completed, they went to Yat's house and ate the food which his wife had prepared.[37]

If Yat's helpers be thought of as the pupils, he taught them to help him by employing the technique of giving. Their drives were hunger and various appetites aroused by the anticipation of a feast; their response was coöperation in the log pulling; the cue was Yat's announcement; and their reward was the feast given by Yat. Yat thus taught people to help him by giving them a feast.

If Yat be thought of as a pupil and the others as the teachers, helping rather than giving is the technique employed. The drive was the wish to get the log to the house tamberan (based upon the prestige which Yat would gain from having contributed a slit gong to the hamlet); the response was gathering food for a feast, announcing a work bee, and coöperating in the log pulling; the cues were those which indicated that the log was properly seasoned, and that there would be enough men in the hamlet who did not have

[37] It might be objected that this case does not represent socialization since it concerns adults who have presumably already learned coöperative work habits. Such an objection can be answered in the following ways. Although the increments in reinforcement get smaller and smaller with each successive reward, there is always a strengthening of the habit with each reward. Thus a habit theoretically can never be completely learned, and the process of socialization continues throughout the life of any individual. Secondly, if a habit does not lead to reward, it becomes extinguished. Thus reward is necessary to maintain habits as well as to teach them, and the maintenance of habits is as crucial to the process of socialization as is the initial learning of them.

pressing work of their own to do; the reward was getting the log to the house tamberan plot. Yat's helpers thus taught him to give a feast by helping him.

Not giving and not helping are also techniques which are frequently used to arouse motivation. Kwoma teachers may punish a pupil by refusing to help him or give to him, after he has made a wrong response, or they may threaten him by promising not to help him or not to give to him if he should make a wrong response. The threat of breaking relationship is effective, not only because it implies aggression, but also because it implies withdrawal of support. Thus War's threat that he would break relationship with Gwiyap if he did not stop taking sago from Payap's plot, implied withdrawal of help and was effective in changing Gwiyap's behavior for this reason as well as because it implicitly threatened the kinds of aggression which kinship restrictions inhibit.

Praising is the third technique of rewarding used by Kwoma teachers. It is an acquired reward on the verbal level. As with other rewards, it may be employed either in conjunction with motivation and guidance or alone. A Kwoma teacher most frequently employs this technique when a pupil has performed an unexpectedly "good" response rather than merely a right one. Kwoma pupils are thus reinforced for excelling, for doing better than others, and this may explain in part why Kwoma individuals strive for superiority and prestige.

One of the phrases frequently employed in praising is *handombas*, "good." This word gains its power to reinforce habits by being frequently used in rewarding contexts. A Kwoma will pat his stomach after a good meal and say "*handombas*," or he will say it when he is greeting a friend, or he will use it to refer to someone or something that he likes. He also uses it to describe tasty food, good workmanship, or someone whom he regards highly. As a result, *handombas* comes to have a relaxing or acquired reward value,[38] and thus has the effect of reinforcing preceding habits when-

[38] See N. E. Miller and John Dollard, *Social Learning and Imitation* (New Haven, 1941), chap. iv.

ever a teacher applies it to a pupil. Since, moreover, a Kwoma teacher seldom punishes, scolds, or threatens a pupil at the same time that he praises him, *handombas* becomes a cue, reducing whatever anxiety may be present, and thus acquires further rewarding value.

A second phrase, *harafa ma malaka*, is applied to men of high prestige who have many privileges that the ordinary person does not enjoy. It comes to mean, therefore, the right to go to the *Nokwi* ceremonies, to have many wives, to have many helpers at work bees, to be deferred to at court meetings, and to be so formidable that no one dare threaten or attack you. When a teacher applies this phrase to a pupil, it symbolizes an advance toward the attainment of these goals and is therefore rewarding. Furthermore, if a pupil is called *harafa ma malaka*, he is never called *karaganda yikafa*, "little child," at the same time, as these are antithetical concepts. Since the latter phrase is used to scold pupils, the former symbolizes non-scolding and thus gains further reward value.

Praising may be exemplified by the following case. Yat speared two pigs in one afternoon, a remarkable feat since a man will often hunt for weeks without success. When he returned to the hamlet, he joined a group of men who were sitting in the house tamberan and told them of his accomplishment. The men praised him for his prowess, referring to his act as *handombas* and to him as a *harafa ma malaka*. Thus Yat was rewarded by these words of praise for whatever hunting technique led to his success.

In conclusion, the following summary of the results of the preceding analyses may be made. The assumption that learning principles apply to the process of culture transmission at Kwoma has led to an organization of the data observed, so that some of the factors which permit, and some of the forces which compel, a Kwoma individual to learn his culture have been isolated and defined. Furthermore, the application of learning theory has brought certain essential details of the process of socialization into sharper relief than might otherwise have been the case. It is evident, also, from the above analysis, that Kwoma teachers have a practical knowledge of the way in which people learn, and use certain teaching techniques which are adapted on the one hand to the principles of learning and on the other to the culture and the necessity of transmitting it. Some of the techniques of teaching which the Kwoma employ stress motivation, others guidance, and still others reward, but all of them are in some way adjusted to the fact that learning only takes place when a person is motivated by a drive to make a response in the presence of cues and gains a reward for so doing. It was further shown that punishing, scolding, threatening, warning, and inciting were used by Kwoma teachers to motivate their pupils; leading, instructing, and demonstrating to guide them; and giving, helping, and praising to reward them.

In accordance with the hypothesis of the basic psychological unity of mankind, learning principles should apply to the process of culture transmission in all societies. Furthermore, since every society is faced with the problem of training the members of the oncoming generation, certain teaching techniques should be present in all cultures, and, certain conditions of social life being present in all societies, some of the techniques observed at Kwoma should be found in other cultures as well. Divergent historical processes and differing environmental conditions, however, may have produced techniques which are unique to a particular culture or to a certain area, may account for the absence of certain techniques in one culture which are found in others, and may have resulted in variations in the use of, and the emphasis placed upon, these techniques from culture to culture. When the data with which to test the above hypotheses have been gathered, it will be possible to construct a general theory of the process of socialization.

CHAPTER VIII

THE INCULCATION OF SUPERNATURAL BELIEFS

THE manner in which supernatural beliefs and practices are transmitted to the oncoming generation is one of the most puzzling problems which a student of socialization has to solve. When a teacher wishes to transmit customs which accord with natural and social laws, he has the support of the environment, which supplies both motivation and reward to validate his teaching efforts. When, however, the teacher's task is to transmit habits which do not accord with these laws, his task should be more difficult. It is the purpose of this chapter to describe and analyze the way in which supernatural beliefs are transmitted at Kwoma and to suggest some hypotheses concerning their transmission in other societies.

A number of factors are responsible for the inculcation of supernatural beliefs. Perhaps the most basic of these is the technique of warning described in the previous chapter. Generalization from real dangers, imitation, the operation of chance, and finally social punishments also play an important part in the process. These factors will be discussed and exemplified in the following pages.

An analysis of the cases in which supernatural beliefs and practices are transmitted at Kwoma indicates that teachers rely in large part upon the technique of warning to inculcate this aspect of the culture. This technique was defined, analyzed, and exemplified in the last chapter. It was shown that a warning consists of a specification of the danger and its source, and of instructions for escape from, or avoidance of, the danger. It was shown that Kwoma pupils learn to heed warnings because when they ignore them they experience pain both from the source specified in the warning and from the teacher who punishes them.

Supernatural Beliefs

The warnings which Kwoma teachers issue may be divided into two categories: realistic and unrealistic. A realistic warning is one which, if not heeded, will result in pain from the source specified, whereas an unrealistic warning is one which, if not heeded, will not result in pain from the source specified.

Realistic warnings are continually employed by Kwoma teachers concerning all the dangers which appear in the natural and social environments. To list all the warnings a person might receive in the course of his life would be to list much of the culture. It is expedient, however, to mention a few of these warnings in order to indicate how strongly the habit of heeding is built up in the Kwoma pupil. During the weaning period a child is warned not to go too far from home lest he get lost, not to eat certain poisonous foods lest he become sick or die, and not to take or destroy the property of others lest he be punished by the owners. During childhood he is warned not to be impolite to relatives lest they scold him, not to walk about in the houses of other people lest they punish him, not to go alone in the swamp lest he be killed by a wild pig or crocodile, and not to hurt a sibling seriously lest he thereby hurt himself. A boy is warned not to stare at the genitals of females lest they punish him, and not to have an erection in front of his *sister* lest she beat his penis with a stick. Girls are warned not to behave immodestly lest they be criticized. An adolescent boy is warned not to be lazy lest no woman choose him for a husband, not to be caught philandering lest he be attacked by the girl's relatives, not to rape a girl lest he be killed by her relatives, not to hunt pigs lest he be killed or injured, and not to trespass on the property of others lest he be forced to pay damages. An adolescent girl is warned not to be lazy lest no one marry her, and not to be unchaste lest her *brothers* refuse to help and protect her. Adults are also frequently warned by friends and relatives throughout their lives.

Whenever a Kwoma child does not heed one of the above-listed warnings, it is highly probable that he will experience the pain specified in the warning and that he will be scolded or beaten by his teachers. Thus a strong habit of heeding whatever warning a teacher may issue is built up in every Kwoma individual. As a result, Kwoma teachers may warn their pupils concerning dangers which do not exist and expect that their pupils will heed. This is in fact the case in the inculcation of supernatural beliefs. By means of warnings Kwoma teachers instill in their pupils an unrealistic fear of *marsalai*, ghosts, sorcery, and blood.[1]

Marsalai are supposed to be huge monsters in the form of snakes or crocodiles which cause rain and wind storms, earthquakes, and other cosmic phenomena. They are supposed to be present at the yam-cult ceremonies and to be responsible for a plentiful yield of this crop. A child is first warned about these monsters early in life. When a Kwoma mother weans her child she warns him not to suckle, lest he be injured by the *marsalai* which has now taken possession of her breast. She sometimes emphasizes this story by putting a bloodsucker on her breast. During childhood a person is warned not to go near or touch certain rocks and waterholes, lest the *marsalai* who dwell therein cause a storm or shoot a sago needle into his foot in anger at being disturbed. He is also warned at this period not to go near the house tamberan during a cult ceremony lest the *marsalai* who are present kill him. He is told that the sounds[2] which he hears are the voices of these monsters. When he is initiated at the beginning of adolescence, he is warned not to look up too suddenly at the cult figures which represent the *marsalai* lest the shock kill him.

Ghosts are believed to be the spirits of dead Kwoma who live on the outskirts of the tribal territory. Either as invisible shadows or in the form of a bird or an animal, they sometimes visit the hamlet of the living, particularly at night or when a death has occurred. It is believed that they sometimes attack a person, that they can cause accidents by frightening him, that they are eager to take souls to the land of the dead, and that they cause nightmares and fits of possession. Most warn-

[1] Kwoma have other supernatural beliefs, but these four provide the most important sources of unrealistic fear.
[2] Gongs, flutes, and bull-roarers.

ings about ghosts are issued during childhood. Boys and girls are warned not to go abroad at night lest they be attacked by ghosts, not to approach the places specified as the land of the dead lest an accident befall them, not to go near the platform on which the dead are exposed lest the ghosts which hover around harm them, and not to whistle at night lest they attract these dangerous supernatural beings. Adolescents are warned not to disobey the commands of a ghost as they are issued through the medium of a possessed person lest they come to harm.

The Kwoma believe that certain people have the power to injure or kill by means of sorcery. They do so either by inserting a magical "poison" into food to be eaten by the victim or by burning in a special clay pot certain materials, particularly food leavings, blood, and semen, which have been associated with the victim. A child is first warned about sorcery during the weaning period, when he is told not to eat food given him by anyone except a close relative, lest there be "poison" in it, and not to eat away from home lest he carelessly spill crumbs with which he can be sorcerized. These warnings are repeated during childhood, and others are added. A boy is warned not to spill the blood of the snakes and marsupials which he kills, lest it be found by a sorcerer and used against him. He is also warned to be careful not to spill his own blood when he cuts himself. Adolescent boys are warned not to have sexual intercourse with a girl who is likely to give his sperm to a sorcerer. Adolescent girls are warned to dispose of their menstrual blood carefully, so that it cannot be used as sorcery material.

The Kwoma believe that food is converted into blood, which remains in the system for a time and then deteriorates. Good (fresh) blood is responsible for the health of an adult and the normal growth of a child. Bad (deteriorated) blood causes sickness and pain and prevents normal growth. It follows from this theory that bad blood must be removed from the system in order to insure good health and normal growth, and that care must be taken not to eat food contaminated with bad blood and thus get it back into the system.

Kwoma children are warned that if they do not allow someone to bleed them when they have a headache, stomach-ache, or sprain, the pain will become worse and they may even become seriously ill. A boy is also warned that if he does not bleed his penis he will not grow up.[3] When the age-grade initiation approaches, a boy is warned that if he does not attend it and have his blood ceremonially let, he will not grow up. Since this operation is performed in a stream, he is warned that if he eats fish he will become sick, for the fish may have been contaminated by his blood. He is warned that if he eats an animal which he has killed with a spear or arrow he will sicken and perhaps die, since his blood enters the animal through his weapon and contaminates its flesh. This warning is reiterated to adults when they begin pig hunting. An adult who plants yams is warned not to eat them lest he become sick, for the seed and produce have become contaminated with his blood.

One other unrealistic warning should be mentioned here, because a case involving it will be discussed later. Adolescents are warned that if they eat sago flour washed by a woman it will make them sick. The normal procedure in processing sago flour is for the woman, either sister or wife, to crush the pith and for the man to rinse the flour from it.

The following case will serve to illustrate the psychological effect that the above unrealistic warnings usually have upon a Kwoma pupil. Kar, Mar, Gwiyap, and I were walking through the swamp one day, and the path passed by a waterhole. Kar warned the rest of us not to pass too near it for it was the dwelling place of a *marsalai*. Mar and Gwiyap heeded and passed by the waterhole at a distance. I, however, did not heed, approached the hole, and poked my walking stick into it. The three Kwoma shouted at me for doing this, warning me to stop and scolding me for my temerity. The fact that Mar and Gwiyap passed by the waterhole at a distance can be analyzed thus: the drive was fear evoked by Kar's warning due to the pain which both Mar and Gwiyap

---

[3] This warning is not made directly but by implication, and the practice is performed in secret. See chap. iv, p. 64.

had previously experienced for not heeding realistic warnings; the response was avoiding the waterhole; the cues were the sight of the waterhole and Kar's instructions; and the reward was the reduction of fear. Since I had not been brought up in Kwoma society, Kar's warning did not evoke fear and I did not make the right response.

Although the technique of warning provides the basis for the inculcation of supernatural fears, several other factors play an important part in this process. One of these factors is the belief that supernatural dangers are similar to real dangers, a fact which strengthens the Kwoma child's fear of them by the principle of secondary generalization.[4]

Since *marsalai* are described as great snakes or crocodiles which live in the swamp, realistic warnings about snakes, crocodiles, and other dangerous animals would tend to generalize to these supernatural monsters. In other words, each time a Kwoma is reinforced for heeding a warning about an animal, particularly a snake or crocodile, he is also somewhat reinforced for heeding warnings about *marsalai*,[5] that is, unrealistic fears. A second source of generalization is that warnings about *marsalai* all concern disturbing their dwelling places. The common word for house is used to describe these supposed dwellings, so that all realistic warnings about trespassing in, and stealing from, the house of human beings also strengthen the warnings about *marsalai*. Finally, *marsalai* are described as being huge. Since large animals and

[4] If two objects are described by the same term, a person tends to respond to them both in a similar manner. Hull has described this as secondary generalization. See C. L. Hull, "The Problem of Stimulus Equivalence in Behavior Theory," *Psychol. Rev.*, XLVI (1939), 9–30. It is also discussed by Miller. See N. E. Miller and John Dollard, *Social Learning and Imitation* (New Haven, 1941), chap. v. Experimental evidence in support of this principle has recently been adduced by Dr. Jane Birge. See J. S. Birge, "The Rôle of Verbal Responses in Transfer" (Doctoral Dissertation, Yale University, 1941). G. P. Murdock has found empirical support for this principle in a study of the generalization of incest taboos by means of common kinship terms.

[5] Kwoma vivify their warnings about *marsalai* by telling children that the sounds they hear at the time of a ceremony are the voices of these monsters. The sounds are in reality produced by gongs, bull-roarers, and flutes, but this theory offers another avenue of generalization from animals to *marsalai* on the basis of the sounds which they both make.

big men are likely to be more dangerous than small ones, generalization on the basis of size also tends to support the warnings issued about these supernatural beings.

Ghosts are described not only as having human form but as actually being the spirits of deceased persons. Kwoma seldom speak of ghosts in general terms, but usually specify the ghost of some particular deceased relative. When a Kwoma dreams of someone who has died, he is told that the ghost of this person has actually visited him in the night. Moreover, living persons are sometimes called ghosts. Thus the similarity between men and ghosts is impressed upon a child. Hence, when he is rewarded for heeding warnings about living persons, this should by generalization strengthen the habit of heeding warnings about ghosts. Kwoma children are told that ghosts can assume the form of birds and animals. Whenever a bird or animal is heard or seen at night, it is often suggested that it may be a ghost in disguise. Thus fear of ghosts may generalize from animals as well as from men.

Fear of food "poisoned" by sorcery has, like food contaminated by blood, a realistic source of generalization from food which is actually spoiled. Kwoma employ the same word (*kafwa sek*) to describe putrifying meat or fruit, and to describe food which they believe is "poisoned." Thus if a child becomes ill after not heeding the realistic warning against eating spoiled food, this should tend to strengthen warnings about sorcery. A second source from which the belief in sorcery may receive generalized support is realistic warnings concerning aggression from human beings. Each time a person is scolded, threatened, insulted, or spanked by another person, such an event should strengthen his fear that he can be harmed by sorcery also.

A realistic source from which fears about blood contamination may spring is less evident. The following suggestions may be made. When sickness results from food which is really contaminated, it should strengthen a person's tendency to avoid food which is supposed to be contaminated. Secondly, the Kwoma word for milk is "breast blood." Children are made to abhor milk at the time of weaning, and this abhorrence may generalize through the common term to the drinking of blood or to eating things believed to be contaminated with it.[6]

Imitation, as well as warning and generalization, is of considerable importance in the inculcation of supernatural beliefs. In the previous chapter it was indicated that imitation took its place along with teaching as one of the two most important mechanisms of culture transmission. Although imitation was not analyzed in detail, it was indicated that a Kwoma pupil is very frequently rewarded for behaving like other persons in the society, particularly those who are in the same sex, age, and kinship category as the pupil. Conversely, Kwoma pupils frequently do not gain rewards and do experience pain when they behave differently from these models. This is particularly true when the model gives evidences of being in a dangerous situation.[7] Thus to behave differently from a model comes to evoke anxiety in a Kwoma pupil, whereas to behave like one comes to have an acquired reward value.[8]

The following case will illustrate the way in which supernatural fears are transmitted by means of imitation. I started to whistle one evening while Mar and Mey were visiting me. Mar warned me to stop lest I attract ghosts, but I persisted. Mar then bolted for his house and Mey fol-

[6] Potable liquids such as coconut milk are classed with water, whereas undrinkable liquids such as milk, urine, and breadfruit sap are classed with blood.

[7] The following case will serve as illustration of pain suffered for not imitating. Awa became possessed one night and began to belabor her sister with a stick. Chinuwa caught hold of Awa to prevent her from harming anyone. Several children from the hamlet, hearing the commotion, gathered to see what was happening. Awa struggled against Chinuwa's restraining arms, finally broke free, and began to lay about her with the stick. All the children except Fit ran out of reach. He delayed for a moment and received a blow from Awa on his legs. He then ran away as the rest had done. Fit, by this event, was at first punished for not imitating the other children and then rewarded for imitating them by escaping further blows. Such a situation as this not infrequently presents itself to Kwoma children.

[8] See N. E. Miller and John Dollard, *Social Learning and Imitation* (New Haven, 1941).

lowed him. Mey's behavior can be analyzed thus: the drive was fear caused both by my whistling and by the sight of Mar starting to run while he remained; the response was running after Mar; and the reward was the reduction of fear. Had not Mar run away first, Mey might have discovered some other means of reducing his fear, but by imitating Mar he learned to avoid ghosts in the same manner as his older *brother*. Kwoma pupils in a similar manner learn to avoid *marsalai*, to protect themselves from the dangers of sorcery, and to escape the dangers associated with blood. Thus imitation is an important mechanism for the transmission of supernatural beliefs and practices.

Chance as a factor in maintaining supernatural beliefs has long been noted by anthropologists and sociologists.[9] The data from Kwoma tend to support this theory. Storms occur so frequently that it would be extraordinary if one did not occasionally occur after a person has disturbed the dwelling place of a *marsalai*, and this would help to prevent the extinction of the habit of heeding. The following case illustrates this point. Yat had cleared a garden site near a large rock thought to be the dwelling place of a *marsalai*. When the time came to burn the dried brush and branches, a necessary step in the process of gardening, he expressed some anxiety lest this might anger the *marsalai* which lived in the rock, but nevertheless went ahead with his burning. That night there was a bad storm with a high wind, and Yat took this as proof of his belief that he had indeed angered the supernatural being. Wof, Gwiyap, and Mar all explained the storm in the same way. The next time that there was a bad storm, I said to Gwiyap: "Yat didn't disturb a *marsalai* today. How do you account for the storm?" Gwiyap replied: "Maybe Yat didn't, but someone else did. Probably it was one of those stupid people from Wanyi."

Chance also operates to support warnings about ghosts. Marok and Kar stayed visiting in a part of the tribe some distance from their home until after dark, thus not heeding

[9] See W. G. Sumner and A. G. Keller, *The Science of Society* (New Haven, 1928), vol. II, chap. xxi.

the warning about walking abroad during the night. On the way home they heard a strange noise, took it to be a ghost, stopped in their tracks, and yelled for help. War and others, who were gossiping in the house tamberan, heard their cries and shouted back instructions to make a dash for the house tamberan. They did this and thus escaped what they believed was imminent danger. The chance occurrence of a strange noise had operated on this occasion to strengthen the fear of walking abroad at night.

An episode which involved Wof illustrates how chance can strengthen sorcery beliefs. He came home one day to find that someone had tampered with his store of sago flour. Believing that someone had taken flour in order to sorcerize him, he asked his first wife if she knew who could have done it. She replied that she had seen his second wife in that part of the room and that it was undoubtedly she who had stolen the food in order to sorcerize him. When Wof accused the younger woman, she denied it. The next day Wof came to my house and asked me if I had any medicine against sorcery, for he felt sick. He said that his head and stomach ached and he knew that someone was trying to sorcerize him. Whether Wof's illness was an attack of malaria, psychological depression resulting from repressed anger at his wives, or some other psychic or physical disturbance, it strengthened his belief in the efficacy of sorcery. He probably guarded his food stores more carefully thereafter.[10]

Chance can operate to reinforce the habit of heeding a warning about blood. Children who let blood from their penises do grow up; after phlebotomy has been practiced pains eventually disappear; and women who menstruate and men who let blood from themselves remain healthy. The following case also illustrates how chance may operate to support the belief in blood contamination. Toward the end of my stay at Kwoma our regular shoot boy left and we appointed Mes to take his place. Previously he had helped around our house and had eaten whatever pigeon meat was

[10] It was, indeed, not long after this that he scolded Ham for walking about his porch and accused him of being a thief of sorcery material.

left over from our table. When he became shoot boy the question arose as to whether he could still eat this meat since he killed it himself. Gwiyap was of the opinion that since he killed the birds with a gun rather than with a spear or arrow his blood would not be transferred and it would be perfectly safe to eat the meat. Yat, his *paternal uncle*, disagreed with this opinion, and held that it would be dangerous. Gwiyap then argued that the former shoot boy had eaten birds that he had shot without getting sick. Yat countered that, although he did not get sick, he had missed many shots and that this was probably due to his having eaten his own kill. Mes decided to heed his *uncle's* warning and ate no more pigeon meat. It happened that Mes was a very good shot and missed extremely few birds. He explained his accuracy as proof of the wisdom of heeding his *uncle's* warning.

Certain forces operate against heeding unrealistic warnings in Kwoma society. One of the most important of these is the fatigue drive. This drive exerts a constant pressure on the pupil not to run away from ghosts, not to bother to avoid the dwelling place of *marsalai*, to be careless about his food leavings, and not to go to the trouble of gathering nettles to scrape his penis to renew his blood. In other words his fears of the supernatural must be strong enough to overcome his indolence. Furthermore, the avoidance of supernatural dangers is frequently incompatible with the satisfaction of some other drive. When Yat discovered that he had cleared his garden too near a *marsalai's* dwelling place, his fear of disturbing the *marsalai* was opposed by his need to raise vegetables in a convenient place in order to satisfy his hunger. Similarly, when a pupil scrapes his penis or practices phlebotomy to let out bad blood these acts are opposed by the pain which they cause; when he does not eat a pig he has killed or yams he has planted, these renunciations are opposed by his hunger for these foods. Likewise a pupil's avoidance of ghosts and fear of sorcery often force him to give up satisfactions which he might otherwise attain.

In contrast to realistic warnings, when a pupil does not heed an unrealistic warning, the pain, except by chance, does not follow from the source specified. This could be expected to result, through the operation of the principle of extinction,[11] in a weakening of the habit of heeding this particular warning and in a functional discrimination between realistic and unrealistic dangers.[12] The fact that these unrealistic warnings are sanctioned by the community normally prevents such an event from occurring. Pupils are punished for not heeding warnings about *marsalai*, ghosts, sorcery, or blood, as is illustrated by the following case. Kwiya and Fit each bought a harmonica from me and began playing it around their house. Their *mother* warned them that this would bring ghosts. Neither of them heeded this warning, so the *mother* took matters in her own hands. She scolded them both severely and forced them to return their harmonicas to me. An even more striking case, perhaps, occurred when Mundik,[13] a youth who had not yet received his keloids of manhood, attended a funeral ceremony, thus ignoring the warning about the danger from the *marsalai* of the cult to those who are not yet initiated. Mundik was attacked and beaten by the members of the cult, and, after being tied hand and foot, was thrown into a near-by dwelling. Had it not been for our presence he might well have been killed.

Since social sanctions are, in the last analysis, responsible for the maintenance of supernatural beliefs, an inquiry might profitably be made into the problem of why parents take the time and effort to force children to heed warnings. It may indeed be asked why they even issue these unrealistic warnings. A detailed answer to the above questions is beyond the scope of this chapter, but a few suggestions can be made. In the first place, since the teachers have been brought up in Kwoma culture they do not distinguish between realistic and unrealistic dangers as such. Hence they believe that if a

[11] See chap. vii, p. 192, n. 30.
[12] If a response to a generalized cue does not achieve a reward, but the response to the original cue continues to do so, the organism learns to discriminate between the two cues and to react only to the one which leads to reward. See E. R. Hilgard and D. G. Marquis, *Conditioning and Learning* (New York, 1940), chap. viii.
[13] Mundik was a Yelagu who was staying with relatives at Kwoma.

pupil does not heed an unrealistic warning he will be injured just as surely as, and perhaps even more severely than, if he ignored a realistic warning. Why they wish to prevent the child from being injured is a complex problem, involving identification, loss of help and support, and sanctions against negligence. The important question is why, if parents make their children heed unrealistic warnings in order to prevent them from being injured, does this habit not extinguish when they observe a child experience no harmful consequences when he disregards a supernatural danger? The following case of the extinction of a supernatural belief indicates that this is a real as well as a logical possibility.

Mar and Gwiyap had both been warned not to eat sago flour washed by a female lest it make them sick. Before they started to work as our houseboys they had heeded this warning and each had worked with one of his *sisters* in the process of extracting sago flour. They had washed the pith while the *sister* crushed it. When they began to work for us, however, we demanded their services in the mornings, when they would otherwise have gone to the swamp to replenish the household flour supply. Awa and Kwiya, the *sisters* who had hitherto worked with them, had no other available *brothers*, and therefore formed a team of their own. They took turns washing and crushing and, of course, produced flour washed by a female. Mar and Gwiyap were somewhat hesitant about trying this flour, but they were faced with the dilemma of either going without flour, which had been a staple in their diet since weaning, or ceasing to work for us, which would have meant losing frequent gifts of trade goods as well as some prestige. They chose to risk disregarding the warnings about the food and hoped that the flour would not be like other bad food they had eaten and which had made them sick. Their parents scolded them for this behavior and warned them again. Since no other painful consequences resulted from their first attempt, they decided to try it again, and, for the remaining six months of our stay, they and the rest of their household ate this supposedly harmful food. After the first few occasions their parents stopped scolding and warning them.

Supernatural Beliefs

Thus, not only can the supernatural fears of pupils extinguish, but so also can the fears of the teachers become reduced in the same way, so that they no longer maintain these beliefs by sanctioning them.

The fact that Kwoma children can learn not to heed, and Kwoma parents to stop issuing and sanctioning unrealistic warnings, raises a serious question. Why does this not occur more frequently? Why, in the course of time, have not all these supernatural beliefs disappeared as a result of this process? The answer to this is suggested by one of the basic postulates of the functional theory of anthropology. Parents continue to issue unrealistic warnings and to sanction them because they form an integral part of one or more systems of beliefs, customs, and organized activities which, as a whole, satisfy a social need.[14]

The belief in *marsalai* forms a large part of the charter[15] of the yam cult.[16] *Marsalai* are believed to be present whenever this cult holds a ceremonial meeting and to bless those who participate. In playing the instruments of the cult, the members are producing a representation of the voices of these beings. After a ceremony, no man who has attended may have intercourse with his wife, because the powerful and dangerous influence of the cult *marsalai* still clings to him, and might injure her. Thus, were the belief in these monsters to disappear, the Kwoma would be forced either to provide a new *raison d'être* for their cult ceremonies or to give them up altogether. It is not necessary here to present a detailed account of the functions of the cult, but a few of them may be mentioned to show how important this institution is in Kwoma society. The most direct function of the cult seems

---

[14] See B. Malinowski, "The Scientific Basis of Applied Anthropology," *Reale Academia D'Italia*, XVIII (1940), 22.

[15] Every institution consists in part of the traditional purposes and reasons for its existence which are believed by the members of the personnel. Malinowski has called this the charter. See B. Malinowski, "The Group and the Individual in Functional Analysis," *American Journal of Sociology*, XLIV (1939), 952-954.

[16] The personnel, norms, and material apparatus of this institution can be gathered from the descriptive chapters. The charter and functions are stressed here because of their importance in this context.

to be that it provides a means of artistic expression. Cult ceremonies furnish the chief opportunity for singing, dancing, rhythmic gong beating, flute playing, and the manufacture of carved figures. Numerous important integrative functions are also fulfilled by the yam cult. It provides one of the bases for the social stratification of men, differentiating four prestige positions: boys who do not belong to the cult, members of the first stage, members of the second stage, and members of the final stage. The yam cult is closely integrated with head-hunting, in that only those who have taken a head can become members of the highest stage. The yam cult excludes women and thus helps to define their status and to maintain the division of labor by sex. Through such exclusion it provides a socially accepted means for men to express their aggressive feelings toward women. It also provides an opportunity for ceremonial license. Finally, the yam cult is associated with agriculture. The cult is thus an important institution, closely integrated into Kwoma culture, and to tamper with its charter by refusing to believe in *marsalai* is something which no pupil or teacher could lightly do.

Beliefs in *marsalai*, in addition to forming part of the charter of the yam cult, provide an explanation for cosmic events and a means of controlling them. Bad rain and wind storms, earthquakes, and rainbows[17] are thought to be produced by these monsters. These beliefs permit a Kwoma to perform certain practices which are thought to control them. In the first place he can avoid disturbing them, and in the second place he can utter an aggressive prayer which he believes will stop the storm or earthquake.[18] Thus, both because beliefs in *marsalai* form an integral part of the yam cult and because they perform other functions as well, Kwoma teachers would be very loath to cease believing in them, even if events made them skeptical of their supposed powers.

[17] Wind storms and earthquakes not infrequently destroy Kwoma dwellings and are thus seriously dangerous.
[18] It is assumed here that any activity in the face of danger is normally more reinforcing than passive acceptance, even though this activity is not effective in averting danger.

Kwoma beliefs about ghosts form part of the charter of the funeral cult. Whenever a person is on the point of death, ghosts are believed to hover around in order to carry the soul to the land of the dead. After death they are believed to guard the body during the months that it is exposed on a platform, until the time when the bones are finally buried under the floor of the dwelling and distributed to the relatives and *friends*. The funeral cult functions directly to provide a means of expressing grief. It is at the first funeral ceremony, which begins when the person dies and ends after the corpse has been deposited on the platform, that the female relatives wail, and that the male relatives talk emotionally of their friendship with the deceased and express their hatred of those responsible for his death.[19] Second, this institution provides an opportunity for mourning. Relatives of the deceased daub themselves with mud and deny themselves some article of diet. Finally, the funeral cult provides for the disposal of the corpse, and thus functions to prevent sickness from contagion. The cult also has integrative functions in that it supports the relationship between relatives and *friends* through the distribution of the bones of the deceased at the time of the second funeral. The second funeral also provides an opportunity for a meeting of the members of the yam cult. Thus, were Kwoma teachers to allow pupils to disbelieve in ghosts, a new rationale would have to be discovered for the funeral cult or its functions would have to be taken over by some other institution.

Besides furnishing a reason for funeral practices, the belief in ghosts provides an explanation for strange noises at night and for dreams, and thus affords a rationale for action. When a Kwoma hears a strange noise at night, he rushes into the nearest house, closes the door, and shouts imprecations and curses at the ghosts, commanding them to return to the land of the dead. He often beats the air with sticks to strengthen his commands. If he has a nightmare he resorts to similar practices; the women may wail and beg the

[19] All deaths are believed to be caused by sorcery.

ghost to leave and not to take the soul of the one who has had the nightmare. The belief in ghosts also offers an explanation for irrational acts, e.g., fits of unexpected anger expressed toward members of the in-group. When such occur, the blame can be transferred to a ghost by means of the theory of ghost possession, thus preventing retaliatory measures which would tend to disrupt the group. Ghost possession also provides a means of group catharsis of guilt and of social control. A ghost is believed to possess a person in order to express his anger at a living relative (usually not the possessed person himself) for some sin which he is committing. In order to make the ghost return to the land of the dead, the proper sin must be confessed by an exorcist as spokesman for the group. The exorcist, a relative of the possessed person, lists the sins of the community one by one until the ghost indicates the reason for his anger by means of an affirmation from the possessed person. The sinner then promises to mend his ways, and the ghost returns to the land of the dead. Thus, exorcising the ghost is a group confession of sins and a means of exerting social control. The belief in the existence of ghosts thus fulfills a variety of functions at Kwoma and can therefore be expected to show a strong resistance to extinction.

A large part of Kwoma medical practice derives from beliefs in sorcery. Whenever anyone becomes seriously ill, his relatives announce this event on their house tamberan gongs and command everyone in the tribe to stop sorcery. If the person continues to be sick, they call a sorcery court, at which accusations are made and denied and evidence is presented. Finally, the relatives of the sick person may visit all those whom they suspect of sorcery and make them drink water as a test. Belief in sorcery thus offers an explanation for sickness which allows for coöperative curing efforts, and is thereby of considerable functional importance to those who have no better theory of disease and no more effective methods of cure. A secondary function of this type of medical practice is that it offers, in the procedures against the supposed sorcerer, a formalized method of expressing aggression[20] which is normally harmless because the sorcerer is seldom if ever discovered.

The belief in sorcery, as well as furnishing an explanation for sickness, functions as a means of social control. It stands, indeed, in lieu of a police force and strong political organization as a preventive of criminal behavior. Theft, rape, murder, and trespass, for example, are inhibited by the fear that these crimes will bring retaliation through sorcery from the person against whom the crime is committed or from his relatives. The fear of sorcery is more potent in preventing crimes than the fear of other forms of retaliation because it is considered as dangerous as realistic modes and more difficult to prevent.

Finally, sorcery provides a means whereby persons can express their aggression against other members of the society without serious consequences. Although the Kwoma probably use this mode of expressing anger only infrequently, the belief in the efficacy of the sorcery mechanism permits one to perform acts which he believes will cause the sickness and death of another person. Thus sorcery beliefs, like those about *marsalai* and ghosts, perform important functions for the members of Kwoma society.

Kwoma informants explain that it is necessary to hold the age-grade ceremony once every five years in order to provide an opportunity for the ceremonial letting of blood that insures health and normal growth to the initiates. The beliefs about blood are thus bound into the system of age-grading, which provides a hierarchy of prestige positions and, like the yam cult, provides opportunities for singing, dancing, flute playing, gong beating, wood carving, and ceremonial license. The taboo against eating pork that one has speared, which is based on the Kwoma theory of blood, prevents private consumption by the hunter and compels him to distribute the meat. This results in quick consumption, an important factor in a damp hot climate where no efficient method for preserving meat is known. The distribution of pork to rela-

[20] The announcement of sickness, the behavior at court, and the testing visits are all aggressive in character.

tives also serves to cement kinship bonds. The belief that a person should not eat yams which he has planted, because of blood contamination, results in exchange planting and thus strengthens the coöperative bonds between relatives. Finally, the beliefs in blood strengthen the rules of incest and exogamy, since it is thought that children of parents with the same blood are not likely to be strong and healthy.

Kwoma beliefs about *marsalai*, ghosts, sorcery, and blood are thus seen to be not isolated unrealistic fears, but theories which are enmeshed and intertwined with many of the important institutions of the culture.[21] It is consequently understandable that a Kwoma teacher should insist that a pupil learn these beliefs and that he should tend to disregard evidence that they are unrealistic. The pupil, too, experiences many of the advantages which these beliefs entail, a fact which aids the teacher in the task of inculcation.

Although the above analysis gives an answer to the question of why these unrealistic fears do not extinguish, it raises an equally serious one: How can such fears ever extinguish? In other words, if culture is integrated and functional, how can social change ever take place? The case of Gwiyap and Mar suggests one possible answer to this question. The belief that sago washed by women is not good to eat has the function of making Kwoma men do their share of the work of extracting sago flour. In other words, it supports an equitable division of labor in this phase of Kwoma economic life. The presence of the ethnographer, introducing trade goods which were highly prized by Gwiyap and Mar, their *sisters*, and their parents, introduced a disturbing element into this adjustment. Mar and Gwiyap were willing to take the chance of becoming sick, their *sisters* were willing to do more work, and their parents were willing to let the customary division of labor lapse in order to obtain these trade goods. Without intention, or even awareness of the event until after its occurrence, the ethnographer, by introducing a new form of wealth

[21] Supernatural beliefs, on a cultural level, are similar to neurotic symptoms in the individual, in that both are based on unrealistic fear, both result in secondary gains, and both resist extinction.

and providing a new means of earning it, had set the stage for the extinction of a supernatural belief.

In sum, a number of factors seem to be responsible for the inculcation and maintenance of supernatural beliefs and practices. Kwoma teachers, having repeatedly warned their pupils concerning real dangers, are enabled to use this technique to teach their pupils to avoid dangers which do not exist. To make these unrealistic warnings more forceful, they describe the supernatural dangers as being similar to the real dangers from which their pupils have experienced pain. Imitation also plays as important a rôle as in the transmission of the other aspects of the culture. Despite all these forces which lead a Kwoma pupil to respect supernatural dangers, the effort and deprivation frequently involved in carrying out magico-religious rituals tend to make him omit them. Since such omissions would soon lead to the extinction of these habits, the sanctions of society, as implemented by punishments from his teachers, provide the ultimate force which prevents the pupil from discovering that these dangers do not really exist and do not have to be avoided. Finally, the teachers themselves continue to inculcate these beliefs because they are integral parts of institutions which as a whole are necessary for the satisfaction of the basic and acquired drives of the constituent members of Kwoma society.

INDEX

ACCULTURATION, xviii, 19–22, 148; influence of whites on head-hunting, 167
Adoption, 122, 151
Age-grade cycle, 9, 65–67, 135
Aged, the, 9 n., 129, 130, 135
Aggression, 30, 34, 36–37, 174 n.; as a basis for prestige, 63; displacement of, 165 ff.; toward affines, 101–102, 155–157; toward co-wife, 157; toward foreigners, 103, 162 ff.; toward *friends*, 60–61; toward maternal relatives, 60; toward non-relatives, 99–101, 159–160; toward parents, 59, 94; toward paternal relatives, 60, 144–145; toward siblings, 57–59, 62–63, 91–96, 104, 128, 145–148; toward spouse, 148; *see also* Breaking relations, Drives
Anger, defined, 174; *see also* Aggression
Anticipation, principle of, defined, 181
Anxiety. *See* Fear
Appetite, defined, 175; rôle of in teaching, 192
Art, 54, 89–91, 131–133
Avoidance, between sexes, 38; *see also* Fear

BEGGING, 42–43
Behrmann, 14 n., 19
Betrothal. *See* Sexual behavior
Birge, J. S., 207 n.
Blood, beliefs concerning. *See* Physiology
Boas, F., xv
Breaking relations, 97–98, 156, 167
Brown, J. S., 183 n.

CANNIBALISM, 118, 164
Cannon, W. B., 174 n.
Ceremonial license. *See* Sexual behavior
Chance, rôle of in maintaining supernatural beliefs, 210–211
Childbirth, 150–151
Cleanliness training, 26, 32, 48
Clothing, 33 n., 66 n., 67, 74–75, 87 n.; *see also* Sexual behavior, modesty
Collecting. *See* Economic activities
Commanding, defined, 196–197
Cooking, 44, 69, 108, 117
Coöperation, 159; in defense, 62; in economic tasks, 9, 12, 68–70, 107–109, 129–130
Courtship. *See* Sexual behavior
Court system, 161–163
Cue, defined, 175
Cult. *See* Yam cult
Cutaneous contact, wish for, 33–34, 50, 125 n.

DEATH, 14, 141–144
Descent, 6, 121
Diffusion, v
Discrimination, defined, 213 n.
Disease. *See* Sickness
Divorce, 149, 150
Dollard, J., xiii, xvi, xviii, 40 n., 173, 174 n., 182 n., 192 n., 195, 199 n., 207 n.
Domesticated animals, care of, 47, 117–118
Drives, acquired, 174; *see also* Aggression, Coöperation, Cutaneous contact, Fear, Guilt, Prestige; basic, 173; cold and heat, *see* Temperature regulation; colon and bladder distension, *see* Cleanliness training; fatigue, *see* Fatigue; hunger, *see* Economic activities; and pain, *see* Fear; sex, *see* Sexual behavior
Du Bois, C., xv
Dyk, W., v

ECONOMIC activities, 9, 12; collecting, 116–117; firewood and water supplies, 44, 117; fishing, 12, 47, 70, 116; gardening, 11–12, 45, 46, 69–70, 107–111; house building, 129–130; hunting, 46, 70–

71, 111–116; sago making, 9, 46, 68–69, 116–117; tool making, 47, 69, 71, 118–119, *see also* Trade
Environment, geographic, 3; flora and fauna, 3, 4; rainfall, 4
Erikson, E. H., xv
Evans-Pritchard, E. E., xv
Extinction, defined, 192 n.; rôle of, in inculcation of supernatural beliefs, 213

FAMILY. *See* Kinship behavior
Family line. *See* Social organization
Fatigue, 173, 212
Fear, 174, 181 n.; of ghosts, 35, 55, 88–89, 135–136, Chap. VIII; of *marsalai*, 35, 53–55, 89–91, 130–134, Chap. VIII; of natural environment, 27–28, 35, 52–53, 88, 130; of social environment, *see* Kinship behavior; of sorcery, 24, 88, 136–138, Chap. VIII; rôle of, in teaching, 181–190
Fieldwork, difficulties of, 24 n., 151 n.; position of the ethnographers in Kwoma social structure, 19–23; techniques employed, xvii, 21
Firth, R., xv
Fishing. *See* Economic activities
Food taboos, 68, 69, 109, 110, 113, 116, 118, 128, 137, 151
Fortes, M., xv
Freud, S., v, xiv, 174 n., 181 n.
Functional approach, xv, 215–220

GAMES and play, 25, 38, 45–47, 50, 54
Gardening. *See* Economic activities
Generalization, psychological principle of, defined, 207 n.
Ghosts, 19, 35, 55, 88–89, 135, 143, 204–205, 208–211, 217–218; possession, 136, 165, 204–205
Gillin, J., xv n.
Gorer, G., xv
Government. *See* Political organization
Guilt, 80, 125, 128

HABIT, defined, 173
Hallowell, A. I., v
Hambly, W. D., xiv
Hamlet. *See* Territorial organization
harafa ma malaka, defined, 63
Hayamakwo, defined, 6
Head-hunting, 5, 12, 164 ff.; homicidal insignia, 116
Hilgard, E. R., 173 n., 192 n.
Hogbin, I., xv, xvii
Homba, defined, 80 n.
Homosexuality. *See* Sexual behavior
Hongwam, defined, 5
House building. *See* Economic activities
House tamberan, defined, 6
Hull, C. L., vi, xviii, 173, 177 n., 181 n., 188 n., 197 n., 207 n.
Hunger. *See* Drives, Economic activities
Hunting. *See* Economic activities

IMITATION, 195–196, 209–210
Incest. *See* Sexual behavior
Industriousness, sanctions on, 72–73
Infanticide, 151
Informants. *See* Personnel
Inheritance, 121
Initiation, into adolescence, *see* Age-grade cycle; into adulthood, 106; into childhood, 38; into yam cult, *see* Yam cult
Institutional approach, 215–220
Intertribal relations, 5, 61, 103, 162 ff.; *see also* Head-hunting, Trade

JUNOD, H. A., xiv

KAFWA *sek*, defined, 26 n.
karaganda yikafa, defined, 63
Kardiner, A., xiv
Keller, A. G., 178 n., 210 n.
Kidd, D., xiv
Kinship, behavior of female ego toward relatives, 156–158; behavior toward affines, 101–102, 155–156; behavior toward *ceremonial father, ceremonial son*, 66–

67, 82, 98, 155; behavior toward child, 151–153; behavior toward co-wife, 165–166; behavior toward foreigners, *see* Intertribal relations; behavior toward *friends*, 60–61, 82, 99, 106, 154; behavior toward maternal relatives, 42, 60, 96–97, 153–154; behavior toward non-relatives, 39–40, 61, 99, 104, 159; behavior toward parent, 29, 32, 35, 36, 38, 41, 43–44, 46, 59, 94, 104, 144–145; behavior toward paternal relatives, 42, 60, 94, 144–145, 154; behavior toward siblings, 36, 42, 56–59, 62, 78–79, 91–94, 104, 145–148, 152–153, 165; behavior toward spouse, 148–149; system, 7 ff.
Kluckhohn, C., xv
Koriyasi, defined, 5 n.

LANGUAGE, as barrier to fieldwork, xviii; learning of, 28; rôle of, in teaching, 194–195
Learning, analyzed examples of, 176 ff.; paradigm of, 173; social conditions of, 172
Lineage. *See* Social organization
Linton, R., xiv

MAGIC, 54–55, 75; *see also* Physiology, Sorcery, Yam cult
Malinowski, B., xiv, xv, 197 n., 215 n.
Malu, 119
Map of Rumbima hamlet, 10
Marquis, D. G., 173 n., 192 n.
Marriage, 106; remarriage, 129; trial marriage, 125; wedding, 125; *see also* Kinship, Sexual behavior
Marsalai, defined, 31 n.; 31, 35, 53, 89–91, 103, 130, 134, 204, 206–208, 210, 212–213, 215–216
Masturbation. *See* Sexual behavior
Material culture. *See* Economic activities
Mead, M., v, xiv, 5 n., 31 n.
Menstruation. *See* Physiology
Miller, N., xiv
Miller, N. E., xviii, 40 n., 173, 174 n., 182 n., 183 n., 192 n., 195, 199 n., 207 n.

Milne, Mrs. L., xiv
Minjama, defined, 89
Motivation, 173–174; *see also* Drives
Mowrer, O. H., xviii, 174 n., 182 n.
Murdock, G. P., xvi, xviii, 207 n.
Murray, H. A., 173 n.
Myths, 80 n., 128

NOKWI, defined, 131

OEDIPUS complex, 140 n., *see also* Kinship, behavior

PAIN, 173; avoidance of, *see* Fear
Pavlov, I. P., vi, 173
Personnel, 14–23; Rumbima hamlet by household (chart), 11; the lineage of Mangwiyow (chart), 13; the lineage of Wasahof (chart), 17
Physical characteristics, 4
Physiology, Kwoma theories of: blood, 29–30, 40, 64, 67–68, 81–82, 109–110, 113, 126, 205–206, 208–209, 211–212, 219–220; death, *see* Death; growth, 64; menstruation, 65; reproduction, 150; sickness, *see* Sickness; sperm, 82
Political organization, 5–6, 12; *see also* Court system, Head-hunting, Kinship, behavior, Sorcery
Population, 5 n.
Pregnancy, 77, 150
Prestige, 30, 37, 63, 81, 100, 130 ff., 164 ff., 174; *see also* Age-grade cycle, Yam cult
Property, rules of, 6, 40–41, 46, 120–124; theft and trespass, 43, 125
Pupil, defined, 178

RADIN, P., v
Raum, O. F., xv
Reed, S. W., xvi
Reinforcement, defined, 173
Religion. *See* Yam cult
Reproduction. *See* Physiology
Response, defined, 173–175
Reward, defined, 173–175

Richards, A., xiv
Richter, C. P., 174 n.

SAFE relations, 98–99
Sapir, E., v
Secret societies. See Yam cult
Sexual behavior, betrothal, 83; ceremonial license, 66, 127; courting, 81–86; during infancy, 26–27; during weaning, 32–33; elopement, 85–86; homosexuality, 51, game, 50–51; incest rules, 77–80, between *brother* and *sister*, 80–81, 84–86, between father and daughter, 127–128, between other relatives, 81, 82–83, 99; marital sex relations, 125–126, extramarital, 126, 128, 165; masturbation, 26–27, 49, 73–74; modesty, 49, 51, 75–77, 86–87, 129; premarital sex relations, 74–79, 87–89; training of boys, 48–51, 73–81; training of girls, 51–52, 86; *see also* Marriage
Sib. See Social organization
Sickness, theory of, 54, 64, 88, 136; treatment of, 24, 27, 29, 31, 35, 52, 88; *see also* Physiology, Sorcery
Social organization, 5–6, 121–122, 147–148; *see also* Kinship
Sorcery, 24, 26 n., 39, 40, 42, 43, 88, 136 ff., 161–162, 205, 208, 211, 218–219
Stimulus, defined, 175 n.
Subtribe, defined, 5 n.
Sumner, W. G., vi, 178 n., 210 n.
Supernatural beings. See Ghosts, Marsalai

TANGWISHAMP, defined, 5 n.
Teacher, defined, 178
Teaching techniques, 179 ff.; demonstrating, 195–196; giving and helping, 197–198; inciting, 191–193; instructing, 194–195; leading, 194; praising, 199–200; punishing, 180–185; scolding, 185–187; threatening, 187–189; warning, 189–191, 202 ff.
Temperature regulation, 27, 33
Territorial organization, 5–6
Thorndike, E. L., vi, 173
Totem ancestors, 6
Trade, 5, 12, 119–120, 162
Trial and error, 177
Tribe, defined, 5 n.
Tug, defined, 6

UNDERHILL, R., v
Urumbanj, defined, 5 n.

WANYI, defined, 6
Warfare, 12, 163–164; *see also* Head-hunting
Waskuk, 5 n.
Watson, J. B., vi
Wedgewood, C. H., xv

YAMBON, 5
Yam cult, 12, 53–54, 89–91, 130–133, 215–216
Yelagu, defined, 5
Yenama, defined, 89
Young, P. T., 174 n.

ZINN, E., xvi, 174 n.